The Church's One
Foundation

To: Allan

From: ~~Handel~~

10 / 20 / 2011

The Church's One Foundation

CHURCH AND BIBLE THEMES

Handel Andrews

To order additional copies of this book, contact:
Xlibris Corporation
1-888-795-4274
www.Xlibris.com
98667

CONTENTS

DEDICATION

This book is dedicated to Ruth Maude Andrews, nee Nurse, my loving mother, whose life was a book of history, the leaves whereof were days, the letters mercies closely joined and the title was God's praise.

FOREWORD

I am deeply honored to have been asked to write the foreword for this religious work of my former teacher and friend. *The Church's One Foundation* speaks volumes. Handel lays bare his assumptions on religious themes and biblical history in a very convincing manner. Although I disagree strenuously with some of his inferences, I am impressed with the data he set forward.

He quotes extensively from authorities on the topics discussed and presents the reader with differing points of view.

He began questioning the foundations of his Christian Faith from a tender age. Thanks to his parents, who instilled a love of learning in him. He used his mental prowess to separate theory from fact. The reader will find this ability highly evidenced in this work.

I was introduced to Handel's religious writings from bi-weekly articles he wrote for the New York based newspaper, Caribbean Impact. The articles, "Think on these things," were written under the pseudonym of Brother Liburd. There were those who objected to some of their determinations and the owners Dennis Nelson, Godfrey Wray and yours truly placed disclaimers.

Like these articles, the present work digs to the root of things. Handel begins his chapter, "Life and Teachings of Jesus", by asking "Did Jesus really live?" and states:

> This question has nothing to do with what the priest says in his homily on Sunday or with what I believe, which, incidentally, is in the historicity of Jesus. It concerns the matter of evidence. Put another way, it is a battle between faith and reason. Faith accepts the biblical record as sufficient evidence. Reason seeks verification from the historical record.

The casual reader might dismiss the words as those of a disbeliever based on the question alone, without considering his statement, "I believe…in the historicity of Jesus." The serious reader will read the entire paragraph and recognize that Handel is a believer who is not afraid to discuss views antithetical to his.

Most of us have firmly held religious beliefs and rarely change. As St. Paul advises, we should always be prepared to give a reason for the hope that we hold. *The Church's One Foundation* transcends race, color and religious doctrine. It will provide answers from various points of view to the questions frequently asked about the Christian's faith.

There is also an inspirational section in the book. The hymns discussed are perennial favorites and will touch many hearts. I was moved by the sincerity of "Tell Mother I'll be there."

When I was a little Christian, my mother, bless her soul, was very happy to see this. However, I became a prodigal and walked away from the saints and their wonderful testimonies. I wanted to experience "the world" and its enchantments.

Many years have passed. I no longer have questions about the hope that lies in me. I no longer look to Kant, Hegel or Marx to solve the problems within my soul. Let the bells of heaven ring and may He who opens the Book of Life on the final day hear me say, "Tell mother I'll be there, in answer to her prayer; Tell mother I'll be there, Heav'n's joys with her to share;

Yes, tell my darling mother I'll be there."

Happy reading!

Sincerely,
EDGAR HENRY
New York.

ACKNOWLEDGEMENTS

I thank the following for their contributions to this literary effort:

My wife, Cleopatra, for her encouragement, suggestions and internet services.

George Davson for his sketches.

Edgar Henry for editing.

The Very Rev. Eddie Alleyne, Rector St. Gabriel's Episcopal Church, for his support.

Ivonne Waldron, Henry Jones, Oswald Bobb, Selwyn Felix, Orin VanRossum, Carlyle Douglas, Haris Edwards, Harold Alves, Birchfield Moore, Everton Griffith, Alfred Hubbard, George Duggan and William Wright for their encouragement.

INTRODUCTION

My heart leaps up when I behold
A rainbow in the sky:
So was it when my life began;
So is it now I am a man;

.... William Wordsworth

I must confess that this introduction is a kind of catharsis. I am cleansing myself of the cynicism, doubt and indifference of adulthood and returning to the days of my boyhood and teenage innocence, when to live was in Christ and everyday brought new spiritual pleasures. I will see again the family, friends, pastors, mentors long since gone, but whose influences remain with me as fresh as they were then.

> Strange that the mind will forget so much of what only this moment has passed, and yet hold clear and bright the memory of what happened years ago—of men and women long since dead .... Can I believe my friends all gone when their voices are still a glory in my ears? No. And I will stand to say no and no again, for they remain a living truth within my mind. There is neither fence nor hedge round Time that is gone. You can go back and have what you like of it, if you can remember. [1]

My mother was a wonderful Christian, who raised my sisters and me to believe in the Word of God as a guide for daily living. Every day she held family worship after we, children, had our baths and before breakfast. She

---

[1]   Tim Dirkss. Reviews Richard Llewelyn's How Green was My Valley.

would read and explain a passage of scripture, after which one of us would say prayers. She would always say, "When you go to school, remember that God is with you and he will help you with your English and sums (arithmetic). Do unto others as you would have them do unto you."

Most parents in our neighbourhood must have taught their children the same lesson, because my elementary school, St. Ambrose, was well behaved. Like every school, there were bad behaved children. Bad behaved girls were wild-caned in their hands. The boys recived bakers' dozens on their backsides.

My father was well read and his library contained books on religion, philosophy and mysticism. My favourite author in his library was Marie Corelli ((1855-1924), the brilliant British novelist, whose books sold more than her illustrious contemporaries, Sir. Arthur Conan Doyle, H.G. Welles and Rudyard Kipling combined.

Life Everlasting remains my favourite Corelli. Forget the creed, dogma, belief, call it what you will, of Corelli. Her words questioned my assumptions about Christianity and challenged me to live according to the true standard of Christ. Here are some words from the prologue of that book.

> From the first dawn of his intelligence, man appears always to have felt the necessity of believing in something stronger and more lasting than himself,—and his first gropings for truth led him to evolve desperate notions of something more cruel, more relentless, and more wicked than himself, rather than ideals of something more beautiful, more just, more faithful and more loving than he could be.

> The dawn of Christianity brought the first glimmering suggestion that a gospel of love and pity might be more serviceable in the end to the needs of the world, than a ruthless code of slaughter and vengeance-though history shows us that the annals of Christianity itself are stained with crime and shamed by the shedding of innocent blood. Only in these latter days has the world become faintly conscious of the real Force working behind and through all things—the soul of the Divine, or the Psychic element, animating and inspiring all visible and invisible Nature.

> It would be impossible to the people of this or any other country to honestly believe the Christian creed, and yet continue to live

as they do. Their lives give the lie to their avowed religion, and it is this daily spectacle of the daily life of governments, trades, professions and society which causes me to feel that the general aspect of Christendom at the present day, with all its Churches and solemn observances, is one of the most painful and profound hypocrisy.[2]

Corelli's harshness aside, I agreed with her then and now that many of us who profess to be Christians do not live according to the teachings of Christ. We sin during the week and attend church on Sunday and ask God to forgive us. Next week we do it all over. Our confession has become a ritual instead of an honest plea. We are hypocrites and the truth is not in us. Thanks to God, there are among us persons of faith, whose justified lives, are testimonies to lives lived in Christ.

I was determined to live according to the teachings of Christ by the grace and mercies of God.

Although my father did not share many of my mother's religious beliefs, he approved of the manner in which she was raising us. She followed the precept, "Train up a child in the way he should go: and when he is old, he will not depart from it." (Proverbs 22:6)

As a child and, later, as a teenager, I worshipped with her at the Pilgrim Holiness Church, in Guyana, South America. It was a bible-believing church, where only the "born again" were accepted to membership. On Sunday, I attended Sunday school and morning services. At 3'0clock I went to Mr. Knapp's Sunday school and at 7 o'clock, I attended evening service. On Wednesday night I went to "testimony meeting", where believers praised God for his goodness.

Tears come to my eyes when I remember that many of them were poor and lived day by day through God's mercies and relatives', friends' and neighbors' kindness . I cannot remember any of them complaining about their lot. There were always smiles on their faces and praises to God

Friday night was Young Peoples' meeting, where Christian youth of the church studied the Word of God and interacted with one another in a Christian way.

My mother's parents had migrated from Barbados. Her father, William Nurse, was a preacher in the Christian Mission and she and her siblings

---

[2]   Marie Corelli, The Life Everlasting, prologue, Fullbooks.com, April 29, 2011.

attended his church. That was before I was born. When I came into this world, she was a Methodist and I was baptized at Trinity Methodist Church, D'urban and High streets in Georgetown, British Guiana.

The minister was the Rev. E.S.M. Pilgrim, a learned and brilliant preacher, who had migrated from Barbados and held an M.A. from Cambridge University. In those days the established churches—Methodist, Presbyterian, Lutheran, Catholic and Anglican—were led by brilliant men with remarkable oratorical skills and amazing knowledge of the word of God. I am fortunate to have heard the best of the lot—Rev. Aaron Theophilus Peters (Ketley and Clarkson churches) Rev. Pat Mathews (Smith's Church Memorial); Dereyck U. Adams (Bedford Methodis); Rt. Rev. Alan John Knight (Archbishop of the West Indies and British Guiana) and Archdeacon Pattison Muir, Rector Christ Church Anglican.

I was particularly impressed by Archdeacon's eloquence and learning and visited him at his manse regularly. He became one of my mentors and my friend. He was a historian and told me about Sir Winston Churchill's "History of the English Speaking People", Arnold Toynbee's "World History" and about Hewlett Johnson, the Red Dean of Canterbury and many other intellectual and religious luminaries.

In those days, white people thought that we, the natives, were "the white man's burden." Archdeacon considered us as human beings, who yearned for conversion. He cared sincerely for his flock and considered himself a leader among equals

I developed a lifelong love of history from my conversations with this great, but humble man. If my love for my mother were not as great as it were, and if I did not enjoy being with her at the Pilgrim Holiness on Sundays, I should have sat at his feet every Sunday.

I never ceased asking Archdeacon questions about God, the church and matters of faith. He answered all my inquiries with a smile. On one occasion, I remember him telling me that it was important to ask questions about the things I hear in church, because it was the only way I could have a clear understanding of Christian doctrine. He also told me that prayer was the single most powerful weapon for personal development, that "more things are wrought by prayer than this world dreams of." He also taught me not to wallow in self-righteousness, but thank God for his free gift of salvation. He loved repeating words attributed to John Bradford (around 1510-1555), "There but for the grace of God go I."

My church was not only a bible-believing church; it was a church that took Jesus' Great Commission seriously. Before his ascension, Jesus commanded his disciples, "Go into all the world and preach the good news to all creation."(Mark 16:15 New Living Translation).

This Commission cannot be fully understood in isolation. It must be considered with other passages. One such is Acts 1:8, "you will receive power when the Holy Spirit comes on you; and you will be my witnesses in Jerusalem, and in all Judea and Samaria, and to the ends of the earth." The message begins in the local church (Jerusalem) and spreads to the surrounding communities and, sometimes, throughout the world.

God used my local church as an agent of instruction, as a way of teaching me how to understand and follow the Scriptures and the Great Commission. The message of salvation was good news and I could not keep it to myself. I became a roadside preacher, presenting God's love to a fallen humanity. I preached love instead of fear, because God is love. Jesus did not come to save the righteous, but sinners to repentance. Mine was not a fire and brimstone ministry. I preached salvation instead of damnation. Instead of eternal hell I preached that, "In my father's house are many mansions" prepared for those who repent.

I went all over Georgetown, the capital of Guyana, preaching repentance unto salvation in Jesus' name. I enjoyed preaching at the road corners, because I met the sinner face to face. I made many calls to "give your heart to Jesus and be born again" and, thanks be to God, many persons were converted.

I took my Christianity seriously and read many books relating to my faith. My cousin, Rev. Leslie Miller, who became General Superintendent of Pilgrim Holiness churches in British Guiana (now Guyana) loaned me History of the Jews by the esteemed Jewish historian Flavius Josephus. He gave me John Bunyan's 'Pilgrim's Progress. Among other books that helped develop my Christian intellect were Charles H. Spurgeon's All of Graceland and A Defense of Christianity; Dwight L. Moody, The Overcoming Life, Victor Hugo's The Hunchback of Notre Dame and John Bunyan's Pilgrim's Progress.

I never missed bible study. My mother was my support. She did not read as much as dad, but she was firmly grounded in the word of God. She prayed with and for me regularly. Her life, not only her words, made me a better Christian. I learned more about the Christian life from her than all the books I ever read. Her life was a book of History, the leaves of which were days; the letters were mercies closely joined and the title was God's praise. She walked the talk.

At the age of 19, I left Pilgrims. I had been repeatedly asking questions about church doctrine and received no adequate answers. Instead of pointing me to the ways of truth, my pastors were more concerned with teaching me a lesson of not to question, only accept. Despite my polite curiosity, they shouted repeatedly, "Sit down, Brother Handel."

The fundamentalism that once entranced me now had little or no effect, because I began applying logical method to things of faith. Many years later, I discovered that faith does not submit to scientific analysis. In St. Paul's wonderful words, "Faith is the substance of things hoped for, the evidence of things not seem." (Hebrews 11:1)

Over the years I visited Lutheran, Anglican/Episcopal, Baptist, Pentecostal and other churches. Eight years ago, I began worshipping at an Anglican Church.

I approach the writing of this book with humility and as a life-long student of the Holy Scripture and its history. Initially, I thought of discussing my themes within the framework of Christianity, Judaism, Islam, Hinduism, Buddhism and other ancient religions. However, discretion had the better part of me and I narrowed my references to Judaism and Christianity in the majority of cases.

Christianity includes a variety of denominations and, necessarily, a variety of views. To describe all of these would require a document much larger than what I contemplate. Therefore, I will, more or less, discuss views best representative of the investigated positions.

I am a man of faith and hold most of the doctrines of the church. However, I believe that my beliefs should not prevent me from discussing other points of view. Consequently, I have presented opinions I agree with as well as those with which I disagree. The reader will decide if I achieved impartiality.

CHAPTER BY CHAPTER DESCRIPTION

Part One

Chapter 1: **In the Beginning**
This chapter asks questions about the origin and development of the universe, earth and man from the standpoints of science, religion and myth and analyses their answers.

Chapter 2: **The Christian Bible**
Discusses the history of the Jewish and Christian bibles; their canons, criteria used in determining same and whether, among other things, the bible is the inerrant word of God.

Chapter 3: **The Christian Church**
Among other things, this chapter traces Church history from the Apostolic Church to modern times, including the two Schisms, persecutions under various Roman Emperors and the birth of denominations.

Chapter 4: **Jewish Sects**
This chapter traces to 70 ACE the history and teachings of ancient Jewish sects.

Chapter 5: **The Life and Teachings of Jesus**
Jesus (Yeshua in Aramaic) is the central figure of Christianity. I discuss the historical and biblical Jesus and his teachings. I also analyze theories about his "missing years."

Chapter 6: **Judaism and Christianity**
This chapter analyses the origin, similarities and differences between these two religions.

Chapter 7: **Jewish Myth and History**
This chapter examines the historicity of biblical stories.

Chapter 8: **John the Baptist's Question**
This is a brief chapter on John the Baptist and the significance of his question, "Are you he that cometh, or look we for another?"

Part Two

Chapter 9: **Question of Evil**
This is an examination of the various theories about the origin of evil.

Chapter 10: **Fruit of the Spirit**
This chapter discusses the Fruit of the Spirit, described in Galatians 5:22.

Chapter11: **Justification**
This is a discussion of a fundamental Christian doctrine and traces its history from earliest times to present.

Chapter 12: **Understanding the End Times**
This is an analysis of Preterism, Millenniumism, the Rapture and the Last Judgment.

Part Three

Chapter 13: **Best loved hymns**
I am a sentimentalist and music has always charmed me. In the words of John Armstrong, "Music exalts each joy, allays each grief, expels diseases, subdues the rage of poison, and softens every pain." This is my testimony through the words of some of the hymns I dearly love.

PART ONE

CHAPTER ONE

In the Beginning

According to Aristotle, philosophy begins with a sense of wonder about the world, and the most profound question a man can ask concerns the origin of the universe.

—William Lane Craig

The actual point of creation, the singularity, is outside the scope of presently known physics.

—J. Narlikar

In the beginning God created the heaven and the earth.

Genesis 1:1

Humans have always asked questions about the origin of the universe, earth and life and have given answers based on science, religion and myth. Each approach has its own method. Scientific method involves hypothesis, observation / experiment and a verified conclusion. The basic step in religion is faith based on the word of God (the bible). There are really no steps in myth, since a myth is a traditional story with or without a determinable basis of fact or a natural explanation.

Science and the Universe

The most popular scientific model about the origin of the universe is the Big Bang.

The Big Bang theory is an effort to explain what happened at the very beginning of our universe. Discoveries in astronomy and physics have shown beyond a reasonable doubt that our universe did in fact have a beginning. Prior to that moment there was nothing; during and after that moment there was something: our universe. The big bang theory is an effort to explain what happened during and after that moment.[3]

According to the Big Bang, "our universe sprang into existence as a "singularity" around 13.7 billion years ago."[4] Before it, matter and energy were contained in a singularity, a point with zero volume and high mass making the density. This singularity is found at the center of a black hole (an area of intense gravitational pressure and must not to be confused with a Black Hole singularity, which is created after the core of a very massive star collapses beyond an imaginary sphere. Matter floated in this vacuum until it exploded, flinging gas and energy in all directions.

Although this phenomenon is referred to as an explosion, it was, more or less, an expansion. After the tiniest fraction of a second, the strong nuclear and electromagnetic forces separated, causing the Universe to begin inflating or expanding. (The universe continues expanding or inflating). The gas began cooling and particles clang together. As cooling continued, the particles decelerated and became more organized, eventually growing into stars. This process took about a billion years. Approximately five billion years ago, some of this gas and matter became the sun of our solar system.[5]

The major evidences supporting the Big Bang are:

First of all, we are reasonably certain that the universe had a beginning.

Second, galaxies appear to be moving away from us at speeds proportional to their distance. This is called "Hubble's Law," named after Edwin Hubble (1889-1953) who discovered this phenomenon in 1929. This observation supports the expansion

---

[3.] Big Bang Theory, All About Science, Colorado Springs, Colorado, 2002, June 2011.

[4] Big Bang Theory

[5] Big Bang Theor

of the universe and suggests that the universe was once compacted.

Third, if the universe was initially very, very hot as the Big Bang suggests, we should be able to find some remnant of this heat. In 1965, Radio astronomers Arno Penzias and Robert Wilson discovered a 2.725 degree Kelvin (-454.765 degree Fahrenheit,—270.425 degree Celsius) Cosmic Microwave Background radiation (CMB) which pervades the observable universe. This is thought to be the remnant which scientists were looking for. Penzias and Wilson shared in the 1978 Nobel Prize for Physics for their discovery.

Finally, the abundance of the "light elements" Hydrogen and Helium found in the observable universe are thought to support the Big Bang model of origins. [6]

Judaea-Christian Universe

Although there are many interesting discussions on this topic in the Jewish Kabala (a discipline and school of thought concerned with the mystical aspect of Rabbinic Judaism) and Duetero-canonical books (books considered by the Roman and Eastern Orthodox Churches to be canonical parts of the Old Testament but are not present in the Hebrew Bible , I will limit my discussion to the Old Testament as found in the King James Version, which states that our universe was created by God in the beginning. Both the Jewish and Christian bibles begin with the sentence, "In the beginning God created the heaven and the earth . . . . ." (Genesis 1:1)

I believe that God has always been and is the Alpha "beginning." God (whatever your concept of this entity) was before time. Therefore, I would interpret Genesis 1:1 as: "By his will, God caused the heaven and the earth." God willed the universe into becoming from nothing (ex nihilo).

Persons who believe that God created the heavens are called Creationists and are usually classified as Young-earth Creationists (YEC) and Old-earth Creationists (OLC). The former interpret the Genesis 1 account literally.

---

[6] Big Bang Theory.

They believe that God created the universe out of nothing within six 24-hour periods 6,000 years ago and rested on the seventh day. The latter also believe that God created the universe within 6 days. However; they interpret the days as ages and believe that the universe is billions of years old.

Science and earth

Scientists believe that the universe began with two elements, hydrogen and helium gas, which formed stars that burned these elements in nuclear fusion reactions.

> Generations of stars were born in gas clouds and died in explosive novas. The conditions in those novas produced the heavier elements we have with us today.........some 5 billion years ago in a perfectly ordinary place in the galaxy, a supernova exploded, pushing a lot of its heavy-element wreckage into a nearby cloud of hydrogen gas and interstellar dust. The mixture grew hot and compressed under its own gravity, and at its center a new star began to form. Around it swirled a disk of the same material, which grew white-hot from the great compressive forces. That new star became our Sun, and the glowing disk gave rise to Earth and its sister planets. [7]

Science hypothesizes that earth formed approximately 4.6 billion years ago. At first, it was very hot and volcanic and no life existed on it. A solid crust formed as the planet cooled and impacts from asteroids and other debris caused craters. As the planet continued cooling, water, which had formed on the surface, filled the basins, creating oceans.[8]

Scientists determined the age of the earth using radiometric dating techniques on rocks and meteorites found on earth. Science Dictionary defines

---

[7]   Andrew Alden, Earth's Formation in a Nutshell, About.com, November 11, 2011.

[8]   Tracy V. Wilson. How the Earth Works, HowStuff Works, 1998-2011, March 9, 2011.

radiometric dating technique as, "A process for determining the age of an object by measuring the amount of a given radioactive material it contains."[9]

If one knows how much of this radioactive material was present initially in an object (by determining how much of the material has decayed) and also knows the half-life of the material, one can deduce the age of the object. The best known example of radioactive dating employs carbon 14, a radioactive isotope of carbon.

Rocks: Ancient rocks older than 3.5 billion years have been found on all of earth's continents. Science Daily 9/26/2008 reported that McGill University researchers had discovered the oldest whole rocks on Earth. These rocks, known as "faux-amphibolites", may be remnants of a portion of Earth's primordial crust—the first crust that formed at the surface of our planet. They were found in Northern Quebec, along the Hudson's Bay coast. Their estimated age, using isotopic dating, is 4.28 billion years.

There have been dates of 4.36 billion years from Western Australia for isolated resistant mineral grains called zircons. There were also dated rocks known as the Acasta Gneiss in the Northwest Territories, which are 4.03 billion years old. However, dating earth from the formation of rocks is unreliable, because earth's rocks have been recycled and destroyed by the collision of totonic plates.

Meteorites: A more reliable way for dating earth is by measuring meteorites found on earth. Science assumes that meteorites and earth formed at the same time. Therefore, the age of meteorites would be the same as the age of earth if it had been completely preserved. So far, 70 of these meteorites have been measured and scientists determine that they were formed 4.54 billion years ago. Thus, according to science, the age of the earth is 4.54 billion years.

Bible and Earth

The bible states that God created Earth on the third day:

> And God said; Let the water under heaven be gathered together unto one place. And let the dry land appear; and it was so. And God called the dry land earth. And the Gathering together of

---

[9]   Radioactive Dating, Dictionary.com., , 2011 November 10, 2011.

waters he called seas. And the evening and the morning were the third day." (Genesis 1:9-10, 13.).

According to this verse, earth was created by divine speech in an instantaneous act during one day, called the third day. Some bible scholars claim the day was 24 hours, while others assert it could have been many centuries in length.

Most OEC accept the 4.5 billion year estimate of the Earth's age currently advocated by most scientists. Some accept this, but believe that a day can represent a 24 hour period or a long time. Others posit a long period of billions of years between the first 24 hour day of creation and the second.[10]

The majority of the Early Church Fathers believed that earth was 6,000 years old or less—St. Barnabas(?-61ACE), Bishop Irenaeus (70-135 BCE), Hippolytus (-235 ACE), and Sextus Iulius Africanus 160-240 ACE), to name a few. Clement of Alexandria (152-217 ACE), Origen (185-254 ACE) and St. Augustine (354-430 ACE) argued strenuously that the earth was much older. However the former position remained the established position until the Enlightenment.

In 1642, Sir John Lightfoot (1602-1675), churchman, distinguished Rabbinical scholar and Vice-Chancellor of Cambridge University, championed the YEC theory and stated that "the moment of creation was 9:00 AM, September 17th, 3928 BC."[11]

> That Lightfoot's day of Creation occurred during 3929 BC can be deduced from the last page of the "Prolegomena" of The Harmony of the Four Evangelists, among themselves, and with the Old Testament (1644). The quoted year of 1644 must be subtracted from 5573, not 5572, to obtain 3929 BC, during which year 1 of the world began at the (autumnal) equinox.

> And now, he that desireth to know the year of the world, which is now passing over us,—this year, 1644,—will find it to be 5572 years

---

[10]   B. A. Robinson, "Estimates of the age of the earth", Religious Tolerance, March7, 2011.

[11]   Kathy A. Miles and Charles F. Pets II, The Age of the Earth, Kathy A. Miles and Charles F. Peters1 2001, March 7, 2011.

just finished since the creation; and the year 5573 of the world's age, now newly begun, this September, at equinox. [IV: 112]

The only date for the equinox given by Lightfoot was in a 'private' undated sermon entitled "The Sabbath Hallowed":

That the world was made at equinox, all grant,—but differ at which, whether about the eleventh of March, or twelfth of September; to me in September, without all doubt. [VII: 372]."[12]

In the 17th Century, one of the most brilliant men of his time, decided to further the 6,000 year view. James Ussher was born 1581 in Dublin, Ireland, died 1656 and was buried in Westminster Abbey on instructions from Oliver Cromwell, then Lord Protectorate of England. Ussher was professor, Vice-Chancellor of Trinity College, Dublin, expert in Church History, Latin, Greek and Semitic languages, member of the Ireland Privy Council and Archbishop of Armagh in the Irish Anglican Church. In the "Annals of the Old Testament, deduced from the first origins of the world" (published in two parts, in 1650 and 1654 respectively and an English translation published in 1658, after his death.), he asserted that the earth was 6,000 years old and was created in 4004 BCE:

1a AM, 710 JP, 4004 BC On the third day Ge 1:9-13 (Tuesday, October 25th) when these waters below ran together into one place, the dry land appeared. From this collection of the waters God made a sea, sending out from here the rivers, which were to return there again. Ec 1:7 He caused the earth to bud and bring forth all kinds of herbs and plants with seeds and fruits." [13]

Because there was no certain knowledge of nations' history preceding the Persian Empire, Bishop Ussher relied entirely on the bible, which he considered inerrant, for his knowledge of these periods. He chose Nebuchadnezzar's death (562 BCE) as the anchor for earlier biblical dates.

---

[12] Ussher-Lightfoot Calendar—Definition, WordIq.com, 2010, March 10, 2011.

[13] James Ussher, .Annals of the World, London 1658, March 6, 2011.

Thus, working backwards from that date, he arrived at 4004 BCE as the date for the creation of earth.

Currently, only a few Fundamentalists hold the YEC age of the earth. The majority of Christians hold the OEC dates.

Science and origin of Man

Evolutionists believe that four billion years ago, particles on earth clang together randomly to form proteins and DNA molecules, and that from that 'particle-clang' process, single-cell life forms grew in the primordial soup of early earth to become humans."[14]

The most prominent scientific theory about the evolution of man proposes that humans and apes derive from an apelike ancestor that lived on earth a few million years ago.

> The theory states that man, through a combination of environmental and genetic factors, emerged as a species to produce the variety of ethnicities seen today, while modern apes evolved on a separate evolutionary pathway.[15]

Charles Darwin (1809-1882) who wrote The Origin of Species (1859) is arguably the most famous biological evolutionist. His theory of human evolution was based largely on observations he made during his 5-year voyage around the world aboard the HMS Beagle (1831-1836). He is erroneously thought to have stated that man is descended from the ape. What he said was that there is a gap in the fossil record and he did not know where man came from.[16]

> The theory of evolution of man is supported by a set of independent observations within the fields of anthropology, paleontology and molecular biology. Collectively, they depict life branching out

---

14   Stuart Wilde, "Where Did Humans Come From (The Fourth Alternative), Stuart Wilde 2009, March 9, 2011.

15   "Evolution of Man - - Theory Concepts", All about Science.org,, Colorado Springs, Colorado 2002, June 2010.

16   Stuart Wilde. Where Did Humans Come

from a common ancestor through gradual genetic changes over millions of years, commonly known as the "tree of life."[17]

The chain of human evolution started with the genus Australopithecus. This creature was not a human, but an intermediate between ape and human. However, both were biologically similar enough to be classified as members of the Homini tribe. Both were two-footed, upright walkers. By comparison, chimpanzees, bonobos and gorillas are primarily quadruped or four-footed.

Australopithecus

According to scientific evidence, earliest australopithecines (group of different kinds of Australopithecus) emerged about 4 million years ago and were common in East and South Africa by 3 million years ago. At least seven species have been identified by fossil record and skull discovery:

Australopithecus anamensis was named in August 1995. The material consists of 9 fossils, mostly found in 1994, from Kanapoi in Kenya, and 12

---

[17]   "Evolution of Man", All about Science.

fossils, mostly teeth found in 1988, from Allia Bay in Kenya. Anamensis existed between 4.2 and 3.9 million years ago,

Australopithecus afarensis existed between 3.9 and 3.0 million years ago. It was named by D. Johanson and T. White in 1978. Perhaps its best known example is ("Lucy"), a 3.2 million year old partial skeleton found in November 1974 at Hadar, Ethiopia

Kenyanthropus platyops, which means "Flat faced man of Kenya", was named in 2001 from a partial skull found in Kenya by Justus Erus, a member of a team led by Meave Leakey, in 1999 at Lomekwi in Kenya. Estimated age is between 3.5 and 3.2 million years. With an unusual mixture of features, it is about 3.5 million years old.

Australopithecus africanus existed between 3 and 2 million years ago and is similar to afarensis. It was discovered by Raymond Dart at the lime mine at Taung near Kimberley, South Africa in 1924.

Australopithecus sediba was discovered at the site of Malapa in South Africa in 2008. Two partial skeletons of a young boy and an adult female, dated between 1.78 and 1.95 million years ago, were found

Australopithecus aethiopicus s existed between 2.6 and 2.3 million years ago. This species is known from one major specimen, the Black Skull, discovered by Alan Walker. A few other minor specimens, which may belong to the same species, had a body similar to that of africanus, but a larger and more robust skull and teeth. It existed between 2 and 1.5 million years ago.

Approximately 2.3 million years ago, the homo genus emerged. Some scientists claim it evolved from the australopithecines. Others say it had moved away from that group and evolved on its own. Different species lived in Tanzania, Kenya, Ethiopia and South Africa.

Species of the Homo Genus:

Sahelanthropus tchadensis was named in July 2002 from fossils discovered in Chad in Central Africa. It is the oldest known hominid or near-hominid species, dated at between 6 and 7 million years old.

Orrorin tugenensis was named in July 2001 from fossils discovered in western Kenya. The fossils include fragmentary arm and thigh bones, lower jaws, and teeth and were discovered in deposits that are about 6 million years old. The limb bones are about 1.5 times larger than those of Lucy, and suggest that it was about the size of a female chimpanzee.

Ardipithecus ramidus was named in September 1994 from some fragmentary fossils dated at 4.4 million years.

Homo habilis lived from about 2.4 to 1.5 million years ago. It was an upright east African hominid having some advanced humanlike characteristics and the first of the homo genus to appear.

Homo erectus / Homo ergastor possessed upright stature but small brain. The former was found in Asia and the latter in Africa. This specie lived 1.8-2 million years ago.

Homo Antecessor existed 800,000 years ago and was found in Spain.

Homo heildelbergensis existed 500,000-100,000 years ago and was found in Africa, India, China and Europe.

Homo neanderthalensis existed 130,000 years ago and was found in Europe, East Asia and the Middle East.

Homo soloensis is a sub-specie of Homo erectus

Homo rudolfensis existed about 1.9 million years ago.

Homo sapiens is the only surviving hominid specie. Modern humans are members of this specie, which has existed since 200,000 years ago.[18]

In 2000, Kenyan and French scientists unearthed fossilized remains of man's earliest ancestor dated at approximately 6 million years. They named the creature Millennium Man. To whatever genus it belongs, it is considered the oldest ancestor of man.

There are two ways of looking at the age of man from the standpoints of science. If we regard Australopithecus as the ancestor of man and include him in the discussion as man, then man is 4 million years old, as old as Australopithecus. If we believe that man emerged when the homo genus emerged, then man is 2.3 million years old, as old as the first homo specie. If we believe that man emerged when Homo sapiens emerged, then man is 200,000 years old, as old as Homo sapiens.

The Bible and Man's Age

Most Christians are Creationists, who believe that human beings were created by God as a developed entity and were not the product of evolution. However, they disagree about the age of the creature.

---

[18]   Jim Foley, Hominid Species, March 4, 2011.

Young Earth Creationists (YEC) believe that humans were created 6,000-10,000 years ago. Until the 17ᵗʰ Century, it was the only view of man's age. The majority of the Early Church Fathers, Martin Luther and John Calvin held this belief. Perhaps the most powerful proponent of this belief was James Ussher, whose biographical details were given earlier.

He arrived at the age of man by adding the genealogies from Adam to Abraham (Genesis 5, 11) and from Abraham to the 17ᵗʰ Century. Calculated literally from the Bible it adds up to 6,000 years. Adding from the 17ᵗʰ Century to present, young earth creationists arrive at the age of man at 10,000 or thereabouts.

Old Earth Creationists (OEC) believe that man is much older than 10,000 years and some agree with the figures of Science.

Sumerian and Babylonian myths

Sumer and Babylon held a common view of the universe, based on water as the originating primordial substance. Sumerian cosmogony began with the primordial sea, Nammu, the mother of all. She created An (sky), a hard metallic shell, which lies on Earth, and Ki (earth). Their union produced Enlil, the god of air, wind and storm. Enlil lifted An away from Ki, filling the space which man inhabits. The space was filled with Lil (atmosphere). Its brighter parts formed the sun, moon, and stars.

Enlil also created all living things, except humans, who were created by his son Enki from clay in the image of the gods.

The Babylonians

Like the Sumerians, Babylonian cosmogony began with the primordial sea, composed of two types of water: fresh, deified in Apsu (male) and salt, deified in Tiamat (female). After a period of time, new gods, the children of Apsu and Tiamat, appeared. These were very noisy and Apsu complained that he could not rest during night or day. Consequently, he planned to kill them. However, they took preventative steps. They killed first Apsu and then Tiamat. Marduk, who became the chief god, split Tiamat's body in two. One half became the firmament and the other half became the Earth. Tiamat's spittle provided rain and clouds. Her head became mountains.

Critique

In this chapter I presented the scientific and religious views of the origin and age of the universe, earth and humans. Many questions remain. Is Science accurate in its calculations? Is religion reasonable in its belief in a Creator and its insistence that man was created complete and not a process of evolution?

Science and the Universe

I discussed the most popular and reasonable scientific model for explaining the origin of the universe—the Big Bang. Its hypotheses are set out in scientific models that describe the Universe as expanding or inflating from a very hot, dense state approximately 13.7 billion years ago.

However, some critics argue that it "is pure presumption, because there are no physical principles from which it can be deduced that all matter in the universe would ever gather together in one location, or from which it can be deduced that an explosion would occur if the theoretical aggregation did take place."[19]

With respect to the very dense state that existed at the beginning, Richard Feynman contends that, "This concept of infinite density is not scientific. It is an idea from the realm of the supernatural, as most scientists realize when they meet infinities in other physical contexts."[20]

Scientists posit that the Big Bang was the beginning of the expansion of space-time from a singularity. However, they have not accounted for the beginning of space-time. Where did it come from? The argument of Big Bang Apologists is that it came from nothing. I do not think such an

---

[19] Origin and Evolution of the Universe, Chapter 1 Origin and evolution of Matter Part 1, Evolution Encyclopedia Vol. 1. Evolution -facts.org, ALTAMONT, TN, March 4, 2011.

20 Evolution Encyclopedia Vol. 1. Origin and Evolution of the Universe.

answer is definitive, since something must have existed before space-time and might have even caused it.

That something could be God, a first cause or a first principle. However, science cannot accept this direction, because it is outside the realm of rational thinking with which science deals exclusively. Hence, science is left with an arbitrary starting point, which, like Intelligent Design, has to be accepted on its own account. In other words, the Big bang is pure speculation.

Creationists and the Universe

Creationists believe that God created the universe. They believe this as a fact based on Genesis 1:1. Time's immemorial question is, If God created the universe, who/what created God? Christians answer that God has always been. Therefore nothing could have created Him. He is the Alpha, the Beginning, and his existence and works must be accepted by faith. "Through faith we understand that the worlds were framed by the word of God, so that things which are seen were not made of things which do appear." (Hebrews 11:3)

Science and Earth

According to Science, earth formed as particles collected within a giant disc of gas orbiting what would become our sun. Once the sun ignited, it blew the extra particles away, leaving the solar system and earth. However, this scientific supposition fails to provide evidence showing how earth formed within the disc and how matter and gas originated.

Creationists and Earth

I disagree with Young Earth Creationists' estimate that Earth is 6,000 years old, because archaeologists have found hominids fossil millions of years old. Lucy, one of these, is dated 3.2 million years and Millennium Man 5 million years. Since these creatures lived on earth, it follows that earth had to be as old as them.

Science and Man

Most scientists conclude that particles on earth clang together randomly to form proteins and DNA molecules, and that from this 'particle-clang' process, single-cell life forms grew to become humans.

One critic of the theory contends that the formation of life would have required hundreds of thousands of proteins and that it would have been impossible for such a large quantity to combine randomly. He also contended that it would have been equally impossible for millions of DNA molecules to come together randomly.

> The chance of particles bumping together to form the right amino acid chain to establish one life-sustaining protein are 10 or 10 with one hundred and thirty zeros. Then the odds that millions of protein molecules happen into existence by chance, just as millions of DNA atoms also happened to become viable at the same instant, and that they bound together to form millions of species of animals, plants and insects here on earth, would be 10 to the power of all the zeros you could put down on a piece of paper between here and a distant galaxy."[21]

I accept that humans are millions of years old. Unlike the scientists (Big Bang and Evolutionary), I believe that man was created by God. I also believe that humans evolved to the Homo sapiens state over a process of time. I believe that all humans spring from a common ancestor created by God.

---

[21]   Stuart Wilde. Where Did Humans Come From?(The Fourth Alternative).

CHAPTER TWO

The Christian Bible

Never yet did there exist a full faith in the divine word which did
not expand the intellect, while it purified the heart; which did
not multiply and exalt the aims and objects of the understanding,
while it fixed and simplified those other desires and feelings.

—Samuel Taylor Coleridge

The word "bible" derives from the Greek word "bilia", meaning books.
It is used twice in scripture (Daniel 9:2 in the Septuagint and Timothy 4:3).
In this article, the term Christian Bible refers to the Jewish and Christian
canonized scriptures found in versions of the Holy Bible. I will discuss
its composition and versions, selection of its canon, "missing books" and
whether or not it is the inerrant word of God.

The Christian Bible is divided into 2 parts—Old Testament, which
is the first part and New Testament, the second part. The Old Testament
was written in Hebrew and Aramaic and the New Testament was written
in Greek (Alexandrian). The original manuscripts of the books included in
the bible are lost and bibles contain translations of copies. The following
are some of the many versions (translations) of the Bible:

The Septuagint

The Septuagint or "LXX" is the Greek (Alexandrian) version of the Old
Testament and is the earliest surviving version of these scriptures. The word
Septuagint is derived from the Latin "Septuaginta", meaning 70 and refers
to a tradition that claims 70 or 72 Alexandrian Jews completed these bible

translations during 285-246 BCE at Alexandria. The names "Septuagint" and "LXX" are of later Latin origin and are not used in the Greek bible. The usual Greek name for the translation is "kata tous ebdomekonta", meaning "according to the seventy." The original Septuagint was a translation of the Torah, the first 5 books of the Jewish bible.

The other books of the Hebrew bible were translated anonymously at a later date in an undetermined order. The later Septuagint contained most of the Jewish Apocrypha, a collection of 14 or 15 Jewish texts.

The books of the Apocrypha are called "Deutero-canonical" by the Roman Church, which uses the word "Apocrypha" to describe the Pseudepigrapha. The Wikipedia Free Encyclopedia defines these as "falsely attributed works, texts whose claimed authorship is unfounded; a work, simply, whose real author attributed it to a figure of the past."[22]

The Latin Vulgate

The Vulgate is a Latin version of the Bible translated, for the most part, by St. Jerome around 383-405 ACE at the instruction of Pope St. Damascus1 (366-384 ACE), who wished to replace the older Latin versions. The Council of Trent (the Ecumenical Council of the Roman Church held at Trento, Capital of the Prince-Bishopric of Trent in the Holy Roman Empire on December13, 1545 and December4, 1563) ruled it the official Bible of the Roman Church.

The Vulgate used today is not the Jerome version (He died without completing his work.). It was created by assembling books from a variety of sources, including Jerome. The Vulgate excludes the 2 books of Esdras.

Wycliffe Bible

In 1384, John Wycliffe (1328-1384), an Oxford Professor and Theologian, produced the first complete translation of the bible into English, using the Vulgate as his source. It was completely handwritten, because the printing press had not yet been invented.

---

[22] "Pseudepigraph", Wikipedia the free encyclopedia, last modified february 17, 2011, March 15, 2011.

He clashed with the Church over his views that its teaching was contrary to the bible, the Eucharist was pagan and that persons should be permitted to read the Bible in their language. Pope Gregory X1 was so angry with him that 44 years after he (Wycliffe) died, he ordered his bones unearthed, crushed and scattered in a nearby river. In 1405 the Oxford synod passed a resolution banning Wycliffe's bible.

The Great Bible

The Great Bible was the first authorized translation of the Bible into English. It was prepared by Myles Coverdale (1488-1569) and completed April 1539. Henry V111, then King of England, authorized it to be read at Church of England services.

The Bishop's Bible

This bible, first published in 1568 and revised in 1572, was authorized by the Church of England and was the base text for the Authorized King James Version.

King James Version

The most widely read of English bibles is the Authorized King James Version. In 1604, James 1, then King of England, authorized a new English translation of the Bible, which was completed in 1611 by 47 scholars of the Church of England. The phrase "Authorized Version" was first used in England in 1824 and the phrase "King James version" first appeared there in 1884.

Other versions

The foregoing described the most important versions of the bible. However, there were many other versions of the English bible corresponding to various changes in the language.

Anglo-Saxon or Old English

Anglo-Saxon or Old English was the language spoken by the Anglo-Saxons and their descendants between the 5th and 11th centuries ACE in, what is now, Britain.

The Wikipedia Free Encyclopedia states that although John Wycliffe is often credited with the first translation of the Bible into English, there were, in fact, many translations of large parts of the Bible centuries before his work. It says that toward the end of the 7th century, the Venerable Bede (673-735), "Father of English History" and Doctor of the Church, began a translation of Scripture into Old English.[23]

The Catholic Encyclopedia, a most reliable source on bible history, does not mention the great historian's translations, but credits him with commentaries on the Pentateuch and the Books of Kings, Esdras, Tobias and the Canticles. It also credits him with interpreting St. Mark, St. Luke, the Acts, the Canonical Epistles, and the Apocalypse.[24]

Aldhelm (640-709 ACE), West Saxon abbot of Malmesbury, the most learned teacher of 7th-century Wessex, a pioneer in the art of Latin verse

---

[23] "English translations of the bible", Wikipedia the free Encyclopedia, last modified February 12, 2011. Retrieved March 15, 2011.

[24] Herbert Thurston, "The Venerable Bede." The Catholic Encyclopedia, Vol. 2, New York: Robert Appleton Company, 1907, March 15, 2011.

among the Anglo-Saxons and the author of numerous extant writings in Latin verse and prose, translated the complete Book of Psalms and large portions of other scriptures into Old English.[25]

Abbot Ælfric(955-1020) " . . . . known as "the Grammarian", the author of the homilies in Anglo-Saxon, a translator of and a writer upon many miscellaneous subjects, also translated Holy Scripture into Middle English."[26]

Middle English

Middle English covers the period 1066-1500. Wycliffe's Bible was the only complete bible translation in the Middle Ages.

Modern English

Modern English was the language spoken in England between 1500 and 1800.

> This was the first major period of bible translation into the English language. It began with the dramatic introduction of Tyndale's Bible and included the landmark King James Version and Douai Bibles. It included the first "authorized version", known as the Great Bible (1539); the Geneva Bible (1560), notable for being the first Bible divided into verses; and the Bishop's Bible (1568), which was an attempt by Elisabeth I to again create an authorized version.[27]

The name given to the English from the 12th Century through 1470 is Early Middle English and Late Middle English covers the period 1470-1550. The period 1485 through the 17th century is usually referred to as the Early Modern English Period. The present-day English language is termed Modern English and covers the period from the 18th century

---

25   "Aldhelm Biography", Biographicon, n.d, March 15, 2011.

26   "Aelfric, Abbot of Eynsham." The Catholic Encyclopedia. Vol. 1. New York: Robert Appleton Company, 1907, March 15, 201

27   "English translations of the Bible", Wikipedia, March 15, 2011.

to present. New versions of the bible emerged during each of the periods mentioned.

The Canonical Books

These are the books approved by the Church for inclusion, and found, in the Christian bible. The earliest extant record of a canonical New Testament dates between 117-138 ACE. The processes by which the Old Testament was composed took many years and cannot be definitely determined.

The Tanakh is the word used in Judaism for the canon of the Hebrew Bible, the Christian Old Testament or Old Covenant. It is also known as the Masoretic Text or the Miqra. These number 39 in most Christian bibles and 24 in the Hebrew bible. The difference in the number of books is due to the fact that in the Jewish Bible several groupings of the books are combined into single books, kept on a single scroll.

The following books comprise the Jewish Bible:

1. Torah (Law) is composed of the first five books:

    a.   Genesis—Bereshith
    b.   Exodus—Shemot
    c.   Leviticus—Vayikra
    d.   Numbers—Bamidbar
    e.   Deuteronomy—Devarim

According to Judaism, Torah was the teaching Yahweh gave Moses to give to the Israelites. It is also called the Pentateuch (five books). It is also called the Written Torah, as distinct from the Oral Torah, which was also transmitted by Yahweh to Moses on Sinai.

2. The Prophets (Neviim) consists of 8 books: The Earlier Prophets and the Later Prophets.

Earlier Prophets

Joshua (Y'hoshua)

Judges (Shophtim)
Samuel (I & II) (Sh'muel)
Kings (I & II) (M'lakhim)
Isaiah (Y'shayahu)
Jeremiah (Yir'mi'yahu)
Ezekiel (Y'khezqel)

Later Prophets:

a. Hosea (Hoshea) Earlier
b. Joel (Yo'el)
c. Amos (Amos)
d. Obadiah (Ovadyah)
e. Jonah (Yonah)
f. Micah (Mikhah)
g. Nahum (Nakhum)
h. Habakkuk (Havakuk)
i. Zephaniah (Ts'phanyah)
j. Haggai (Khagai)
k. Zechariah (Z'kharyah)
l. Malachi (Mal'akhi)

Ketuvim"Writings" or "scriptures", also known by the Greek title "Hagiographa", consists of 11 books:

The poetic books
Psalms
Proverbs
Job

The "Five Scrolls":

Song of Songs (Shir Hashirim
Ruth (Rut)
Lamentations Eikhah
Ecclesiastes (Kohelet)
Esther (Esther)

The rest of the "Writings":

Daniel (Dani'el)
Ezra-Nehemiah (Ezra v'Nechemia)
Chronicles (I & II) (Divrei Hayamim)

Books quoted but not included in the Hebrew Bible:

The Book of the Wars of Yahweh (Numbers 21:14).
The Book of the Just (Jasher) (Joshua 10:13).
The Annals of King David 1 Chronicles 27:24
More about David written by Nathan the prophet; a book by
    Samuel the Seer (not 1-2 Samuel), and a book by Gad the
    Seer (1 Chron. 29:29).
A biography of Solomon in the history of Nathan the prophet;
    Visions of Iddo the seer (2 Chronicles 9:29).
The Annals of the Kings of Israel (1 Kings 14:19, 2 Chron. 33:
    18; cf. 2 Chron. 20:34).
The Annals of the Kings of Judah (1 Kings 14:29, 15).7
The Acts of Solomon (1 Kings 11:41).
Iddo's History of Judah (2 Chron. 13:22).
Annals of Jehu son of Hanani 2 Chron. 20:34
An unknown and untitled work of Isaiah(2 Chron. 26:22).
An unknown lament for Josiah by Jeremiah (2 Chron. 35:25).

The Apocrypha

The term "apocrypha", which means "hidden", "spurious", "missing"
"lost" or of uncertain origin, refers to books written between 400 BCE
and the 1st and 2nd centuries ACE and not included in most versions of
the Christian Bible. Most of these books were included in the King James
Version ((1611). In 1615, George Abbott, then Archbishop of Canterbury
(1611-1633), forbade issuing a bible without the Apocrypha upon
punishment of one year's imprisonment.

In 1885, Edward White Benson, then Archbishop of Canterbury
(1882-1896), ordered them removed from the King James Version. They

are still omitted from that version. However, some are found in the Catholic Bible. In the case of the Book of Jasher, it has always been completely suppressed. Two others, Jubilees and the Book of Enoch, are only found in Ethiopian Orthodox bibles.

There is an Old Testament Apocrypha and a New Testament Apocrypha. Most of the Old Testament apocrypha appear in the Septuagint and The Latin Vulgate Bible (Douai bible is its English translation), but are omitted in the Jewish, King James and other Protestant bibles.

Kevin P. Edgecomb observes with respect to the terms apocryphal, canonical and non-canonical:

> The terms "canonical, "non-canonical", "apocrypha," and "pseudepigraphal" are often confusing when cited in contemporary investigations of ancient Jewish and Christian literature. They are all anachronistic terms that later Christian communities used to describe literature that did or did not eventually find acceptance in the Hebrew and Christian Bibles. Initially most of those writings, if not all of them, functioned as sacred literature in one or more Jewish or Christian religious communities.[28]

Old Testament Apocrypha (OTA)

The original OTA were:

"1 Esdras" appears in the Latin and Septuagint bibles. "Esdras" is the Greek word for "Ezra" and most scholars assert that the book borrows heavily from the Book of Ezra, the book of Chronicles and the book of Nehemiah.

"2 Esdras" appears only in the Latin Bible. It is a Jewish apocalypse, first written in Greek about 100 ACE. Around 120 ACE, it was edited by an unknown Christian and translated into Latin. This book was not included in Septuagint manuscripts; consequently the Greek text is lost. The book consists mostly of dialogues between Ezra and angels sent to

---

[28]   Kevin P. Edgecomb, "SBL Notes, part two", Biblicalia, n.d., March 15, 2011.

him to answer his urgent theological questions about the problem of evil, and specifically, the failures and afflictions of Israel. The Book tells of how the Hebrew Scriptures were destroyed in the Babylonian exile and then perfectly restored by the miraculous inspiration of Ezra as he dictated all of the books to five scribes over a period of forty days. He also dictated 70 secret books that are to be reserved for the wise.

"Song of the Three Holy Children" (including The Prayer of Azariah) is an embellishment of the ordeal of Shadrach, Meshach, and Abednego recorded in the canonical book of Daniel. It consists of prayers and hymns of the type which the three young men might have made to God during their ordeal.

The "Book of Tobit" ("Book of Tobias" in the Roman bible) is included in the Roman and Septuagint bibles. It was written around 170-200 ACE in Hebrew or Aramaic as a didactic romance. It tells the story of Tobit, a devout Jew in exile in Assyria and his son Tobias. Despite his devoutness, he was blinded and prayed for death. The book also tells of Sarah, a widow whose seven husbands had each been killed by the demon Asmodeus on their wedding night. She also prayed for death.

God sent the angel Raphael to Earth to help them Tobias married Sarah and, with Raphael's help, overcame the demon and restored his father's sight.

"The Prayer of Manasseh" appears in both the Latin and Septuagint bibles. It is a psalm of repentance, composed to suit the situation of Manasseh, the king of Judah, who was carried captive to Babylon. It was rejected by the Roman Catholics at the Council of Trent in 1546.

"Judith" is included in the Roman and Septuagint bibles. It was written in Hebrew (now lost) around 150 BCE and translated shortly after into Greek. It is the story of a beautiful young widow named Judith (meaning "Jewess") who saved her city from a military siege. She went out to the enemy commander's camp, allured him, got him drunk and then cut off his head while he slept. She returned with his head and displayed it to her people, exhorting the men to go to battle and defeat the enemy. They went and were victorious.

The "Rest of Esther" (chapters 10-16) appears in both Roman and Septuagint bibles. It is credited to anEgyptian Jew writing around 170 BCE.

"First Maccabees" was written in Hebrew about 100 BCE and translated into Greek shortly after. Jerome testified to having seen the Hebrew text, which is now lost. The book is generally regarded as a historical account of events during the Hasmonean revolt during 175-135 BCE. It is regarded by historians as a source of accurate information. It is included in Catholic and Orthodox canons, but rejected by Protestants as apocryphal.

"Second Maccabees" is included in both Roman and Septuagint bibles. It is not a sequel to First Maccabees; but purportedly a history of the Jewish revolt against Antiochus IV and concludes with the defeat of the Syrians in 161 BCE. Probably written around 124 BCE by an Alexandrian Jew in Alexandria, most scholars consider it as fanciful and unhistorical. The writer's interests are religious rather than historical and he seeks to advance religious ideas current among the Jews of Alexandria during the first century BCE.. Some statements in the book support the Roman Catholic teachings on purgatory, prayers for the dead and the intercessory work of glorified "saints."

"Sirach" (also titled "Ecclesiasticus") is included in Roman and Septuagint bibles. "Ecclesiasticus", originally called "The Wisdom of Jesus son of Sirach", or simply "Sirach", was written first in Hebrew about 200 BCE by Joshua Ben Sirach and translated into Greek by his grandson around 135 BCE. The book consists mainly of proverbs and other wise sayings about common life, combined in discourses about religious life and faith. It was called "Ecclesiasticus" (the "churchly" book) because it was often read in church services and was regarded as the greatest of the apocryphal books.

"Baruch" is included in Septuagint and Roman bibles. It is a five-chapter book, containing exhortations against idolatry, a celebration of the Law as God's "wisdom" and encouragements and promises to faithful Jews. It was edited about 150 BCE.

"Epistle of Jeremiah" is included in Roman and Septuagint bibles and is often printed as chapter 6 of "Baruch." It is presented as a letter from Jeremiah to the Jews exiled in Babylon It is generally regarded as written around 200 BCE against pagan idolatry

"The Story of Susanna" does not appear in any version of the bible. It is a short story about how two old men, who used to indulge in excessive sex, tried to compel a beautiful and virtuous young wife, Susanna, to have sex with them. When she refused, they publicly accused her of adultery. At a trial, they gave false testimony and Susanna was condemned by the council of elders. However, Daniel the prophet, being divinely inspired concerning the facts, exposed the two men in a second trial, after which they were condemned and put to death. This story was inserted between chapters 12 and 14 in the Septuagint version of the "Book of Daniel."

"Bel and the Dragon", like "Susanna", is not found in any version of the bible. It is a combination of two stories which were also attached at the end of Daniel in the Septuagint. Bel related the story of Babylonian idol by that name, to which Daniel refused to give an offering. When he was challenged, he told the Persian king that the vain idol had no need of offerings because it could not eat anything. The king ordered the priests of Bel to disprove Daniel face death.

They tried to deceive the king by entering the temple of Bel at night through a secret entrance and ate the food-offerings themselves. Their scheme was exposed by Daniel, who had spread ashes on the temple floor, revealing their footprints. The priests of Bel were slain and their temple destroyed.

In the story of the "Dragon", Daniel refused to worship an actual living "dragon," and accepted a challenge to slay the dragon without sword or staff. He fed the dragon a concoction of pitch, fat and hair, which caused it to burst open and die. As a result, Daniel's enemies threw him into the lion's den. The hungry lions did not eat him, because they were filled after being fed with food brought from Israel by the prophet Habakkuk. Both of these stories were written circa 150-100 BCE.

Other Apocrypha

The "Book of Jasher"[29] or "Book of the Upright" (Sefer haYashar in the original Hebrew) is a most fascinating book that parallels Genesis in many respects and makes many passages and incidents in Genesis easier to understand. Interestingly, it was well known to ancient Hebrews, but was suppressed. The Prophet Joshua referred to it:

> And the Sun stood still, and the Moon stayed until the people had avenged themselves on their enemies. Is this not written in the Book of the Upright(Sēper haiYāšār)? (Joshua 10.13)

Second Samuel also mentions it:

> To teach the Sons of Judah the use of the bow; behold it is written in the Book of the Upright (Sēper haiYāšār)." (2 Samuel 1.18)

---

[29] Book of Jasher, J.H. Parry and Company, Salt Lake City, 1887, March 9, 2011.

The opening verse of the book is, "And God said, Let us make man in our image, after our likeness, and God created man in his own image." (Jasher 1.1)

This verse was once the beginning of the Hebrew Bible. Scholars are divided on a date when "Jasher" was written. Based on the fact that Joshua and Samuel quoted it, leads me to conclude that it was written earlier than these books. Joshua was written sometime between the 8th and 7th Century BCE and 2 Samuel (originally combined with 1Samuel in a single volume) was edited in the 6th Century BCE.

Most scholars consider the book authentic and accurate in its details. It was first translated from the Hebrew in 800 ACE and suppressed shortly afterwards, but "rediscovered" in 1829 ACE.

"Jasher" contains 91 chapters, written in correct and fluent Hebrew and describes Israelite history from Adam to that of the Judges in Israel. Three-fourths of the work is devoted to the pre-Mosaic period, one-fifth to the Mosaic period, and only three pages to later history

The book goes into more details than does Genesis about the Creation, the family of Adam, Enoch, Noah, Abraham, Moses and many early Israelites. As a case in point, did you know that Moses once ruled Ethiopia, which is called Kush in the bible? According to the "Book of Jasher":

> So Moses took the city by his wisdom, and the children of Cush placed him on the throne instead of Kikianus king of Cush. And they placed the royal crown upon his head, and they gave him for a wife Adoniah the Cushite queen, wife of Kikianus." (Jasher 73:30-36)[30]

Two other books bear the name of Book of Jasher. One is a Hebrew treatise on ethics and another, published in 1751, claims to have been translated from Hebrew into English by Flaccus Albinus Alcuinus. The latter is sometimes called Pseudo-Jasher to distinguish it from the third "Book of Jasher", which I have been describing.

The "Book of Enoch"[31] is, arguably, the most important of the "missing books." It is believed that Enoch, Noah's great grandfather, wrote it. Some believe that Noah took it with him into the ark.

---

[30]   Book of Jasher, J.H. Parry and Company, Salt Lake City, 1887, March 9, 2011.

[31]   BOOK OF ENOCH, Andy McCracken, Modern English   translation with introduction and notes. Exodus 2006, March 9, 2011.

Second and Third Century Church Fathers such as Justin Martyr, Bishop Irenaeus, Origen and Clement of Alexandria used and quoted it.

Although most scholars believe the book was written during the second century BCE, others believe it was written much earlier. It went out of circulation sometime between the 4th and 5th centuries ACE. In 1773, James Bruce, the famous Scottish explorer, returned to Scotland after spending 12 years in North Africa and Ethiopia. He returned with three Ethiopic copies of the lost book. In 1821 Richard Laurence published its first English translation. The famous R.H. Charles edition was published in 1912. In the following years several portions of the Greek text surfaced. With the discovery of cave 4 of the Dead Sea Scrolls, seven fragmentary copies of the Aramaic text were discovered.

The book is divided into the following five major sections:

1. "The Book of the Watchers" (chapters 1-36)
   The fallen angels, "Watchers," have sexual intercourse with women, who birth a race of giants, whose wickedness caused God to destroy them with a great flood. Once their demonic spirits have been released from their dead bodies, these demons wreak havoc in the world until the end time of judgment.

2. "The Book of the Similitudes or Parables" (chapters 37-71) Enoch's visions are interpreted by angels. This section primarily concerned with a figure called "the messiah"; "the righteous one"; "the chosen one" and "the son of man."

   And there I saw One who had a head of days,
   And His head was white like wool,
   And with Him was another being whose countenance had the
       appearance of a man,
   And his face was full of graciousness, like one of the holy angels.
   2) And I asked the angel who went with me and showed me all
       the hidden things, concerning that 3) Son of Man, who he
       was, and whence he was, (and) why he went with the Head
       of Days? And he answered and said unto me:
   This is the son of Man who hath righteousness,
   With whom dwelleth righteousness,
   And who revealeth all the treasures of that which is hidden."
       (Enoch 46:1-2)

The figure described in these verses is God's agent for the final judgment and vindication of the upright.

3. "The Book of Astronomical Writings" (chapters 72-82). This section describes visions of earthly and heavenly events. Enoch describes to his son Methuselah his journey through the stars above the earth, guided by the angel Uriel.

4. "The Book of Dream Visions" (chapters 83-90). Enoch tells Methuselah 2 visions he had. The first is of the sky falling and, as a result, the earth cataclysmic disasters. The second describes the history of humanity from the creation of Adam to the final judgment. In it, humans are represented as animals and angels are represented as human beings.

5. "The Book of the Epistle of Enoch" (chapters 91-107). This letter is written by Enoch for later generations. Noah tells Methuselah to gather all his brothers to hear about the future. Righteousness and wickedness are contrasted throughout to show that God will reward goodness and truth but punish evil and sin.

The "Book of Jubilees" [32]was purportedly written in the 2nd century BCE, and is a revelation given by God to Moses through the medium of an angel. It provides an instructive account of the biblical history of the world from creation to Moses. It is divided into "jubilees" (periods) of 49 years. Because each of these periods is forty-nine years, the Ethiopians called it MAZHAFA KÛFÂLÊ, i.e. the "Book of Jubilees." Incidentally, the only complete version of Jubilees is in Ethiopian and forms part of the canon of the Ethiopian Orthodox Church

The narrative follows the pattern of Genesis and parts of Exodus and offers little new information apart from the names of Adam and Eve's daughters - Azura and Awan - and nine sons not mentioned in Genesis. Jubilees also states that Cain later married Awân and Seth married Azûrâ, thus accounting for their descendants.

---

[32]   Book of Jubilees, translated R. H. Charles, Society for Promoting Christian Knowledge, London, England, 1917, March 3, 2011.

The New Testament

The New Testament or New Covenant is the second half of the Christian Bible and comprises the "Canonical Gospels", "Acts of the Apostles", the "Epistles" and the "Book of Revelation."

The Canonical Gospels

This is the name given to the 4 Gospels found in the New Testament of most Christian Bibles and were written in Greek by various persons after 45ACE.

"Matthew's Gospel" is attributed to a 1st Century anonymous Jewish Christian, probably based in Palestine. The Gospel used Mark's Gospel as its source. It is closely associated with Jewish tradition and was probably written for Jewish Christians. Messianism, which runs throughout Jewish thought, is the main focus of this gospel. It presents Jesus as the Messiah, using 62 references from the Old Testament. Since one of the essential attributes of the Messiah was that he should be a descendant of King David, Matthew begins his book by tracing Jesus' genealogy to that king.

The "Gospel according to Mark" was written around 70 ACE by an anonymous Greek. Some traditions hold that the book was written by John Mark, a follower of St. Peter, from whom he got most of his information about Jesus. However, modern scholars generally believe that it was written after Peter's death. It is the first Canonical Gospel written and only the "Gospel of Thomas" was written earlier.

The Gospel was probably written for a Roman audience. At the time it was written, christians were being persecuted throughout the Roman Empire and it was written to strengthen their faith. As a result, more of Jesus' suffering is recorded in Mark than in the other canonical writers. Roughly one-third of it describes Jesus' passion.

Traditionally, the "Gospel according to Luke" has been attributed to Luke, a physician and travelling companion of the Apostle Paul. However, contemporary research suggests that it was written by an anonymous Greek during the later decades of the 1st Century. This Gospel and "Acts of the Apostles", probably written by the same writer, were once combined in one volume. It is the longest of the canonical gospels.

It was probably written for a Christian Gentile audience. The "Theophilus" to whom the book is dedicated, refers to no particular person. In Greek, the term simply means "friend of God." Like Matthew, Luke uses Mark as its source. One of the writer's aims was to strengthen the faith of those who questioned Jesus' second coming, because of its delay. Another theme in Luke is that Jesus was the perfect man, who sacrificed himself for the salvation of mankind. Salvation, a prominent theme in Luke, is not used by Matthew or Mark.

"John's Gospel" differs from the aforementioned gospels in important respects. They are referred to as "synoptical", in the sense that they share common themes, points of view and narrative. John's gospel does not share these. It was written anonymously by a Greek or a person versed in Greek philosophy and did not even bear John's name in the original version. "According to John" was attached when the 4 Gospels were combined in one collection. Modern scholars date the gospel to 90-100 ACE.

The primary aim of the gospel is to present Jesus as the Messiah, the Son of God, through whom one gains eternal life (John 20:30-31). A very important question about the book is why it omits so many significant events in the life of Jesus. These include Jesus' birth, baptism, and temptation, Gethsemane and Ascension. The consensus is that they were excluded, because they did not directly impact on John's main theme of Jesus' divinity.

The letters or Epistles of St. Paul

These are the fourteen New Testament books that bear the Apostle Paul's name plus "Hebrews." Scholars disagree on which books he wrote. However, most agree that he wrote the "Epistles to the Romans", "Philippians", "Galatians", "Philemon", "1st and 2nd Corinthians" and "1st Thessalonians." Most scholars also agree that he did not write "Hebrews", "1 and 2 Timothy" and "Titus." They are divided on the others.

The writings began as letters to churches and individuals, intended to deal with local church problems and were read during service. Later they evolved into Epistles or Apostolic letters published for and read by the public. They were written sometime (Paul's death is usually given as 64 ACE) between 51 and 64 ACE.

The letters detail Paul's ministry and take theological positions that are the foundation of today's Christianity. Although Paul places emphasis on Jesus as the head of the church, his teachings are radically different from Jesus'.

The canonical gospels present Jesus as a Jewish Messiah, but Paul transformed him into a universal Savior. Other themes in his epistles include: the cross (1 Corinthians 1:17-18, Galatians 6:14, Philippians 2:8; the Resurrection: (I Corinthians 15); Jesus' return: I Thessalonians4:13, 2Thessalonians2:1-15.

Revelation

"Revelation" is the last book in most Christian Bibles and the last to be included in the New Testament canon. The traditional view is that it was written by John, the Apostle, when he was exiled on the island of Patmos. The current view among scholars is that it was written around 70 or 96 ACE somewhere in Asia Minor by an Asian Christian, probably from Ephesus. It is the only apocalyptic book included in the New Testament.

It is addressed directly to 1st Century churches in 7 cities of Asia (a Roman province in, what is now, Western Turkey), who were threatened by false teaching, persecution, idolatry and complacency. Most scholars divide the book into two parts: the first contains what I have just described and the second part consists of visions and symbols.

Revelation lends itself to various interpretations. One is that certain names, like "Babylon" and "Mother of Harlots", referred to the Roman Empire as the persecutor of the Church. The "beast" was the Roman Army, agent of God's judgment (Armageddon) on the Jews. Another interpretation, focusing on the second part, is that the prophecies foretold the fall of the Roman Empire. Another view of the second part is that its prophecies refer to events that would unfold shortly before the second coming of Jesus.

New Testament Apocrypha

Here is a list of the New Testament Apocrypha:

> The Epistles of Jesus to Abgarus
> Epistle of the Apostles
> The Epistles of Jesus to Abgarus
> Acts of Andrew
> Acts of Andrew and Matthias

Acts of Barnabas
Epistle of Barnabas
Gospel of Barnabas
Gospel of Bartholomew
Martyrdom of Bartholomew*
Apocryphon of James
Book of James (protevangelium)
First Apocalypse of James
Second Apocalypse of James
Acts of John
Acts of John the Theologian*
Apocryphon of John (long version)
Book of John the Evangelist
Revelation of John the Theologian*
Secret Gospel of Mark
Acts and Martyrdom of St. Matthew the Apostle*
The Martyrdom of Matthew
Gospel (Acts) of Nicodemus (aka The Acts of Pontius Pilate)
Acts of Peter
Acts of Peter and Andrew
Apocalypse of Peter
Gospel of Peter
Letter of Peter to Philip
Acts of Philip
Gospel of Philip
Acts of Thaddeus (Epistles of Pontius Pilate)*
Teaching of Thaddeus
Acts of Thomas
Apocalypse of Thomas
Book of Thomas the Contender
Consumation of Thomas
Gospel of Thomas
Acts of Paul
Acts of Paul and Thecla
Acts of Peter and Paul*
First Infancy Gospel of Jesus Christ
The Gospel of Mary
History of Joseph the carpenter
Narrative of Joseph of Arimathaea Shepherd of Hermas

Clement
Diatession
Gospel of the Lord (Marcion)
Epistles of Pontius Pilate
Revelations of Stephen
Gospel of the Ebionites
Gospel of the Egyptians
Gospel of the Hebrews
Gospel of the Nazaraeans

Most of these books make interesting reading. However, I will discuss only The Epistle of Jesus Christ and Abgarus, Epistle of Barnabas, Gospel of Thomas, Shepherd of Hermas and Gospel of Mary.

"The Epistles of Jesus Christ and Abgarus" [33]is correspondence that Abgarus, King of Edessa, made to Jesus, inviting him to Edessa to cure his sickness. It purports that Jesus sent a letter to him declining the invitation, but telling him that after his ascension one of his disciples will visit him and cure his illness. Eusebius, Bishop of Caesarea, Bishop of Palestine, was the first person to mention this correspondence. The Bishop, writing in the 4th Century ACE, examined the records of the City of Edessa in Mesopotamia, where Abgarus reigned, and found them written in the Syrian language. A translation in Greek is included in his Ecclesiastical History

"The Epistle of Barnabas"[34] is a 21-chapter Greek document whose authorship is undetermined. Some believe it was written by Barnabas, Paul's disciple and travelling companion. Others argue that it was written by Barnabas of Alexandria, an early Church Father. Some also believe that it was written by an Alexandrian Jew named Barabbas. The majority of scholars regard the work as anonymously written between 70 and 131 ACE. It is written allegorically and aims to give an accurate knowledge of salvation through Jesus Christ.

"The Gospel of Thomas"[35] is completely preserved in a Coptic papyrus manuscript discovered in 1945 at Nag Hammadi, Egypt. It is generally believed to have been written between 60-140 ACE. Its author is unknown.

---

[33] Epistle of Jesus Christ and Abgarus, Globusz Publishing, 2001-2011, March 9, 2011.

[34] Peter Kirby, Epistle of Barnabas,February 2006, March 14, 2011.-,

[35] Gospel of Thomas , Scholars Version translation in The Complete Gospels, The Jesus Seminar , n.d., March 9, 2011.

The Gospel is not a narrative of Jesus' life, but a collection of his sayings. It pre-dates the canonical Gospels. The major difference between it and them is that it does not describe Jesus' life, but his "secret teachings."

Here are the gospel's introductory words:

> These are the secret sayings that the living Jesus spoke and Didymos Judas Thomas recorded. And he said, "Whoever discovers the interpretation of these sayings will not taste death."

The book contains more than 110 of these sayings, each introduced by "Jesus said." Helmut Koester, Professor of New Testament Studies and Winn Professor of Ecclesiastical History Harvard Divinity School, says that " . . . what is typical about these sayings is that in each instance, these sayings want to say that if you want to understand what Jesus said, you have to recognize yourself. You have to know yourself, know who you are."[36]

"The Shepherd of Hermas" [37] is a 2nd century Christian literary work. It comprises five visions given to Hermas, a former slave; twelve mandates or commandments and ten similitudes or parables. Its author has been accepted as Hermas, the brother of Pius 1, bishop of Rome. Irenaeus, bishop of Lugdunum (now Lyons, France) and Tertullian, an early Christian writer and first to write Christian Latin literature, quoted it as scripture. It was bound with the New Testament in the Codex Sinaiticus and was listed between the Acts of the Apostles and the Acts of Paul in the stichometrical list of the Codex Claromontanus.

"The Gospel of Mary"[38] was originally written in Greek in the second century ACE, but its two existing copies are fragmentary. The Gospel can be divided into two parts. The first section describes the dialogue between the risen Jesus and his disciples. The second section contains

---

[36]   "From Jesus to Christ: the story of the Gospel of Thomas", FRONTLINE (WGBH educational foundation), April 1998. March 4, 2011.

[37]   Shepherd Hermas, Early Christian Writings", Peter Kirby, February 2, 2006, March 9, 2011.

[38]   Gospel of Mary Magdalene, introduced by Karen L. King, ranslated by George W. Macrae and R. McL. Wilson, Douglas M. Parrott, ed., The Nazarene Way of Essenic Studies, n.d., March 7, 2011.

Mary's description of special revelation given to her by Jesus. At Peter's request, she tells the disciples about things that were hidden from them. The basis for her knowledge is a vision of the Lord and a private dialogue with him.

It should be noted that the Catholic Old Testament contains 7 apocryphal books omitted in the Protestant Bible. These include: "Tobit", Judith, Baruch (with letter of Jeremiah), Sirach (or Ecclesiasticus), Wisdom and 1 and 2 Maccabees.

Canonization

To this point I have discussed the composition of the Hebrew, Greek, Roman and British bibles and given brief descriptions of some of the books found in them. The manner in which a book was included in the bible is known as canonization and the books included comprise the canon.

The word "canon" is derived from the Greek word "kanon", meaning reed or measurement. Therefore, a canonical book is one that meets the standard for Holy Scripture. The word, as a standard collection of Scripture, was not used until the 4th century ACE.

The determining event regarding the canon occurred at the Council of Carthage (now Tunisia in North Africa) on August 28, 397 ACE. The council determined that the only books that were divinely inspired and that could be read in church were: (The Old Testament) Genesis, Exodus, Leviticus, Numbers, Deuteronomy, Joshua the son of Nun, Judges, Ruth, four books of Kings, two books of Paraleipomena, Job, the Psalter, five books of Solomon, the books of the twelve prophets, Isaiah, Jeremiah, Ezechiel, Daniel, Tobit, Judith, Esther, two books of Esdras and two books of the Maccabees. Of the New Testament: four books of the Gospels, one book of the Acts of the Apostles, thirteen Epistles of the Apostle Paul, one epistle of the same [writer] to the Hebrews, two Epistles of the Apostle Peter, three of John, one of James, one of Jude, one book of the Apocalypse of John (Revelation).

Jewish Canon

There is no agreement as to when the Jewish canon was set. Nevertheless, there are many suggestions to the effect. Some bible scholars suggest that the Tanakh (Jewish bible) canon developed in stages: The Torah was canonized around 400 BCE, the Prophets around 200 BCE and the Writings around 100 ACE.

Other scholars affirm that after the destruction of the temple in 70 ACE, the rabbinical school of the Pharisees in Jamnia (also known as Jabneh or Yavneh) became a center of religious thought. Around 70 or 90 ACE, it met at a council and determined what books to include as scripture.

Most scholars reject this option, arguing that no evidence exists for such a council. They further assert that general agreement existed since the first century ACE concerning the Old Testament's content. The only claim that can be made with certainty is that by 200 ACE, the Jewish canon had been set.

Old Testament Canon

The Old Testament Canon, with variations in sequence and compilation, includes the Jewish Bible (Tanakh or Masoretic text). However, the canons of the Eastern and Roman Churches include books excluded from the Jewish bible. Protestant bibles include only those books in the Jewish bible. This begs the question as to what criteria were used in determining the Jewish and other canons.

Criteria for determining the OT Canon include:

(1) The deity must have spoken to prophets or holy persons and His words were recorded.
(2) The words must be faithfully transmitted.
(3) Authenticity must be established by means of blessings for honor, and curses for dishonor, in transcription.
(4) The literature must have been preserved in a sacred place.

Criteria used for determining the Eastern and Roman Canons were:

(1) Early dating, use by Early Church Fathers

(2) Divine authority and inspiration

(3) Conformity with accepted church teaching and

(4) Value to the Church.

These criteria are not collectively exhaustive, since other factors, political and cultural, also determined the formation of the canon.

Additionally, some of the books excluded from the Hebrew and Protestant bibles were used by Jewish prophets and Early Church Fathers. Why were they excluded? They might have been excluded, because those who compiled the canon had personal reasons for so doing.

New Testament Canon

"The Canon of the New Testament, like that of the Old, is the result of a development, of a process at once stimulated by disputes with doubters, both within and without the Church, and retarded by certain obscurities and natural hesitations, and which did not reach its final term until the dogmatic definition of the Tridentine Council".[39]

Richard Carrier puts this process of canonization in perspective:

It took over a century of the proliferation of numerous writings before anyone even bothered to start picking and choosing, and then it was largely a cumulative, individual and happenstance event, guided by chance and prejudice more than objective and scholarly research, until priests and academics began pronouncing what was authoritative and holy, and even they were not unanimous. Every church had its favored books, and since there was nothing like a clearly-defined orthodoxy until the 4th century, there were in fact many simultaneous literary traditions.[40]

---

[39] George Reid, "Canon of the New Testament", The Catholic Encyclopedia, Vol. 3, New York: Robert Appleton Company, 1908, March 15, 2011.

[40] Richard Carrier, "The Formation of the New Testament Canon", Copyright© Internet Infidels® 1995-2011, March 22, 2011.

Development of Canon

Around 135 ACE, Basikides, a religious teacher in Syria, wrote a dozen books of commentary on the Christian Gospels (all lost) entitled Exegetica.

Marcion (85-160 ACE) wrote the first canon of the New Testament in 140 ACE. It consisted of ten Pauline Epistles and one Gospel, which Tertullian (160-220 ACE) later identified as the Gospel of Luke.

The term "New Testament" (kainê diathêkê) was first used in an anti-Montanist treatise, written by an unknown author in 192 ACE and quoted by Eusebius.[41]

Tatian (110-180 ACE), a Syrian-Christian writer, in 160 ACE. , selected the four Gospels in the Christian canon. From these four gospels, he "composed a single harmonized "Gospel" by weaving them together, mainly following the chronology of John. This is called the Diatessaron ("That Which is Through the Four") and it became for a long time the official Gospel text of the Syriac church, centered in Edessa." [42] There are no complete versions of this work. Theophilus of Antiochus (?-183/185) treated Tatian's Gospels as Holy Scripture equal to the Jewish prophets.

Lodovico Antonio Muratori (1672-1750 ACE), a distinguished Italian historian, antiquary, Roman Catholic priest and one of the foremost scholars of his age, "discovered the Muratorian Canon, a scrap of early Christian literature (c.a.d. 190) containing the earliest known list of the New Testament books."[43] He published it in 1740 ACE. Most scholars believe the original was written around 170 ACE.

It lists and describes most of the current New Testament scriptures.

> The author notably omits the Epistle to the Hebrews, the Epistle of James, and the letters of Peter, but he mentions favorably the Wisdom of Solomon, the Shepherd of Hermas, and the Apocalypse of Peter, which were omitted by the later church.[44]

---

[41]   The Formation of the New Testament canon, March 15, 2011.

[42]   The Formation of the New Testament CanonI, March 15, 2011.

[43]   "Muratorian Fragment",   New World Encyclopedia,   New World Encyclopedia, n.d., March 7, 2011.

[44]   "Muratorian Fragment."

In 244 ACE, Origen ((185-254 ACE), scholar and theologian, declared the Tatian Gospels to be the only trustworthy, inspired Gospels. He lists the four Gospels, Paul's 13 letters, one letter each of Peter and John and the Revelation.

In 367 ACE, Pope Athanasius I of Alexandria (293-373 ACE), became the first person to list the 27 books that comprise the New Testament.

In 382 ACE, Pope Damasus commissioned St. Jerome (347-420 ACE), the leading biblical scholar of his time, to provide a Latin translation of the Bible from the different translations then in use. The following year, Jerome delivered to the Pope his revised Latin translation of the Gospels. The remainder of the New Testament was revised from older Latin versions. Interestingly, Jerome's revised New Testament contained the identical books on Athanasius' list.

In 393ACE, a church synod at Hippo Regius in North Africa endorsed the lists of Athanasius and Jerome, excluding The Epistle to the Hebrews. However, in 397 ACE, the Third Synod of Carthage approved the lists, including the Epistle that had been previously omitted.

Is the bible inerrant?

When the bible is described as "inerrant word of God", the meaning is that the original handwritten copy was free from errors in word and content. Since all originals of bible manuscripts are lost, some bible scholars contend that translations of the originals contain accidental copyist errors or intentional additions/deletions by forgers. However, conservative and fundamentalist Christians believe that inerrancy extends to the translations and, thus, the copies we have are inerrant as the originals.

Catholic' Position

The official position of the Roman Church on the bible is that it is the inerrant Word of God. This concept, known as absolute inerrancy, is the belief that the bible in its original autograph copy in Hebrew, Aramaic or Greek is without error.

The FIRST VATICAN COUNCIL (1869-1870) supports the view that the bible is inerrant

> The complete books of the old and the New Testament with all their parts, as they are listed in the decree of the said council and as they are found in the old Latin Vulgate edition, are to be received as sacred and canonical.

> These books the Church holds to be sacred and canonical not because she subsequently approved them by her authority after they had been composed by unaided human skill, nor simply because they contain revelation without error, but because, being written under the inspiration of the Holy Spirit, they have God as their Author.[45]

The books to which the Council refers are those of the Old Latin Vulgate, begun by Saint Jerome, who was commissioned by Pope Damasus I in 382 ACE to make a revision of the then existing Latin versions of the bible. That translation, with the canon authorized at the Council of Trent (1545-1563) was "written under the inspiration of the Holy Spirit." They are, therefore, inerrant, because "they have God as their Author."Since God is the author of the bible, the question of the truth or falsity of a biblical passage is irrelevant. The only question concerns its meaning.

THE SECOND VATICAN COUNCIL (1962-1965) reaffirmed the views of the First Vatican Council that the bible was superintended by God and was, consequently, inerrant:

> For holy mother Church, relying on the belief of the Apostles (see John 20:31; 2 Tim. 3:16; 2 Peter 1:19-20, 3:15-16), holds that the books of both the Old and New Testaments in their entirety, with all their parts, are sacred and canonical because written under the inspiration of the Holy Spirit, they have God as their author and have been handed on as such to the Church

---

[45]   "First Vatican Council", Dei Filius (Dogmatic Constitution on the Catholic Faith, April 24, 1870), Session III, Chapter 2, "On revelation", March 15, 2011.

herself.(1) In composing the sacred books, God chose men and while employed by Him (2) they made use of their powers and abilities, so that with Him acting in them and through them, (3) they, as true authors, consigned to writing everything and only those things which He wanted. (4)

Therefore, since everything asserted by the inspired authors or sacred writers must be held to be asserted by the Holy Spirit, it follows that the books of Scripture must be acknowledged as teaching solidly, faithfully and without error that truth which God wanted put into sacred writings[46]

Westminster Confession of Faith (WCF)

In 1643, the English Parliament called upon the learned clerics of the Church of England to meet at Westminster Abbey to advise "on issues of worship, doctrine, government and discipline of the Church of England. Their meetings, over a period of five years, produced the confession of faith, as well as a Larger Catechism and a Shorter Catechism."[47]

Over the past centuries since its issuance, many denominations hold it as their official position on the inerrancy of the bible, among other things. These include Baptists, Congregationalists and Presbyterians.

Like the Council of Trent, the First and Second Vatican Councils, the WCF recognized that the bible was written under the inspiration of the Holy Spirit and that in its original autograph writing in Hebrew, Aramaic and Greek, it is the true Word of God.

The Old Testament in Hebrew (which was the native language of the people of God of old), and the New Testament in Greek (which, at the time of the writing of it, was most generally known to the nations), being immediately inspired by God, and, by His

---

[46] Dei Verdum, Dogmatic Constitution on Divine Revelation - CHAPTER III, paragraph 11," SACRED Scripture" , March 4, 2011.

[47] "WESTMINSTERCONFESSION OF FAITH, 3rd Edition with Corrections", Committee for Christia Education & Publications, Presbyterian Church in America, Lawrenceville, GA., 2000, March 15, 2011

singular care and providence, kept pure in all ages, are therefore authentical . . ." [48]

The word "inerrant" is not used in the WCF, which uses the sentence, "given by inspiration of God." (1.2) I understand the sentence to mean "supervised by God." Since God cannot err, it follows that what He supervises cannot contain an error. Therefore, the WCF's position is that the bible, having been supervised by God, t is free from error.

In another section the WCF states, "The authority of the Holy Scripture, ... dependeth not upon the testimony of any man, or church; but wholly upon God (who is truth itself) the author thereof." (1.4) God not only supervises, but is the author of the bible. Since the error-free God cannot author error and He is the author of the 66 books of King James Version (referenced in the WCF), it follows that these books are error free.

Chicago Statement on Biblical Inerrancy

In October 1978, 300 evangelical scholars met in Chicago at a three-day conference sponsored by the International Council on Biblical Inerrancy. Among attendees were Kenneth Kantzer, Harold Lindsell, John Warwick Montgomery, J. I. Packer, Robert Preus, James Boice, Norman L. Geisler, John Gerstner, Carl F. H. Henry and R. C. Sproul.

They formulated the "Chicago Statement on Biblical Inerrancy", a document which defined Evangelical teaching on the subject.

The Short Statement is:

1. God, who is Himself Truth and speaks truth only, has inspired Holy Scripture in order thereby to reveal Himself to lost mankind through Jesus Christ as Creator and Lord, Redeemer and Judge. Holy Scripture is God's witness to Himself.

2. Holy Scripture, being God's own Word, written by men prepared and superintended by His Spirit, is of infallible divine authority in all matters upon which it touches: it is to be believed, as God's instruction, in all that it affirms: obeyed, as God's command, in all that it requires; embraced, as God's pledge, in all that it promises.

---

[48]   "Westminister Confession of Faith" 1:8

3. The Holy Spirit, Scripture's divine Author, both authenticates it to us by His inward witness and opens our minds to understand its meaning.

4. Being wholly and verbally God-given, Scripture is without error or fault in all its teaching, no less in what it states about God's acts in creation, about the events of world history, and about its own literary origins under God, than in its witness to God's saving grace in individual lives.

5. The authority of Scripture is inescapably impaired if this total divine inerrancy is in any way limited or disregarded, or made relative to a view of truth contrary to the Bible's own; and such lapses bring serious loss to both the individual and the Church.[49]

Sentences such as (1) "inspired Holy Scripture", (2) "Holy Scripture, being God's own Word, written by men prepared and superintended by His Spirit", (3) "Scripture is without error or fault" (4) "total divine inerrancy" are affirmations of bible inerrancy.

I believe that the bible (whether Roman, Orthodox, or Protestant) is, within limitations, the inerrant word of God. I believe that holy men, under special conditions, received inspiration from God for their writings. In this respect, they gave first, to the Jews, and then to the Gentiles, certain codes of behavior and worship. I also believe that some of these writings are allegorical.

Most historical and scientific statements and descriptions in the bible came from the knowledge of the writer, essentially based on the period in which he lived and the state of scientific development and knowledge. Consequently, some statements on these subjects do not stand the test of time.

I will cite Joshua's "long day" as an example. In Joshua 20:12-13, Joshua commanded the sun and moon to stand still, thereby extending the day so that the battle could be won.

In bible times, the earth was considered to be the centre of the universe and that the sun and other revolved around the earth, and day and night was caused by this rotation. As such, Joshua's command that the sun and moon "stand still" would be reasonable within such a framework. The

---

[49] "CHICAGO STATEMENT ON BIBLICAL INERRANCY", Southwestern Baptist Theological Seminary, Fort Worth, TX. 2009, March 9, 2011.

sun and moon would stop rotating around the earth, and daylight would continue.

Since Galileo (1564-1642), the view is no longer that the earth is the center of the universe. The sun is now proven to be the centre of the universe and the moon and earth rotate around it. Joshua's long day violates the principle of conservation of angular momentum of rotating bodies, a fundamental law of physics. The moon, also, cannot simply stop in its orbit; it would fall towards the earth.

Many biblical historical accounts have been proven false. An example is Moses. His history is found in four books of the Torah—"Exodus", "Leviticus", "Numbers" and "Deuteronomy." However, there is no historical proof that he existed. The biblical story resembles a Babylonian story of Sargon the Great. Archaeologists have found cuneiform tablets dating to 1000 BCE describing the story of Sargon the Great, a Babylonian King, ,who ruled Sumer around. 2334-2279. He was saved as a baby when his mother made a basket out of rushes, sealed it with tar and placed it in a river. The basket containing the baby was found by a princess who later raised him in the palace. Israelites who were enslaved in Babylon were familiar with the story and later adopted it.

The selection of books in the canon was not ordered by God, but by the tastes of man. As such, bias, prejudice and expediency determined its composition. Some very edifying books (Enoch, Jubilees) are omitted from every canon except the Ethiopian. Jasher, one of the greatest books ever written and which was known to many holy men of old, is completely suppressed.

Conclusion

This sketch of the Christian Bible is intended to give the believer strength in his/her faith. In the final analysis, I believe that all scripture aims at teaching how to please God. The Old Testament teaches it through the Law. The New Testament teaches it as salvation through Jesus' sacrifice. The Christian bible, like holy books of all religions, asks its believers to approach it with faith. Much good will come by studying it as a description of the workings of God throughout the ages. Whether it is the infallible, inerrant word of God is more the critic's concern than it is the Christian's. To the Christian, it is the word of God.

The bible contains the noblest, finest creations of the human mind. Shakespeare's "Hamlet," Goethe's "Faust", Khayyam's "Rubbyait", Hugo's wonderful "Hunchback of Notre Dame", Shelley's "Prometheus Unbound" fall short in inspiring me the way the Bible does. The teachings of this book tells the creature that he is the special concern of the Creator, who at times spoke to men of old, some of whom recorded their thoughts, dreams, visions in what we call the Bible.

CHAPTER THREE

The Christian Church

Do not hold aloof from the Church; for nothing is stronger than the Church. The Church is your hope, your salvation, your refuge. It is higher than the heaven; it is wider than the earth. It never grows old, but is always in full vigor. Therefore, indicative of its solidity and stability, Holy Scripture calls it a mountain; of its purity, a virgin; of its magnificence, a queen; of its relationship to God, a daughter.

—Homily on Eutropius

For many centuries, the term Christian Church refereed to the Roman and Eastern Churches until the Eastern Church separated and until the Protestant Reformation. I will not discuss every branch of church history, a task that requires volumes instead of a chapter. I will describe those aspects of the subject that provide an understanding of the ideas, events and persons that shaped church history from its Apostolic beginnings to modern times.

I discuss the spread of Christianity, limiting myself to Europe and Africa. I also describe the persecution of Christians by Roman Emperors and by the Roman Church. I touched on theology, specifically those disputes within the Roman church and those between Rome and the Eastern Church. I also describe some of the main present-day denominations and examine the fundamental differences among them.

Part One
Upper Room-Council at Nicaea

In the "General Introduction" to his classic work History of the Christian Church, Philip Schaff states:

> History has two sides, a divine and a human. On the part of God, it is his revelation in the order of time (as the creation is his revelation in the order of space) and the successive unfolding of a plan of infinite wisdom, justice, mercy, looking to his glory and the eternal happiness of mankind. On the part of man, history is the biography of the human race and the gradual development, both normal and abnormal, of all its physical, intellectual and moral forces to the final consummation at the general judgment.[50]

The Christian Church is the assembly of Jesus' followers and can be conveniently divided into the universal and local church. The former is composed of those persons who accept Jesus as their Savior, the community of believers. The latter is composed of various denominations, such as the Roman (Catholic) Church, the Orthodox Church (sometimes called the Eastern Orthodox) and the Protestant Church. Despite doctrinal and other differences among them, denominations are united in their acceptance of Jesus as their head.

Apostolic Church Period

Christian church history began in Palestine with Jesus' followers after his ascension. Most historians date it from Pentecost (the Jewish harvest festival of Shavuot, which commemorates God's giving the Ten

---

[50]   Philip Schaff, History of the Christian Church, The Electronic Bible Society, Dallas, TX, 1998, March 8, 2011.

Commandments to Moses at Mount Sinai) in 30 ACE to 100 ACE when John the Apostle died.

After Jesus' ascension, many of his followers remained in Jerusalem and formed a closely-knit group known as the Nazarenes or Jesus' Followers, terms they did not use to describe themselves. They called themselves "Believers", "The Faithful" and "Saints".

Christian church history began with this group in an upper room after some of them returned from the Mount of Olivet (Acts 1:12-14) and not on the Day of Pentecost, as many affirm. Jesus had commanded his disciples that they should remain in Jerusalem for the promise of the Father, when they would receive power after the Holy Ghost came upon them.(Acts 1:4,8) That happened on the day of Pentecost (Acts 2:1-4). This event was not the beginning of the Christian Church, but the beginning of the outreach of the Christian Church that assembled earlier in the upper room, aforementioned.

Initially, the Nazarenes numbered approximately 120 members (Acts 1:13-16), including Jesus' mother and his brothers. The leaders were Simon Peter, James, the oldest brother of Jesus, and John. "And the Lord added to the church daily such as should be saved." (Acts 2:47) Eventually, the church numbered 3,000 to 5,000 believers.

The Nazarenes were Jews, who prayed in the temple at Jerusalem and "had all things common; and sold their possessions and goods, and parted them to all men, as every man had need." (Acts 2:44-45)

They continued worshipping daily in the temple and breaking bread from house to house. (Acts 2:46) After they were expelled from the synagogue for preaching Jesus' return, they continued believing the sacredness of Jewish scriptures, practicing baptism, using incense, keeping an altar, observing Jewish holy days, observing the Sabbath and circumcision. They also held the Jewish view that God was one and indivisible. To them, Jesus was the Messiah not God.

Evangelism in the Apostolic Period

The Nazarenes and their converts spread the good news beyond Jerusalem. Their earliest Christian missions from Jerusalem followed the path of the Phoenician tin trade. It spread from the cities and towns along the Phoenician / Syrian coast to Antioch along the main Phoenician settlements of Cyprus, Crete, Sicily, Cyrenia Massilia (Marseilles), Sardinia,

Spain and ultimately Southwest Britain. Before St. Paul set out upon his later journeys, all the main Phoenician colonies and trading ports possessed Christian missions.[51]

Peter preached in Pontus, Galatia, Cappadocia, Asia and Bithynia (1 Peter 1:1). St. Andrew preached in Scythia (Russia), Turkey and Sebastpolis, Nicea, Nikomidea to the south of the Black Sea and Greece.

St. Bartholomew preached in India, Yemen, and Armenia. St. Matthew preached in Persia and Ethiopia. St. Thomas preached in Odessa and India. St. Simon preached in Babylonia and Syria. John and St. Philip preached in Asia Minor. St. Paul preached in Syria, Tarsus, Antioch, Cyprus, Galatia, Ephesus, Greece in Philippi, Thessalonica, Corinth, Italy, Spain and Rome.[52]

Deaths of the Apostles

In 44 ACE, James the Greater, son of Zebedee and brother of John, the Apostle, was executed by Agrippa, King of Judaea (41-44 ACE).

In 62 ACE, James, the Just, was martyred; either by being stoned to death after he had been sentenced to death by the High Priest Ananus, or by being thrown from the top of the Temple in Jerusalem by the Pharisees.

Legend has it that Matthew died as a martyr in Ethiopia in 60 ACE.

Thaddaeus was crucified in Edessa; Greece in 72 ACE. St. Thomas was martyred either in Persia or India.

Simon Peter was crucified 54-68 ACE at Rome.

Andrew, brother of Peter, was crucified in Edessa, Greece, but the date of his crucifixion is unknown. John, son of Zebedee, died in 98 ACE of natural causes.

The deaths of John the beloved, Bartholomew and Simon the Canaanite are unknown.

[51] "Spread of Christianity into early Brittan", Historical Stuff, n.d., March 15, 2011.

[52] "HOW DID CHRISTIANITY SPREAD THROUGHOUT THE WORLD?"n.p., n.d., March 5, 2011.

Persecution in 1ˢᵗ and early 2ⁿᵈ centuries

The first persecution against Christians started in 64 ACE in the reign of Nero Claudius Caesar Augustus Germanicus, commonly known as Nero (37-68 ACE). Fire destroyed a large area of Rome in July, 64 ACE. The people believed that Nero had set the fire, but he blamed the Christians and ordered their punishment. Cornelius Tacitus (56-117ACE), the great Roman historian wrote:

> Consequently, to get rid of the report, Nero fastened the guilt and inflicted the most exquisite tortures on a class hated for their abominations, called Christians by the populace. Accordingly, an arrest was first made of all who pleaded guilty; then, upon their information, an immense multitude was convicted, not so much of the crime of firing the city, as of hatred against mankind. Mockery of every sort was added to their deaths. Covered with the skins of beasts, they were torn by dogs and perished, or were nailed to crosses, or were doomed to the flames and burnt, to serve as a nightly illumination, when daylight had expired. Nero offered his gardens for the spectacle, and was exhibiting a show in the circus, while he mingled with the people in the dress of a charioteer or stood aloft on a car. Hence, even for criminals who deserved extreme and exemplary punishment, there arose a feeling of compassion; for it was not, as it seemed, for the public good, but to glut one man's cruelty, that they were being destroyed.[53]

Peter and Paul were crucified and beheaded respectively in 67 ACE. It is generally recorded that the next series of persecutions occurred during the reign of Titus Flavius Domitianus (81-96 ACE), commonly known as Domitian. However, there is little or no supporting evidence for this claim.

---

[53] Cornelius Tacitus, The Annals, book 15, chapter 44, Alfred John Church, William Jackson Brodribb, Ed., Perseus Digital Library, n.d., March 8, 2011.

Christianity and the Mystery Religions

When Christianity spread to Rome in the first century ACE, mystery cults were in their heyday. The Greek word "mystêrion" denotes initiation: a 'mystery' is something into which you are initiated.

They were called mystery religions because of their secrecy, specifically, their rituals were only revealed to initiates. Those accepted into membership were called "mystes." The person who introduced the applicant was known as "mystagogos." The leaders of the cults were "hierophantes ", persons who knew and revealed higher knowledge.

Some of the more popular cults were the cult of the "Great Mother" Cybele, a Syrian goddess", the cult of Isis and Osiris, which came from Egypt, cult of Dionysius from Greece and , the most popular, the cult of Mithra from Persia.

> They were appealing in the turbulent times of the Roman Empire because they also claimed to save their adherents from the worst that fate could throw at them in this world while promising immortality in the next. To achieve immortality and union with god required a period of preparation in which the initiate followed the religion's precepts in an effort to become holy. Once this period was over, the initiate performed a ritual, usually one of great emotional intensity, in which he or she was baptized into a new life. Ultimately this led to unity with the religion's god who had died and risen from the dead.[54]

Depending on one's perception on the interaction between these mystery religions and Christianity, the latter either merged with some of the former or, at least, was greatly influenced by them.

Mithraism

Mithraism was a pagan religion consisting mainly of the cult of the ancient Indo-Iranian Sun-god Mithra.

---

[54]   Jeff Anderson.," Christianity and the Mystery Religions", Jeff Anderson, 1999, March 15, 2011.

> It entered Europe from Asia Minor after Alexander's conquest,
> spread rapidly over the whole Roman Empire at the beginning of
> our era, reached its zenith during the third century, and vanished
> under the repressive regulations of Theodosius at the end of the
> fourth century.

> The origin of the cult of Mithra dates from the time that the
> Hindus and Persians still formed one people, for the god Mithra
> occurs in the religion and the sacred books of both races, i.e. in
> the Vedas and in the Avesta.[55]

Vexen Crabtree contends that, "Christianity grew out of a mixture of
Persian Mithraism, Judaism and the works of individuals such as St. Paul
who gave us written records of this synthesis."[56]

There are, indeed, some striking resemblances in symbolism and
worship between Mithraism and Christianity. Like the Roman Church,
Mithraism had seven sacraments, including baptism and communion with
bread and water. Mithras was born of a virgin on December 25th and his
birthday was celebrated in the Festival of Light. Mithraism also taught
immortality of the soul, the last judgment and the resurrection.

Based on the available evidence, I cannot conclude that Christianity
copied or stole from Mithraism. The reader must decide for himself/herself
based on the data presented.

One of the Christian cults certainly influenced by mystery systems was
Gnosticism.

The Original Catholic Encyclopedia provides the following description
of Gnosticism:

> A collective name for a large number of greatly-varying and
> pantheistic-idealistic sects, which flourished from some time
> before the Christian Era down to the fifth century, and which,
> while borrowing the phraseology and some of the tenets of the
> chief religions of the day, and especially of Christianity, held
> matter to be a deterioration of spirit, and the whole universe a

---

[55]   John Arendzen, "Mithraism", The Catholic Encyclopedia, Vol. 10, New
York: Robert Appleton Company, 1911, March 9, 2011.

[56]

depravation of the Deity, and taught the ultimate end of all being to be the overcoming of the grossness of matter and the return to the Parent-Spirit, which return they held to be inaugurated and facilitated by the appearance of some God-sent Saviour.[57]

Although the Encyclopedia speaks of the Gnostics "borrowing the phraseology and some of the tenets of the chief religions of the day, and especially of Christianity", the fact was that they were a branch of Christianity.

The term "Gnosticism" derives from the Greek "gnosis", meaning knowledge. Like all mystery religions, Gnosticism held that only certain persons could obtain the secret knowledge of the cosmos and life. These persons were called pneumatics or psychics.

Gnostics believed that matter was gross and that the world was created by the demiurge, an evil god, separate to the real God. Through esoteric knowledge, man can escape materiality. Some Gnostic sects regarded Jesus as an embodiment of the real God, who became incarnate to bring Knowledge (gnosis) to mankind. However, there were others who regarded him as a false prophet, who preached a different knowledge to that given to him by John the Baptist.

In the following excerpt, Professor Schaff refers to those who believed that Jesus was God incarnate.

> Gnosticism is a heretical philosophy of religion, or, more exactly, a mythological theosophy, which reflects intellectually the peculiar, fermenting state of that remarkable age of transition from the heathen to the Christian order of things.[58]

Gnostics also wrote Gospels, purporting to be sayings of Jesus Christ. Some of these are the Gospel of Thomas (written sometime between 60 ACE and 140 ACE), Gospel of Mary (120-180 ACE) and Gospel of Peter (sometime in the 2nd century ACE). I discussed these and other Gnostic Gospels in chapter 2.

---

[57]   John Arendzen, "Gnosticism", The Catholic Encyclopedia, Vol. 6, New York: Robert Appleton Company, 1909, March 3, 2011.

[58]   Phillip Schaff, History of the Christian Church, vol.2, ante-Nicene Christianity, The Electronic Bible Society, Dallas, TX, 1998, March 8, 2011.

The Apostles' Creed

There was an urgent need in the 2nd Century to define church belief and oppose "heresies" being promulgated by the Gnostics and other sects in the Church. The Apostles' Creed was such an attempt. Despite its title, it was not written by the apostles. It is not known who wrote it; but it was first mentioned in the "Interrogatory Creed of Hippolytus" in 205 ACE. Christian thinkers, such as Irenaeus of Lyons (125-203 ACE), Bishop of Lugdunum in Gaul), Justin Martyr (103-165), Tertullian (160-220 ACE) knew it. However, no one has credited any of them with its composition.

The Creed exists in two main forms-the earlier, shorter Latin Form (around 140 ACE) and the received Form, which was developed sometime during the 5th and 7th centuries ACE.

The Latin Form:

> I BELIEVE in God the Father almighty
> And in Christ Jesus, his only Son, our Lord
> Who was born of the Holy Spirit and the Virgin Mary
> Who was crucified under Pontius Pilate and was buried
> And the third day rose from the dead
> Who ascended into heaven
> And sitteth on the right hand of the Father
> Whence he cometh to judge the living and the dead.
> And in the Holy Spirit
> The holy church
> The remission of sins
> The resurrection of the flesh
> The life everlasting.

16th century version:

> I BELIEVE in God the Father almighty,
> I also believe in Jesus Christ his only Son, our Lord,
> conceived of the Holy Spirit, born of the Virgin Mary.
> suffered under Pontius Pilate, crucified, dead and buried; he
>   descended into hell,
> rose again the third day,
> ascended into heaven,
> sat down at the right hand of the Father,

thence he is to come to judge the living and the dead.
I believe in the Holy Ghost,
the holy catholic Church, the communion of saints,
the remission of sins,
the resurrection of the flesh and life eternal."

The modern English version:

I believe in God, the Father almighty,
creator of heaven and earth.
I believe in Jesus Christ, God's only Son, our Lord,
who was conceived by the Holy Spirit,
born of the Virgin Mary,
suffered under Pontius Pilate,
was crucified, died, and was buried;
he descended to the dead.
On the third day he rose again;
he ascended into heaven,
he is seated at the right hand of the Father,
and he will come again to judge the living and the dead.
I believe in the Holy Spirit,
the holy catholic church,
the communion of saints,
the forgiveness of sins,
the resurrection of the body,
and the life everlasting. AMEN."[59]

The first 2 lines of the creed, "I believe in God the Father Almighty, Maker of Heaven and Earth." attacked the Gnostic view that the world was not created by the true God, but by an evil God.

Gnostics believe there is a true, ultimate and transcendent God, a being who is beyond all created universes and who never created anything in the sense in which the word 'create' is ordinarily understood. Instead this God 'emanated' or brought forth from

---

59   "Apostles Creed", n.p, n.d., March 22, 2011.
60   Dan Sewell Ward, "Gnostics", Dan Sewell Ward, 2003, March 9, 2011.

within Himself the substance of all there is in all the worlds, visible and invisible. However, much of the original divine essence has since been projected from their source and in the process has undergone some distinctly unwholesome changes in the process.

One aeonial being who bears the name Sophia ('Wisdom') is of great importance to the Gnostic world view. In the course of her journeyings, Sophia came to emanate from her own being a flawed consciousness, a being who became the creator of the material and psychic cosmos, all of which he created in the image of his own flaw. This being, unaware of his origins, imagined himself to be the ultimate and absolute God. Since he took the already existing divine essence and fashioned it into various forms, he is also called the Demiurgos or 'half-maker[60]'

"And in Jesus Christ, His only Son, Our Lord, Who was conceived by the Holy Ghost, Born of the Virgin Mary." This part of the Creed defined the position of the writer(s) that Jesus was God in man, born miraculously. Most of the Jewish Christians, like some Gnostics, believed that Jesus was the Messiah, but not God incarnate. The Gnostic Gospels portray him as a wise teacher, whose teachings could only be understood by a few.

"(Jesus) was crucified, died, and was buried; he descended to the dead. On the third day he rose again; he ascended into heaven." There were dying and rising gods in Mystery Religions. Some examples are Dionysius, Mithras, Adonis, Osiris, Attis and Bacchus. Some have argued that the Creed's writers were acquainted with these and copied their resume. I disagree with these and believe that the writers of the Creed did not copy the views of the Mystery Cults, but were confidently affirming their conviction that Jesus was crucified, died, buried and on the third day was resurrected and ascended into heaven. They believed in St. Paul's words, "And if Christ be not risen, then is our preaching vain, and your faith is also vain." (1 Corinthians 15:14)

" . . . the resurrection of the body, and the life everlasting."The central tenet of Gnosticism was that matter was gross and that someday the enlightened few would be freed from the taint of matter and the shackles

---

[60]   Dan Sewell Ward, "Gnostics."

of the body, and return to the heavenly realm as Pure Spirit. As such, they completely rejected the Creed's profession that the body would be resurrected. The creed also professes that there will be everlasting life (to believers). Gnosticism believes in eternal life as pure spirit.

At first, the Creed was used as a declaration of faith before baptism, which was the defining act of salvation in early Christianity. These days it continues being recited at baptism in Liturgical churches. It is also currently used by many Christian denominations to state their main beliefs.

Post-Apostolic/ Ante-Nicene Period

The post-Apostolic or ante-Nicene period covers the end of the first century ACE to the First Council of Nicaea (325 ACE).

Among eminent Post-Apostolic Church Fathers mention must be made of Polycarp (69-155 ACE), Bishop of Smyrna; Irenaeus of Lyons (125-203 ACE), Bishop of Lugdunum in Gaul); Justin Martyr (103-165); Tertullian (160-220 ACE), a prolific Carthaginian writer and Origen (185-254 ACE).

The church spread throughout the Roman Empire and beyond during this period. At the beginning of the 2nd century, it had spread to various cities in Greece, Asia Minor, Syria and India. By the mid-third century ACE, there were 100 Episcopal sees (Cathedrals of bishops) in Italy and, by its close; Christianity had spread to Britain, Gaul (France), Spain, Germany, the Iberian peninsula, Carthage (Tunisia) and Alexandria. Gentile Christians far outnumbered Jewish ones and the Jewish element declined to such an extent that scholars term the period "Gentile Christianity."

Ante-Nicene /Post-Apostolic persecutions

Persecution of Christians continued in the Roman Empire under Marcus Lupus Nerve Trains, commonly known as Trajan (53-117 ACE), Emperor from 98 ACE to his death. By his order, Ignatius, bishop of Antioch, was thrown into the Coliseum around 108 ACE and eaten by lions.

The persecutions continued under Hadrian (117-138) and Antonius Pius (138-161). Among those who were martyred during this period was Germanicus of Smyrna (?-156 ACE), who was torn apart by beasts during the Smyrna public games.

Polycarp, bishop of Smyrna, was killed during Antonius Pius' reign. The story is told that, at age 88, he was warned that he would be killed for his religion. He hid in a farmhouse, but was seen by an angry mob, intent on killing him. When the governor begged him to renounce his faith and pledge loyalty to the Roman gods, he refused and reportedly said, "Fourscore and six years have I served Him, and He has never done me wrong; How then can I now blaspheme my King and Savior?"

According to legend, the soldiers prepared to nail him to the stake, but he assured them that nails would not be needed and he was tied instead. The fire was lit and the flames flared, but parted around him. Finally, a soldier killed him with a sword. Twelve other Christians, who accompanied Polycarp, were also put to death on the same day.

Persecution of Christians continued under the co-emperors Marcus Aurelius Antoninus Augustus, generally known as Marcus Aurelius (121-180 ACE) and Lucius Aurelius Verus (130-169 ACE). The latter died in 169 ACE and Marcus ruled as sole Emperor until his death. That he did not stop the persecutions is most disappointing, since he was a humanistic philosopher, whose writings rank among the finest of any period. I recognize that he was tutored in philosophy hostile to "Christian superstitious beliefs" and knew nothing of Jesus and never read any of the Gospels. Whatever little he knew about Christianity came from his observation of the lives of his Christian servants. Historians assert that what he saw was a kind of supernatural devotion, which was repugnant to a man of reason as he was. Being a patriot and defender of Roman values, he could not and did not change the established laws against the Christians.

Some scholars, among them Tertullian, instance him as applying those laws mildly. Others state that he was as cruel as those who preceded him. Although there were many persecutions during his reign, none can be directly traced to him. The persecution in Lyons, France in 177 ACE, when 48 Christians were executed, was the doing of the provincial administration.

The next major set of Christian persecutions was during the reign of Gaius Messius Quintus Decius, who ruled from 249 to 251 ACE. Christian writers of the period state that Empire-wide persecution of Christians began under him. The state required all citizens to sacrifice to the state gods. Proof was accepted in the form of a libellus, a certificate from a temple confirming the act. There were so many persecutions during Decius's reign that no accurate estimate has ever been given.

Persecutions continued during the joint Emperors Gaius Aurelius Valerius Diocletianus, commonly known as Diocletian (284-305 ACE) and Marcus Aurelius Valerius Maximianus Herculius, commonly referred to as Maximian (286-305 ACE).

In 302 ACE, Galerius asked Diocletan to begin a general persecution of Christians. Diocletan agreed and it started February 24, 303 ACE. It was called "The Great Persecution" and officially ended in 313 ACE.

Four edicts were issued: The first edict ordered the destruction of Christian literature and places of worship across the empire and prohibited the assembling of Christians for worship. Christians were to be deprived of the right to petition the courts and not allowed to respond to actions brought against them in court. Christian senators, veterans and soldiers were to be deprived of their ranks and imperial freedmen were to be re-enslaved. This edict was the only legally binding edict in the Western part of the Empire. However, progressively harsher legislation was devised in the Eastern part.

The second edict ordered the arrest and imprisonment of all Christian lay readers, deacons, bishops and priests.

In a third edict, issued November, 303 ACE, Diocletian declared a general amnesty for all Christians who agreed to sacrifice to the gods.

In March 304 ACE, the fourth edict ordered all persons—men, women and children—to gather in a public place and offer a collective sacrifice. If they refused, they were to be executed.

May1, 305 ACE, Diocletian and Maximian resigned as Senior and Junior Emperors. Caesar Flavius Valerius Aurelius Constantinus Augustus, commonly known in English as Constantine I, Constantine the Great, or Saint Constantine (276-337 ACE) and Gaius Galerius Valerius MaxiMaximianus (260-311 ACE) known as Galerius became joint Senior Emperors. During this period, relations between the Church and Rome improved dramatically, due mainly to the aforementioned Constantine.

In 311 ACE, Emperor Galerius issued The Edict of Toleration, which ended the Great Persecution. This was followed by The Edict of Milan (313 ACE), a letter signed by emperors Constantine, emperor in the West and Licinius (Valerius Licinianus Licinius 263 325), emperor in the East..The edict proclaimed religious toleration in the Roman Empire. Constantine's second and third edicts prepared the way for legal recognition of Christians and their protection.

Before I discuss the Nicene Council, one of the seminal events in Church history, I will discuss the history of the African church, since it played a central role in the dispute.

Christianity in Africa

The Christianization of Africa cannot be discussed within the context of the entire continent. The writer must choose to discuss those countries that best exemplify the Christian tradition on the vast continent. A good starting point is North Africa, specifically Egypt.

Tradition holds that Saint Mark first went to Egypt sometime between 41 and 44 ACE and returned in 64 ACE to preach. His first convert was Anianus, who became Patriarch of Alexandria after St. Mark's martyrdom at Alexandria in 68 ACE. Egypt's patriarchal succession remains unbroken. This makes the Egyptian (Coptic) one of the oldest Christian churches.

Egyptian Christians were also the first in Christendom to establish a school for the study of Christianity, the Didascalia in Alexandria. Its curricula were not limited to Christian studies or to Christians. Many Greek and Roman students and scholars attended the school, where science, mathematics, physics, chemistry, astronomy and medicine were some of the subjects taught.

Very little is known about the school's beginning, but its first head was Pantaenus (around 180 ACE.), who was later sent to India as a missionary by Demetrius I, Patriarch of Constantinople (189-232 ACE), eleventh bishop after St. Mark. After Pantaenus left the school, his pupil Clement of Alexandria (150-.215 ACE) succeeded him. Clement is credited with being the first systematic teacher of Christian doctrine. Origen (185-254 ACE), one of the most renowned writers of the Christian Church, was one of his students.

In the first years of the third century, under Septimus Severus, the Alexandrian Christians were relentlessly persecuted. Clement fled to Palestine and became bishop of Jerusalem.

In the 250s and early 300s ACE respectively, Roman persecution of Christians in Egypt was brutal. The fact that they worshipped openly, unlike their Roman counterparts who worshipped underground, increased the severity.

Despite being persecuted, Christianity expanded to the remotest parts of Egypt and beyond. Egyptians christianized Nubia in the Sixth century ACE.

When Alexandria fell to the Arabs in 640 ACE, the Islamisation of Egypt began and, within 100 years, most of Egypt had converted to Islam. The Coptic Church survived in a weakened state through the centuries.

NUBIAN CHRISTIANITY

When independent Nubian kingdoms emerged in the sixth-century ACE, many of their subjects had already been converted to Christianity by Egyptian missionaries from the Egyptian Coptic Church.

In the sixth century ACE, Nubia was divided into three kingdoms: a northern, called Nobatia, which extended roughly from the First Cataract south to the Third; a central, called Makuria, which extended from the Third Cataract south to the Sixth and a southern called Alwa, which extended from the Sixth Cataract southward up the Blue Nile to the land between it and the Abyssinian (Ethiopian) kingdom of Axum.

The Arab armies that had subdued Egypt attempted to conquer Nubia in 642 and again in 652. The Nubians repulsed them in the first confrontation; but were subdued in the second. A peace treaty was signed. It was agreed that the Arabs would not attack Nubia if the Nubians paid an annual tribute of 360 slaves and allowed a mosque to be built in the center of their capital at Old Dongola. The contract was signed and remained in effect for six centuries.

Nubia had two Christian kingdoms, each with its own rule. There were thirteen Episcopal sees and every settlement had at least one church. There were also several monasteries. [61]

Ethiopia

Christianity arrived in Ethiopia in the fourth century ACE, when Meropius, a Christian merchant from Tyre, was shipwrecked off the Ethiopian coast enroute to India. He died, but his two nephews, Frumentius and Aedesius who accompanied him, were washed ashore and taken to the Royal palace. They became King Ella Amida's private secretary and royal cupbearer respectively. When the king died, Frumentius became regent for the infant prince Ezana and he and Aedesius were allowed to evangelize the country. After Ezana came of age, Frumentius and Aedesius left Ethiopia. On their way home, they travelled through Egypt. Frumentius stayed in Alexandria; but Aedesius returned to Tyre, where he remained and was ordained a priest.

---

[61]   "Nubian Civilization", n.p., n.d, March 7, 2011.

Frumentius asked Athanasius (293-373 ACE), Bishop of Alexandria, to send missionaries to Ethiopia. In 329 ACE, Athanasius sent him and ordained him the first abuna or bishop of the Ethiopian Orthodox Church.

The Ethiopians referred to Frumentius as Abba Selama, meaning "Father of peace." He erected his Episcopal see Episcopal see at Axum, baptized King Ezana, who had succeeded to the throne, built many churches and spread Christianity throughout Ethiopia.

Towards the end of the 5th century ACE, monks from either Syria or Egypt built monasteries there. They also encouraged the translation of the Bible into Ge'ez, then the native language. Although Ge'ez is no longer a living language, the Ethiopian church continues to use it as its liturgical language.[62]

Carthage (now Tunisia)

I cannot definitely state when Christianity went to Carthage (now Tunisia) or who took it. However, at the beginning of the 3rd century ACE, a flourishing church existed in the Roman colony. The best example of this was that Victor 1, Roman Pope (189-198/199 ACE) was born and grew up, there.

Ancient African Christian scholars

Two names are prominent in ancient African Christian scholarship —Quintus Septimius Florens Tertullianus (Tertullian. 160-ca. 220 ACE) and St. Cyprian (?-258 ACE).

Tertullian

Tertullian was born in Carthage in the Roman province of Africa. He has been called the "father of Latin Christianity", because he is the first writer to produce an extensive body of Christian work in Latin. He is the

---

[62] "Christianity in Ethiopia", EthiopiaFamine.com, n.d., March 22, 2011.

oldest extant Latin writer to use the term "Trinity" and to give a formal exposition of a Trinitarian theology. He is credited with 31 extant treatises, all in Latin. His Montanistic writings got him into trouble with the Roman church, which he left towards the last ten years of his life.

Montanism was a religious movement of the second century ACE, which the Roman Church deemed heretical. It arose around 172 ACE in Phrygia (a kingdom in the west central part of Anatolia, in what is now modern-day Turkey) under the leadership of one Montanus and two female prophets, Prisca and Maximillia, whose utterances were taken as coming from the Holy Spirit.

The Montanists believed in the imminence of the Day of Judgment. They also believed that a fallen Christian cannot be redeemed. The movement died around 220 ACE as a sect, except in isolated areas of Phrygia, where it continued until the 7th century. Tertullian kept his Montanist beliefs, but in 213 ACE he left the Church and formed "Tertullianists", a sect named after, and led by, him.

St. Cyprian

St. Cyprian was born at Carthage, where he was baptized around 246. Shortly after his baptism he was ordained deacon and soon thereafter presbyter. Sometime between July 248 ACE and April 249 ACE he became Bishop of Carthage, a position he held until his death in 258 ACE.

In 250 ACE, Roman Emperor Decius issued an edict against Christians to renounce their faith and offer sacrifices to Roman gods. Many Carthaginian Christians refused and were put to death. At the beginning of the persecution, Cyprian fled and supervised his church through a trusted deacon. He was accused of cowardice and infidelity in Rome. His response was that, as head of the Church, he needed to be safe in order to lead his flock.

When he returned to Carthage, after 14 months absence, his church was in uproar. During the persecution, many Christians had fallen away ("lapsi"), but were accepted after the persecution ended. Cyprian and those who supported him in the clergy believed they should show genuine repentance before being readmitted.

Felicissimus, who had been ordained deacon by the presbyter Novatus during the absence of Cyprian, opposed all action taken by Cyprian's representatives. Cyprian deposed and excommunicated him and 5 other bishops, who supported him. Novatus disregarded Cyprian's actions.

In May 251, Cyprian called a synod to discuss the situation. The synod agreed that all lapsi who repented their guilt should be admitted to penance, which should last a period commensurate to their guilt. This decision was confirmed by a synod under Pope Cornelius (251-martyrdom 253 ACE) in Rome in the autumn of the same year.

Novatus continued opposing Cyprian, but with the support of most of the African bishops, Cyprian emerged victorious. Cyprian convened 2 other synods (255 and 256 ACE) both of which condemned heretical baptism. In Rome, baptism done by heretics was considered valid. In Carthage such baptism was regarded as invalid. Carthage and Rome kept their respective practices until 314 ACE at the Synod of Arles, when Carthage agreed to conform to the Roman practice.

Cyprian was martyred in 258 ACE.[63]

The Donatists

During the Diocletian persecution (303-305 ACE), Christian leaders in Carthage were ordered to hand over their Christian scriptures and writings to be burned. Those who complied were called "traditores" meaning those who hand over, from the Latin "tradere", to hand over. Those who did not comply but confessed Christ before the authorities were called Confessors and were either martyred or imprisoned. The church hierarchy, including its bishop and archdeacon, were "traditors" and forbade food being taken to imprisoned Confessors.

Upon the death of Mensurius(?-311 ACE), bishop of Carthage, Caecilianus was consecrated bishop of Carthage by Felix, bishop of Aptunga. This was distasteful to the Confessors, because Felix was a "traditor" and, in their opinion, unsuited to perform such functions.

The majority of the Carthaginian clergy supported by bishops in neighboring Numidia, ordained Majorinus bishop of Carthage (311-315 ACE). Majorinus held that those who had surrendered their books to the authorities during Diocletian's persecution should not be accepted into the church and that sanctity was a requirement for church membership and the administration of sacraments.

---

63   John Chapman, "St. Cyprian of Carthage", The Catholic Encyclopedia, Vol. 4, New York: Robert Appleton Company, 1908, March 22, 2011

In 313 ACE, a Church Council was called in Rome to resolve the conflict. Nothing was resolved and another council was held the following year in Arles (ancient Arelate, in the south of Roman Gaul, now France). Constantine, while a junior emperor, presided over the session. It ruled that the validity of ordination and baptism did not depend upon the merit of the administrator but in the act itself. Thus, the council ruled that the Donatist beliefs constituted heresy and, when the Donatists refused to alter their positions, Constantine launched a fierce persecution against them.

When Majorinus died in 315 ACE, Donatus replaced him and held the position until 355 ACE. Although the name Donatists was given to his followers, it was Majorinus who first articulated the positions credited to Donatus.

Despite declaring the views of the Carthaginian Christians heresy and exiling Donatus in 347 ACE, Donatism flourished in Carthage until the Muslim conquest of North Africa in the 7th century ACE, when Christianity in the region was wiped out.[64]

The First Nicene Council

The first Council at Nicaea[65] is the most important event in the history of the Christian Church. As a result of its decisions, Jesus was no longer the son of God, but became very God. I will trace the events that led to the Council, its decisions and its significance to Christian theology.

Background to the Nicene Council

There was no general consensus in the Church about the divinity of Jesus until the Nicene Council. Half the bishops and priests believed that Jesus was the Son of God but not God himself. The other half believed that he was God in the flesh. Around 320 ACE, a priest from Antioch named Arius was appointed priest at Alexandria.

---

[64] John Chapman, "Donatists", The Catholic Encyclopedia. Vol. 5, New York: Robert Appleton Company, 1909, March 22, 2011

[65] "Council of Nicaea", The Nazarene Way of Essenic Studies, March 9, 2011.

He taught that if the father begat the Son (Jesus), then the Son had a birth, therefore there was a time when the son did not exist. Since God has no beginning (He is the beginning) and the Son had one, the Son (Jesus) could not be God. However, Arius conceded that since Jesus had come into existence by God's will, he was superior to man.

Alexander, the Bishop of Alexandria, opposed Arius and argued that the Father and the son were of one substance. In 320ACE, he called a meeting at Alexandria, which was attended by 100 African bishops and excommunicated Arius for teaching "heresy."

Arius appealed to two of his friends, Eusebius of Caesarea and Eusebius of Nichomedia, a friend of Emperor Constantine. The latter convinced the emperor to convene a General (Ecumenical) Council of all the bishops to settle the dispute. Of 1800 bishops in the Church, 300 attended. The sessions were held at Nicaea in Bithynia (now Northwest Turkey) and lasted from May 20-July 25, 325 ACE.

Eusebius of Nichomedia advanced Arius' position and Athanasius, (Alexander's Secretary and later Bishop of Alexandria upon Alexander's death in 326 ACE), advanced the opposing position. After days of arguments and a deadlocked Council, Emperor Constantine intervened and sided with Athanasius. His action was surprising, since he had been supporting Arius all along and his friend was Arius' defender. He ordered everyone present to sign a document (known as the Nicene Creed) stating that Jesus was of the same substance as the Father. The penalty for refusing was banishment. All, except 17 Arians, signed.

The Document read:

> We believe in one God, the Father Almighty, maker of all things visible and invisible; and in one Lord Jesus Christ, the Son of God, the only-begotten of his Father, of the substance of the Father, God of God, Light of Light, very God of very God, begotten, not made, being of one substance with the Father. By whom all things were made, both which be in heaven and in earth. Who for us men and for our salvation came down [from heaven] and was incarnate and was made man. He suffered and the third day he rose again, and ascended into heaven. And he shall come again to judge both the quick and the dead. And [we believe] in the Holy Spirit."

Most historians agree that the majority of those who signed did so because of the Emperor's threats. Constantine banished Arius and bishops who had refused to sign the document.

Within months, many clergy and laity recanted the Nicene Creed. By 329 ACE, Constantine recalled Arius from exile and reinstated those bishops who had been deposed. Shortly before he died, Constantine was baptized by an Arian bishop. Despite the pronouncements by the Church that he repented and died a Christian, historical evidence proves that he died a Sun worshipper.

Arianism flourished under the new Emperor Contantinus Flavius Claudius Constantinus, Constantine's son (emperor 337-340), also known as Constantine II. It declined after his death.

Additions to the Creed

In May 381 ACE, Emperor Theodosius called a General Church Council at Constantinople to provide for a succession in the patriarchal See of Constantinople, to confirm the Nicene Creed, to reconcile the semi-Arians with the Church and to outlaw the Macedonian heresy (named after Macedonius 1, bishop of Constantinople 342-346 ACE and 354-360 ACE. It asserted that the Son and God were of the same substance, but not of the same essence. It also denied the divinity of the Holy Spirit and taught that the Holy Spirit was a creation of the Son and a servant of the Father and the Son.)

The council was not intended to be an Ecumenical Synod and was not summoned by the Pope, nor was he invited to it. No diocese of the West was present either by representation or in the person of its bishop; neither the See of Rome, nor any other see. It was attended by 150 Eastern bishops and lasted from May through July 381 ACE.

It was presided over at first by Meletius, the bishop of Antioch who was bishop not in communion with Rome and who died during its session. Its second president was Gregory of Nazianzen, who was at that time liable to censure for a breach of the canons. After his resignation, Nectarius, who became Bishop of Constantinople, presided until its conclusion.

The canons of the Nicene Council were not placed in their natural position after those of Nice in the codex which was used at the Council of Chalcedon, although this was an Eastern codex.

Its Creed was not read nor mentioned, so far as the acts record, at the Council of Ephesus, fifty years afterwards.

The 325 ACE Creed ended, "We believe in the Holy Spirit." That Creed with additions was ratified by the Council at Constantinople. The addition read:

> The Giver of Life,
> Who proceeds from the Father;
> Who with the Father and the Son together is worshipped and
>   glorified;
> Who spoke by the prophets.
> And in One, Holy, Catholic, and Apostolic Church.
> I acknowledge one baptism for the remission of sins.
> I look for the resurrection of the dead, and the life of the world
>   to come.

The next addition to the Nicene Creed occurred in 589 ACE at the third council of Toledo. At that council the famous Latin phrase "filioque" ("and the son") was inserted into the creed after the words. "We believe in the Holy Spirit, The Giver of Life, Who proceeds from the Father."

It was not until 1014 ACE that the Toledo addition was admitted to the Roman church. The Eastern Church objected to the "filoque clause" and continues to omit it from its creed. The present form of the Nicene Creed recited in Western Christian churches read:

> We believe in one God the Father, the Almighty, creator of heaven and earth, and of all that is, seen and unseen.

> We believe in one Lord, Jesus Christ, the only Son of God, eternally begotten of the Father, God from God, Light from Light, true God from true God, begotten, not made, of one being [substance] with the Father. Through him all things were made. For us and for our salvation he came down from heaven; by the power of the Holy Spirit he became incarnate from the Virgin Mary, and was made truly human. For our sake he was crucified under Pontius Pilate; he suffered death and was buried. On the third day he rose again in accordance with the Scriptures; he ascended into heaven and is seated at the right hand of the Father. He will come again in glory to judge the living and the dead, and his kingdom will have no end.

We believe in the Holy Spirit, the Lord, the giver of life, who proceeds from the Father [and the Son]. With the Father and the Son he is worshipped and glorified. He has spoken through the Prophets.

We believe in one, holy, catholic, and apostolic Church. We acknowledge one baptism for the forgiveness of sins. We look for the resurrection of the dead, and the life of the world to come. Amen.

Christianity in Britain

At this stage, I will discuss the origin and development of Christianity to Britain. Keith Hunt states:

> Christianity was first introduced into Britain 'by Joseph of Arimathaea, A.D.36-39; followed by Simon Zelotes, the apostle; then by Aristobulus, the first bishop of the Britons; then by St.Paul. Its first converts were members of the royal family of Siluria—that is, Gladys, the sister of Caradoc, Gladys (Claudia)and Eurgen his daughters, Linus his son, converted in Britain before they were carried into captivity to Rome; then Caradoc.[66]

I doubt that Joseph of Arimathea brought Christianity to Britain or that St.Paul's first British converts were the British Royal Family. I also dismiss other British legends concerning who brought Christianity to Britain. The important point is that Christianity did reach the British shores.

The earliest religious practices in Britain were Druidic and when Christianity reached Britain it encountered Druids. Druidism was a polytheistic cult whose gods and goddesses were believed to inhabit local springs, caves, forests and mountains and and became the personification of natural objects and events.

The early British Christians, like their brethren in Rome and elsewhere, were fatally persecuted by their Roman colonizers. When Christianity

---

[66] R.W. Morgan, "Christianity came to Britain - When? #1 And those who brought it!", Restitution Of All Things, n.d., March 15, 2011.

became the official religion of the Roman Empire, this ceased and they used their influence to outlaw pagan practices, such as ritual sacrifice and worshipping idols. Pagan temples were also destroyed.

When Rome withdrew from Britain in 410 ACE, Angles and Saxons conquered and settled in the South of England. They forbade the worship of Christianity. However, the rest of England remained Christian, but was isolated from the Roman Church.

In 596 ACE, Pope Gregory 1 (590-604 ACE) sent a Church mission to England. It was headed by St. Augustine, a Benedictine monk, whose claims to jurisdiction over the British church were rejected by the British bishops. However, he succeeded in re-establishing Christianity in parts of the south of Britain. In the meantime, the north was being Christianized Celtic missionaries.

Representatives of the north and south of England met at the Synod of Whitby in 664 and combined to form the Church of England, with dual bishoprics at Canterbury and York. For the next 402 years the Church of England remained in communion with, but not under the jurisdiction of, Rome. When the Normans, who were strict Roman Catholics, conquered England in 1066, they imposed Roman jurisdiction on the English church. In 1534, the church repudiated Papal jurisdiction and recovered its autonomy.

> Contrary to widespread belief, the circumstances of the annulment of the marriage of King Henry VIII to Catherine of Aragon were merely the occasion, but not the cause, of this break with Rome. Henry founded no new Church; he merely restored rightful autonomy to an old one.

> During Henry's reign there were no radical alterations in English religion. The clergy remained unchanged and the Church's principal service, the Mass, continued to be in Latin, although Henry supported the Archbishop of Canterbury, Thomas Cranmer, in ordering the use of English for the Lord's Prayer, the Ten Commandments, the Apostles' Creed and the Bible Readings.[67]

---

[67]   A Short History of the Anglican Church, A Short History of the Anglican Church, the Anglican Church of Canada, Christ Church, Rawdon, Quebec, March 30, 2011.

King Charles 1 was executed January 30, 1649, ending the civil war and abolishing Anglicanism. The parish churches were handed over to Presbyterians or Congregationalists, and Anglicanism went underground. In 1660, the monarchy was restored and jurisdiction of the churches returned to the Anglicans.

Part Two
The post-Nicene period

To this point, I have discussed events in church history from the apostolic period leading up to the Nicene Creed and its additions and the schisms. I will now turn to the post-Nicene (325-590 ACE).

Notable Events of the Period

In 330 ACE, Byzantium was refounded as Constantinople (New Rome), the capital of the Roman Empire.

In 367 ACE, Athanasius of Alexandria wrote a Paschal letter, listing for the first time the canon of the New Testament.

In 407 ACE, John Chrysostom died in exile.

In 431 ACE, Nestorianism was declared heretical by the First Council of Ephesus. The doctrine had been advanced by Nestorius(386-451 ACE), Patriarch of Constantinople (428-431 ACE). It asserted that Jesus was two distinct persons, closely and inseparably united and that Mary was not the Mother of God, but Mother of Christ.

In 484 ACE, the Synod of Beth Lapat , Persia, a Council of the Church of the East, declared Nestorianism as official theology of the Assyrian Church of the East. That action separated the Church of the East from the Byzantine church.

The Monophysites were a form of Noestorians. The established church position on Christ was that he had two natures (human and divine) and two wills corresponding to the two natures. This position was opposed by the Monophysites , who asserted that He had only one nature, his humanity being absorbed by his Deity. This teaching was declared a heresy by the Council of Chalcedon (451 ACE) and the Second Council of Constantinople (553 ACE). The latter demanded that the formulation decided upon in 451 be accepted. The Monophysites refused.

In 533 ACE, Mercurius, a priest of the Basilica di San Clemente on the Caelian Hill, was elected Pope of Rome and took the name of John II, becoming the first pope to change name upon election.

In 579 ACE, 400 Christians were slain by the Lombards in Sicily. In 580 ACE, Monte Cassino was sacked by Lombards and its monks fled to Rome.

Mediaeval Christianity (Gregory I to Gregory 590-1073 ACE).

Philip Schaff observed:

> The MIDDLE Age, as the term implies, is the period which intervenes between ancient and modern times, and connects them, by continuing the one, and preparing for the other. It forms the transition from the Graeco-Roman civilization to the Romano-Germanic, civilization, which gradually arose out of the intervening chaos of barbarism. The connecting link is Christianity, which saved the best elements of the old, and directed and moulded the new order of things."[68]

Monothelitism

During the first half of the 6th century, Byzantine emperor Heraclius (emperor 610-641 ACE) tried to unite the Metophysites and the Chalcedonians (supporters of the decisions at the Chalcedon synod) with a compromise formula. Known as Monothelitism, it posited that Christ possessed two natures (human and divine) but one will and one divine-human "energy." His human will was absorbed within his divine will. This compromise position was rejected by all sides in the dispute.

Constans II (641-668 ACE, Byzantium emperor) was concerned about the effect religious disputes were having on the Empire. He issued an imperial edict, the Type of Constans, which outlawed any discussion on the topic of Christ possessing either one or two wills, or one or two energies.

---

[68]   Philip Schaff, History of the Christian Church, vol.4, March 15, 2011.

Other significant events during the period

In 640 ACE, the Library of Alexandria, Egypt, the center of Western and Eastern learning, with 300,000 ancient papyrus scrolls, was completely destroyed. This was a tragic event, because the works of many Christian writers were also destroyed.

In 641 ACE, Muslim Arabs captured Alexandria and in 642 ACE, they conquered Egypt.

In 648 ACE Pope Theodore I of Rome excommunicated Paul 111, third Patriarch of Constantinople, called a council at the Lateran in 649 ACE and condemned the Ecthesis of Emperor Heraclius Typos of Emperor Constans II.

In the 720s, Leo 111, the Byzantine Emperor banned the pictures and paintings of Christ, saints and biblical scenes. Pope Gregory 111, Pope of Rome, held two synods at Rome and condemned Leo's actions.

In 754 ACE, the Iconoclast Council at Hieri ruled that holy portraits were heretical. In 787 ACE, the Seventh Ecumenical Council declared this finding as heretical

In 731 ACE, English church history was written by the Venerable Bede.

Further conversion of nations

Professor Schaff points out that "mediaeval Christianization was a conversion of nations under the command of their leaders. It was carried on not only by spiritual means, but also by political influence, alliances of heathen princes with Christian wives, and in some cases (as the baptism of the Saxons under Charlemagne) by military force."[69]

Charlemagne (747/748 r-814 ACE) was a Christian and the greatest Medieval king. He spread Christianity through conquest. He was King of the Franks from 768 and Emperor of the Romans from 800 to his death. He was crowned Holy Roman Emperor by Pope Leo III in 800 ACE.

He was a protector of the Church in her temporal affairs. In 773 ACE, Pope Hadrian 1 appealed to him for aid against Desiderius, the Lombard King, who was invading the Papal States. In 771, Charlemagne had divorced his wife, Desiderius' daughter. Charlemagne led a victorious expedition

---

[69]   Philip Schaff, History of Medieval Christianity, vol.4, March 15, 2011.

into Italy, assumed the crown of Lombardy and annexed northern Italy. In 787-788 he annexed Bavaria.

His next campaign was against the Avars, Asiatic nomads who, during the late 6th and 7th centuries, had formed an extensive empire largely inhabited by conquered Slavs living on both sides of the Danube. Charlemagne's campaigns in 791, 795 and 796 conquered a block of territory south of the Danube in Carinthia and Pannonia.

He opened a missionary field that led to the conversion of the Avars and their former Slavic subjects to Christianity.

When he died in 814 ACE, Christian missionaries spread their faith throughout Europe.

The earliest large Christian kingdom in Europe was Great Moravia. Its exact location is still disputed. Some scholars locate it on both sides of the Morava river, the area of modern western Slovakia and in Moravia and Bohemia (modern Czech Republic). Others state that it could have included parts of modern Hungary, Poland, Austria, Slovenia, Croatia, Serbia, Romania, Ukraine and Germany.

Great Moravia was first evangelized by Roman missionaries from Bavaria, who conducted services in Latin. In 863 ACE, the Moravian ruler, Rastislav, asked Byzantine Emperor Michael III to send teachers who would preach Christianity in the Slavic language. The emperor sent two brothers, Byzantine officials and missionaries Cyril and Methodius (later made saints). Although they were Greeks, they knew the Slavic language. Cyril developed the first Slavic alphabet and translated the Gospel into the Slavonic language. The Slavonic liturgy was later outlawed by Rome and Latin rites were imposed.

In 880 ACE, Pope John VIII issued the Bull Industriae Tuae, by which he set up an independent ecclesiastical province in Great Moravia with Archbishop Methodius as its head and Slavonic was recognized as the fourth liturgical language, besides Latin, Greek and Hebrew.

Bulgaria, a pre-eminent Slavic state, remained Greek Orthodox. Its ruler, Boris 1, was baptized in 865 ACE.

A Danish king, Harald Bluetooth, became the first Scandinavian ruler to convert to Christianity. He was baptized around 960 ACE.

In 966 ACE, Mieszko 1, first ruler of Poland, adopted Roman Catholicism and made it the state religion.

In 975 ACE, Hungarian king Gezá and his family were baptized in the Roman Catholic faith, beginning a lasting link between Hungary and Rome.

In 996 ACE, Olaf 1, a Norwegian king, was also baptized and Iceland became a Christian nation around1000 ACE.

By the beginning of the 11th century, most European nations were Christian and with the burgeoning feudal system, the Roman Pope was virtually the head of Europe. "As a great feudal lord with moral pretensions, holding the ring between secular sovereigns, the pope can be seen as Europe'sheadmaster."[70]

Bishops and abbots, recruited from the noble families holding the great fiefs, formed part of the small feudal aristocracy. The Pope was a great feudal Lord and gave his approval to conquests in hope of gaining money and land after victory.

A case in point is the Norman Conquest. Although the Angle-Saxons had converted to Roman Christianity during the Roman Britain period and had an established abbey (Westminister), the Roman Pope approved William the Conqueror's campaign against them.

In 1059 ACE, the Pope also gave his approval to the Normans to attack Sicily, by giving them feudal rights over territory not as yet theirs.

Decline of Papal morality

Following the death of Pope Nicholas I in 867 ACE, the Christian church was corrupted. Kings and emperors appointed bishops and abbots, often without regard to spiritual qualification. This practice, known as simony, referred to the selling of ecclesiastical offices. Additionally, clerical marriage and concubinage, called Nicolaitanism, undermined priestly celibacy."[71]

Others have called the period the Papacy's dark ages. A succession of popes were elected and controlled by prominent aristocratic families and Emperors of Rome. In 955 ACE, Pope John XII (955-963 ACE) became Pope on the orders of Duke Alberic II of Spoleto, ruler of Rome, and his

---

[70] "HISTORY OF FEUDALISM", History World, History World, n.d., March 15, 2011.

[71] "History of Europe Timeline, northwest Europe 9th to 12th century A.D." History World, n.d., March 15, 2011.

father. The Pope was such a womanizer that during his tenure, the papal palace was described as a brothel. [72]

On December 4, 963, Emperor Otto I, Emperor of Italy, deposed Pope John XII because he found him unworthy. He installed Leo VII (963-964) as his successor. John X111(965-972 ACE) was, "for the most part, an embarrassment to the Roman Catholic Church and remains so even to this day. His pursuit of women was so extensive and unashamed that the Latern Palace came to be known as a little more than a brothel."[73]

Benedict VI(973-974) came to a violent end. Apparently after Otto 1, his protector, died, the citizens of Rome rebelled against him and he was strangled to death by a priest.[74]

John XV (985-996) was noted for his greed and nepotism.

In the 11th Century, better Popes emerged. Nicholas II(1058-1061ACE) tried to reform the election of Popes. In 1059, he called a synod at the Lateran palace to that effect. It decided to ensure that papal elections were in the hands of cardinals and removed from the influence of secular rulers and Roman mobs.

Alexander II (1061-1073) attempted to reform the Roman curia and the papacy, but he was opposed by powerful interests that sought their own enrichment.

St. Gregory VII (1073-1085) issued decrees banning clerical marriage, concubinage and simony.

Urban II(1088-1099 continued Pope Gregory v11's church reforms.

The Great Schism

Before leaving the 11th Century ACE, I will discuss an event of immense importance to the Church. The Bishop of Rome was considered first in the order of hierarchy among other bishops. This resulted from Rome's position as the capital of the Roman Empire. When Constantinople became the capital of the Byzantine State, its Patriarch (Bishop) assumed the second position in the hierarchical structure of the church. The third canon of the

---

[72]   Austin Cline, "Popes of the 10th Century. Part 2: History of the Roman Popes." About.com guide, about.com, n.d., March 15, 2011.

[73]   " Popes of the 10th Century." o March 15, 2011.

[74]   Popes of the 10th Century. March 15, 2011.

Second Ecumenical Council (381) recognized this when it stated that, "Let the Bishop of Constantinople, however, have the priorities of honor after the Bishop of Rome, because of its being New Rome."[75]

On July 6, 1054 ACE, the Eastern Church split from the Roman (Western) Church, an event known as the Great Schism. For centuries, relations between the churches were less than cordial. Michael Cerularius, Patriarch of Constantinople (1043-1059 ACE), attacked the Roman Church for using unfermented bread (azymes) in the Sacrifice of the Mass and other practices. Relations between the two Churches grew considerably worse at the beginning of 1054. At that time, Pope Leo ix (149-1054 ACE), Roman Pope, sent a letter to Michael Cerularius. In the letter the Pope cited the Donation of Constantine, a forged document supposedly issued by Constantine 1, Emperor of Rome. In the forged document, the Emperor is said to have granted to Pope Sylvester1(314-335 ACE) and his successors, as successors of St. Peter, dominion over lands in Judea, Greece, Asia, Thrace, Africa, as well as the city of Rome, with Italy and the entire Western Roman Empire, while Constantine would retain imperial authority in the Eastern Roman Empire from his new imperial capital of Constantinople.

Most historians believe that the Pope considered the document genuine.

In January 1054, the Patriarch closed churches in Constantinople that practiced Roman rites. Meanwhile, at the beginning of April 1054, the Pope sent a legation, headed by Cardinal Humbert, to the Patriarch setting out certain demands and reminding the Patriarch that the Roman Church was head of the Church and he (the Pope) was the representative of St. Peter.

Although the Pope died April 19, 1054 ACE, his mission continued its business. The meetings between the two sides were conducted in poisoned atmospheres and reached no agreement. Before leaving Constantinople, Cardinal Humbert excommunicated the Patriarch, who, in turn anathematized the Cardinal. To this day, the Church of Rome (Roman Catholic) remains separate from the Eastern Church (Eastern Orthodox).

---

[75] "Second Ecumenical Council, canon 3", OrthodoxWiki Encyclopedia, Last modified May 16, 2010, March 15, 2011.

Twelfth to fifteenth Century Disputes

Medieval Inquisition

"Medieval Inquisition" was a series of Roman Catholic judicial institutions established to combat heresy. They lasted from 1184 through the 1230s and included the Episcopal Inquisition (1184-1230s) and later the Papal Inquisition (1230s). It was in response to large popular movements throughout Europe considered apostate or heretical to Christianity. One of these was Catharism.

The Cathars was a large sect of Christians who broke with the Roman Church in the Middle Ages, because, in their opinion, the Church had grown lax. It arose in the 11th century, probably an offshoot of a small surviving European Gnostic community that immigrated to the Albigensian region in the south of France and flourished there during the 12th and 13th centuries. The followers of the sect were also called Albigenses, named after the town of Albi in Languedoc, where they lived.

> They did not believe in one all-encompassing god, but in two, both equal and comparable in status. They held that the physical world was evil and created by Rex Mundi (translated from Latin as "king of the world"), who encompassed all that was corporeal, chaotic and powerful; the second god, the one whom they worshipped, was entirely disincarnate: a being or principle of pure spirit and completely unsullied by the taint of matter. He was the god of love, order and peace.[76]

They were vegetarian, non-violent, believed in the equality of sexes, recognized women priests, practiced chastity and believed in reincarnation.

In 1165 ACE, they were condemned by an ecclesiastical council at the Languedoc town of Albi. However, such actions were meaningless, because the Cathari were supported by powerful nobles and some bishops.

In 1206 ACE, the Pope, Innocent 3, asked the nobles of Languedoc to help him destroy the Cathari. Many refused and those who supported the Cathari were excommunicated.

---

[76] "Cathars", Net helper, 2011, March 15, 2011

Raymond VI of Toulous, a powerful count, refused to assist and was excommunicated in May 1207ACE. When the Pope asked Philippe, king of France, to punish those nobles who refused to assist, the king refused. Count Raymond met with the papal legate, Pierre de Castelnau, in January 1208. The meeting was unproductive. The papal legate was murdered the following day.

The Pope excommunicated Languedoc and offered its lands to anyone who would defeat its nobles. The Southern nobles joined the crusade. In 1233, Pope Gregory IX established the papal Inquisition, sending Dominican friars to South France to conduct inquests concerning heresy, specifically Catharism.

The usual procedure was that, upon arrival, an inquisitor gave a month of grace to those wishing to confess to heresy and recant. Those who confessed and recanted were given a light penance. Those accused of heresy, who did not recant, were brought to trial. The trials were conducted secretly in the presence of a representative of the bishop and a number of local laymen. The accused and his /her witnesses were usually tortured.

The usual punishment for those found guilty was penance, fine, and imprisonment. A guilty verdict also meant the confiscation of property by the civil ruler, who might turn over part of it to the church.

> Cathar resistance boiled down to a few chateaux in the Pyrenees,
> including Montségur and Quéribus, which were taken in 1244
> and 1255 respectively. The Inquisition remained active in this part
> of the kingdom for almost another century, until Catharism was
> completely eradicated. The last "bon homme" Guilhem Bélibaste,
> was burnt at the stake in Villerouge-Termenès in 1321. [77]

An interesting footnote about Château de Montségur, the most famous Cathar Castle, is that in a field below the Castle over 200 Cathars were burned alive, having refused to renounce their faith.

The Reformation

In the sixth century ACE, the Roman church would be spilt over Martin Luther's disagreement with its practices, his demand for overall church

---

[77] Peter Wronsk, " MONTSEGUR | History Part 1", Peter Wronski 2002, March 15, 2011.

reform and his theological positions. This period of dispute is known as the Reformation, the Protestant Revolt or the Protestant Reformation.

Martin Luther was born at Eisleben, Saxony in Germany in 1483 and died there in1546. In 1501, he began attending the University of Erfurt, studying liberal arts. In 1502, he earned a Bachelor's Degree in Philosophy and in 1505 received his Master's in the same subject. The same year, he entered the Black Monastery in Erfurt, joining the Augustinian Hermits, an order of mendicant monks.

In 1507, he took his monastic vows and began studying theology at the University of Erfurt. In 1512, he was awarded the Doctorate in Theology at the University of Wittenberg. In October that year, he was received into the senate of the theological faculty of the University of Wittenberg and given the title of Doctor in Bible. He held this position for the rest of his life. Luther was appointed the Augustinian vicar for Meissen and Thuringia, an appointment which gave him charge over eleven Augustinian monasteries in his area.

Pope Leo X needed funds to build St. Peter's Basilica and saw the selling of indulgences as an income generator. In early1517, he announced that new indulgences were available for purchase. As an incentive, he claimed that purchasers would receive valuable religious merit. This merit, which could be distributed at the Pope's discretion from the treasury of merit of the saints, would reduce the penalty of sin in this and the next life.

John Tetzel, a Dominican monk, was given the task for the sale of these extra indulgences. He was a talented, but unscrupulous individual. He promised not only a reduction in punishment for sin, but complete forgiveness and a return to the state of perfection enjoyed immediately following baptism. He also promised purchasers that their relatives in purgatory would be quickly released.

In October 31, 1517 ACE, Luther wrote a letter to Albert, Archbishop of Mainz and Magdeburg, condemning the practice of selling indulgences and the attendant claims. He enclosed a copy of the 95 Theses on the Power and Efficacy of Indulgences (Latin Disputatio pro declaratione virtutis indulgentiarum Latin in which it was written). He also posted a copy on the door of the Wittenberg Castle Church, which was a kind of bulletin board for the University.

The document is a detailed set of propositions concerning church practice and doctrine, specifically, the sale of indulgences. The Catholic Encyclopedia defines indulgence as,

. . . . the extra-sacramental remission of the temporal punishment
due, in God's justice, to sin that has been forgiven, which
remission is granted by the Church in the exercise of the power
of the keys, through the application of the superabundant merits
of Christ and of the saints, and for some just and reasonable
motive.[78]

The Theses was widely copied and printed. Within two weeks it
had spread throughout Germany and within two months throughout
Europe.

It defined the nature of true repentance, established the limits of Papal
power and argued that the canons of the Church apply only to the living;
salvation lies with God alone and Indulgences should not have too great
an importance attached to them, especially compared to the Word and the
Gospel; grace is free to all and cannot be limited to those who purchase
indulgences.

In March1518, the Disputation at Heidelberg began. It was a debate
of Luther's ideas at a meeting of the Augustinian chapter. Luther joined the
debate in April. Several of the brothers accepted his way of thinking.

In May of that year, the papal court began an inquisition in Rome
in response to Luther's ideas. Luther was tried on charges of heresy in his
absence.

On August 5, 1518, Emperor Maximilian denounced Luther as a
heretic and, on August 7, 1518, Luther was ordered to go to Rome within
60 days to answer charges of heresy. In lieu of going to Rome, he went to
Augsburg for an interview with Cardinal Cajetan. The Cardinal told him
to recant, but he refused.

On October 20, 1518 ACE, he fled Augsburg, but returned to
Wittenberg on October 30, 1518 and sought the protection of Elector
Frederick 111 of Saxony.

In November, 1518, Pope Leo X issued a letter detailing the Church's
teaching on Indulgences, which Luther had contradicted. Luther prepared
for exile. However, Frederick decided not to banish him, despite requests
by the Pope.

---

[78] William Kent, "Indulgences", March 9, 2011. The Catholic Encyclopedia.
Vol. 7, New York: Robert Appleton Company, 1910, March 3, 2011.

In January 4, 1519, Luther was interviewed by papal chamberlain, Carl von Miltitz in Altenburg and on January 6, 1519 he agreed to make certain concessions, including sending a letter of apology to the pope. On March 3, 1519, he wrote a letter to Pope Leo X, in which he explained that his intention was not to undermine his or the church's authority.

On January 9, 1520, Rome resumed its inquisition of his ideas. The Pope allowed Luther 60 days to recant. On November 20, 1519, Luther apologized to the Pope personally in a letter. However, he continued denouncing what he saw as false doctrine and corruption.

In June 1520, Pope Leo X issued the Papal bull Exsurge Domine (Arise O Lord), outlining forty-one errors he found in Luther's 95 theses and other writings related to or written by him.

In December 10, 1520, Luther burned the bull of excommunication and other papal documents. In February 1521, Emperor Charles V summoned Luther before the Diet (assembly) of Worms, Germany, which met April 17, 1521. The clerk pointed to a set of books of Luther's and asked him if he would recant the ideas therein contained. Luther asked for a recess.

At the following day's session, he said,

> Unless I am convicted by Scripture and plain reason—I do not accept the authority of popes and councils, for they have contradicted each other—my conscience is captive to the Word of God. I cannot and I will not recant anything, for to go against conscience is neither right nor safe. God help me.[79]

Frederick 111 of Saxony decided to support Luther and arranged for bandits to capture him on his way returning home from Worms and taken to safety in Wartburg Castle. He stayed there for 11 months, May 4, 1521 to February 29, 1522.

In May 26, 1522, the Edict of Worms was signed by the emperor and issued. It condemned Luther's teachings and placed him under the ban of the Empire.

---

[79] Martin Luther, "Excerpts from his statement at the Diet of Worms", translation H.C. Bettenson, Documents of the Christian Church (1903, March 6, 2011.

On March 6, 1523, The General Council of the Diet of Nurernberg ordered Luther and his followers to stop publishing. It outlawed the preaching of anything other than what followed established Roman Catholic doctrine.

On April 1, 1523, the "General Council of the Diet of Nuremberg" General Council of Diet of Worms to enforce the Edict of Worms.

On July 1, 1524 the first Protestant martyrs were burned in Brussels.

On October 9, 1524, Luther stopped wearing the religious habit.

In August 1526, the First Diet of Speyer was held in the city of Speyer, Germany under Archduke Ferdinand I of Austria, in the name of his older brother the Emperor Charles 5, who intended to attend, but was prevented by other commitments. He instructed Ferdinand to seek a reconciliation of the two sides.

Ferdinand asked that the Edict of Worms be executed and that heresy and rebellion be put down, and that any final decisions on religion be postponed until the meeting of a general council.

> The Diet came with the consent of Ferdinand to the unanimous conclusion, Aug. 27, that a general or national council should be convened for the settlement of the church question, and that in the mean time, in matters concerning the Edict of Worms, "every State shall so live, rule, and believe as it may hope and trust to answer before God and his imperial Majesty. [80]

Although the decision concerning religion was only a temporary measure, the planned general council was postponed twenty years. In the mean time, Protestant princes interpreted the wording as permitting independent action and made the best use of it.

The First Diet of Speyer suspended the Edict of Worms. In April 1526, Luther wrote the great hymn, "A mighty fortress is our God."

In February 17, 1546 the great Protestant reformer died of heart attack

---

[80]   Philip Schaff, History of the Christian Church, chapter 8

Ulrich Zwingli

Luther's reformation ideas spread to neighboring Switzerland, which, at the time, was a confederacy of thirteen city-states called cantons. Some cantons

> broke from the Catholic Church and became Protestant while other cantons remained firmly Catholic. Of the cantons that adopted Luther's new movement, the most important and powerful was the city-state of Zurich under the leadership of Ulrich Zwingli. [81]

Ulrich Zwingli (1484-1531 was born at Wildhaus in Switzerland to a prominent middle class family. He studied music, scholastic philosophy and the humanities at Vienna, Bern, and Basel. He received a Master of Theology in 1506.

In 1519, Zwingli began his duties as priest of the Grand Minster in Zurich, "where he preached powerful sermons based on the Scriptures. In these sermons, he denounced the mercenary trade, dropped his own papal subsidy and attacked ecclesiastical abuses, rejected the veneration of saints, cast doubts on hellfire and argued that unbaptised children were not damned. He also married, breaking his vow of celibacy."[82]

In 1522, he argued that the Bible, not the Roman Church and tradition, was the only source of Christian authority and that things not prescribed in the Bible had no place in the church's life.

In 1523, he published "Sixty-Seven Theses", outlining his major religious positions, which resembled Luther's in the "Ninety-Five Theses." The only area of disagreement was the Lord's Supper (Communion). Whereas Luther believed that Christ is literally present in Holy Communion, Zwingli held that it is a symbolic meal.

In 1524, Zwingli used his influence to remove pictures, statues and relics from the city's churches.

---

[81] Richard Hooker, "Reformation: Ulrich Zwingli", Richard Hooker, 1996, March 4, 2011.

[82] "Ulrich Zwingli, Huldrych Zwingli, Swiss Reformation", BELIEVE web-page, n.d., Last updated January 7, 2011, March 15, 2011.

In 1525, the Catholic mass was replaced with a Zwinglian communion using both bread and wine as symbols of Christ's body and blood.

Zwingli also opposed the Anabaptists in Zurich who rejected infant baptism and was killed in Kappel in 1531, when the Catholic cantons of southern Switzerland attacked Zurich.

According to Richard Hooker,

> Zwingli tends to be passed over quickly in world history textbooks for several reasons; the most glaring reason is the simplicity of his theology. In comparison to Luther and Calvin, both of whom wrote a stultifying amount of stuff on every topic under the sun, Zwingli stuck to a single theme throughout his arguments and writing.
>
> Zwingli's theology and morality were based on a single principle: if the Old or New Testament did not say something explicitly and literally, then no Christian should believe or practice it. [83]

John Calvin

Jean (John) Calvin (1509-1564) was born at Noyon in France. He was a scholar, theologian and father of the French Reform Movement. Richard Hooker paid this significant compliment to him:

> The spirit of Zwinglianism reached its fullest development in the theology, political theories, and ecclesiastic thought of John Calvin. Perhaps even more so than Martin Luther, Calvin created the patterns and thought that would dominate Western culture throughout the modern period. American culture, in particular, is thoroughly Calvinist in some form or another; at the heart of the way Americans think and act, you'll find this fierce and imposing reformer. [84]

Calvin graduated as a Doctor of Law in 1531 and self-published a commentary on Seneca's Treatise on Clemenc.

---

[83] Richard Hooker, Reformation: Ulric Zwingli

[84] Richard Hooker, "Reformation; John Calvin."

In 1533, he fled Paris, because he feared that he might have been imprisoned due to his contacts with individuals opposed to the Roman Church. From 1533-1536 he lived outside France under assumed names.

In 1536, he went to Geneva and began lecturing and preaching. In 1538, he was asked to leave because of theological conflicts with the Catholic hierarchy there.

He went to Strasbourg and was pastor to French refugees until 1541, when he returned to Geneva and remained until his death.

In 1538, he began writing commentaries on the Bible and finished his massive account of Protestant doctrine, The Institutes of the Christian Church. This, his magnum opus, is considered "the most famous theological book ever published."[85]

When he returned to Geneva, he worked to change the city and church into a Christian commonwealth. He produced the Ecclesiastical Ordinances in 1541, outlining steps necessary to effect his plan. He also produced the Catechism of the Church of Geneva and, in 1542, Form of Ecclesiastical Prayers and Hymns.

If I were asked what was Calvin's greatest contribution to Protestantism, I should unhesitatingly answer it was his Institutes.

In it, he outlined the basic beliefs of Protestantism. In my chapter "Justification, I discuss his views on this crucial Christian theme.

> The core of Calvinism is the Zwinglian insistence on the literal reading of Christian scriptures. Anything not contained explicitly and literally in these scriptures was to be rejected; on the other hand, anything that was contained explicitly and literally in these scriptures was to be followed unwaveringly. It is the latter point that Calvin developed beyond Zwingli's model; not only should all religious belief be founded on the literal reading of Scriptures, but church organization, political organization, and society itself should be found on this literal reading.[86]

Although Martin Luther died a Catholic, a movement grew from his teachings. Zwingli and Calvin followed the path he followed and movements grew from their teachings. Other leaders followed in other European

---

85 Richard Hooker, "Reformation John Calvin."
86 Richard Hooker, "Reformation: John Calvin."

countries and formed parts of the Protestant Reformation. Thenceforward the European church was split between the Roman Church and this new upstart movement.

The Council of Trent

Cardinal Alessandro Farnese (1468-1549), who became Pope Paul III, (1534-his death) summoned distinguished prelates to Rome to discuss the matter of holding a General Council of The Church. Representatives of Charles V (1500-1558), Holy Roman Emperor (1519-56) and king of Spain (as Charles I, 1516-56); Ferdinand 1 (1503-1564), Holy Roman Emperor from 1558, king of Bohemia from 1528 and Hungary from 1526, king of Croatia, Dalmatia, Slavonia etc and other Catholic rulers favoured such a council. However, the Protestant rulers, including Henry V!!!, King of England, and Francis I, King of France, met at Smalkald, Germany, in December, 1535, and rejected the proposal.

After 2 postponements, the General Council met at Trento (then capital of the Prince-Bishopric of Trent, in what is now Italy) from December 13, 1545 to December 4, 1563 over 25 sessions of 3 periods.

Council fathers attended the first through eighth sessions in Trent (1545-1547), and the ninth through eleventh sessions in Bologna (1547) during the pontificate of Pope Paul III (1534-1549). Under Pope Julius III (1487-1555), the council met in Trent (1551-1552) for the twelfth through sixteenth sessions. The seventeenth through twenty-fifth sessions of the Council were held under Pope Pius IV (1499-1565) in Trent (1559-1563).

According to the Catholic Encyclopedia, the main object of the Council was,

> . . . . the definitive determination of the doctrines of the Church in answer to the heresies of the Protestants. A further object was the execution of a thorough reform of the inner life of the Church by removing the numerous abuses that had developed in it."(Catholic Encyclopedia, Council of Trent) By its own standards, the council succeeded.[87]

---

[87]   Johann Peter Kirsch, "Council of Trent." The Catholic Encyclopedia, Vol. 15,New York: Robert Appleton Company, 1912, March 30, 2011.

Denominations formed after the Reformation

The Anglican Communion

The international association of national and regional Anglican churches is called the Anglican Communion. The word "Anglican" means "of England". Thus, the Anglican Church is also known as the Church of England. In some countries, including the United States, the term "Episcopal" is used for "Anglican."

The Anglican Communion is an association of these churches in full communion with the Church of England (which may be regarded as the mother church of the worldwide communion) and specifically with its principal primate, the Archbishop of Canterbury. The status of full communion means, ideally, that there is mutual agreement on essential doctrines, and that full participation in the sacramental life of each national church is available to all communicant Anglicans.[88]

It is the third largest communion in the world, after the Roman Catholic and Eastern Orthodox Churches. The leadership of the Anglican Communion comprises three international bodies-The Lambeth Confrences; the Anglican Consultitive Council and the Primates Meeting.

The Lambeth Conferences are meetings of bishops of the Anglican Communion convened by the Archbishop of Canterbury every ten years. The first was convened in 1867. Resolutions passed at these conferences are not binding on members.

---

[88]   "The Anglican Communion", Wikipedia, last modified March 29, 2011, March 30, 2011.

The "Anglican Consultitive Council" (ACC) was created by a resolution of the 1968 Lambeth Conference. The council, which includes Anglican bishops, clergy and laity, meets every two or three years in different parts of the world.

> The role of the ACC is to facilitate the co-operative work of the churches of the Anglican Communion, exchange information between the Provinces and churches, and help to co-ordinate common action. It advises on the organisation and structures of the Communion, and seeks to develop common policies with respect to the world mission of the Church, including ecumenical matters.[89]

The "Primates' Meeting" was established in 1978 by Archbishop Donald Coggan (101st Archbishop of Canterbury) as an opportunity for "leisurely thought, prayer and deep consultation" and has met regularly since. It meets in various member countries of the Anglican Communion.

Anglican Communion Beliefs

The Communion has two main wings: the Evangelical wing, which is closest to denominations such as Methodist and Presbyterian and the Anglo-Catholic, which has common ground with Roman Catholic and Orthodox Churches. This latter is sometimes called "High Anglican."

Generally speaking, the "39 Articles of Religion", the Bible in English, the English Book of Common Prayer, "the Apostles", "Nicene" and "Athanasian" Creeds summarize the beliefs of the Anglican Communion.

"39 articles"

The "39 articles" (Articles) were agreed upon by the Archbishops, Bishops and all the clergy of the Provinces of Canterbury and York, London,

---

[89] "Anglican Consultitive Council", the Anglican Communion Office, 2011, April 30, 2011.

in 1562. There are two editions of the 39 Articles: a 1563 one in Latin and a 1571 edition in English.

In 1571, clergy were ordered to subscribe to them by Act of Parliament. The Church of England still requires its ministers to publicly avow their faithfulness to these Articles."[90] Other Communion members are not required to do so.

Some affirmations of the "Articles" are: the sufficiency of the Holy Scriptures for salvation (article 6); as a result of Adam's fall, man cannot on his own will do good works acceptable to God and can only do these by the grace of God by Christ (article 10); sacraments are signs of grace and God's good will towards us (article 25); Transubstantiation is not proven by Holy Scripture (article 28).[91]

English Book of Common Prayer

The Book of Common Prayer (BCP) is the common title of a number of prayer books used in the Anglican Communion. It contains the words of liturgical services of worship. The first BCP was written by Thomas Crammer, then Archbishop of Canterbury, and other clergy, from orders of King Edward VI. It was published in 1549. A revised version followed in 1552. Another edition was published in 1559. The 1662 edition, whose authorship is disputed among scholars, remains the official prayer book of the Church of England.

The full title of the 1662 Book of Common Prayer is The Book of Common Prayer and Administration of the Sacraments and other Rites and Ceremonies of the Church according to the use of the Church of England together with the Psalter or Psalms of David pointed as they are to be sung or said in churches and the form and manner of making, ordaining, and consecrating of bishops, priests, and deacons.

Over the years, there have been many revisions and alterations to the 1662 BCP in various domains of various countries. These include: Episcopal, Church of England, Episcopal Church of Scotland, Church of

---

90   "The 39 Articles of Religion (1562)", The Victoria Web, last modified December 2001, March 31, 2011.

91   "The 39 Articles - full text", Britain Express, London, England, n.d., March 31, 2011.

Ireland, Church in Wales, Anglican Church of Canada, Anglican Church of Australia, Anglican Episcopal Church of Brazil, Anglican Church of Congo, Anglican Church of Ghana and Anglican Church in Korea.[92]

> The Book of Common Prayer is many books in one. We have scarcely turned the title-page, for instance, before we come upon a ritual of daily worship, an order for Morning Prayer and an order for Evening Prayer, consisting in the main of Psalms, Scripture Lessons, Antiphonal Versicles, and Collects. Appended to this we find a Litany or General Supplication and a collection of special prayers.

> Next, we have a sacramental ritual, entitled, The Order for the Administration of the Lord's Supper or Holy Communion, ingeniously interwoven by a system of appropriate prayers and New Testament readings with the Sundays and holydays of the year. This gives us our second volume. Then follow numerous offices which we shall find it convenient to classify under two heads, namely: those which may be said by a bishop or by a presbyter, and those that may be said by a bishop only. Under the former head come the baptismal offices, the Order for the Burial of the Dead, and the like; under the latter, the services of Ordination and Confirmation and the Form of Consecration of a Church or Chapel.[93]

The Baptist Church

The Baptist movement might have originated from the Anabaptists, the English Separatists or the Perpetuates.

The Anabaptist movement was part of the "Reformation" and its followers were called radical reformers by mainstream reformers. The movement began in Switzerland in 1525 and was led by Conrad Grebel

---

[92] "The Book of Common Prayer", part of Anglican Resource Collection, last updated: August 30, 2008, March 31, 2011.

[93] Rev. William Reed Huntington, D.D., D.C.L, ,A short history of the Book of Common Prayer, Copyright Thomas Whittaker, 1893, March 31, 2011.

and George Glaurock. Shortly afterwards, it spread to Holland and Germany. The movement comprised different congregations with differing doctrinal opinions and practices. The central points of agreement were separation of church and state and adult baptism by immersion upon confession of faith.

Baptist might be a shortened form of Anabaptist, which would lend credence to the argument that they evolved from the Anabaptist movement.

English Separatists were a 16th century group of Anglicans who separated from the Church of England over, what they considered, its doctrinal errors and abuses. The first Baptist church sprang from a Separatist congregation of Gainsborough, Lincolnshire in 1606. Its leaders were John Smyth (1570-1612), Thomas Helwys 1575-1616) and John Murton (1585-1626).

Such congregations, separate from the Church of England, were illegal and James1, King of England, had vowed to deal harshly with such lawbreakers. The congregarion increased rapidly and its leaders decided to form an additional group. The original group in Gainsborough continued being led by its founders and another group was formed in Scrooby Manor, led by John Robinson, William Brewster and William Bradford.

Later, this last group became the nucleus of the Pilgrim Fathers who sailed to America on the Mayflower.

Within a year, John Smyth, Thomas Helwys and John Murton fled to Holland. In 1609, Smyth repudiated his former baptism, was baptized by the Mennonites and became a member. John Murton and Thomas Helwys remained Baptists and returned to their Gainsborough congregation.

The Gainsborough and Scrooby Manor congregations were called General Baptists, because they believed in General Atonement, that Jesus died for everyone and whoever believed in him would be saved.

There was another distinct set of Baptists, who were called Particular Baptists. Like their General Brethren, their origin is not clearly defined. Some assert that they developed from Continental Calvinistic congregations who migrated to England in the 1630's. Others contend that they developed directly from dissident radical congregations in London during the 1630's. They believed that Jesus' salvation was for only the Elect. Like the General Baptists, they believed in adult baptism by immersion.

Baptist Church in America

The first Baptist church in America was founded by Roger Williams (1603-1683) in 1639, but he left shortly afterwards to conduct open air meetings, because he believed God was too large to be housed under one roof.

The first national organization of Baptists was "The General Missionary Convention of the Baptist Denomination" in 1814. The Baptist Church in America is composed of various Baptist denominations. These include American Baptist Churches USA, Baptist Bible fellowship, Reformed Baptist, Seventh Day Baptist, Southern Baptist Convention, the largest Baptist denomination.

There is a vibrant Baptist church in Canada. Its denominations include: Association of Regular Baptist Churches, Baptist General Conference of Canada, Canadian Baptist Ministries, Convention of Southern Baptists, Landmark Missionary Baptist Association of Quebec and Fellowship of Evangelical Baptist Churches in Canada.

Baptist churches are autonomous and have no uniform system of beliefs and practice. Therefore, I will only describe areas of consistency. As stated earlier, all Baptist churches practice believer (adult) baptism by immersion as opposed to infant baptism. They believe that baptism is a right for only believers, because it is a sign of one's profession of faith. An infant cannot have such profession.

They also believe in the final perseverance of the believer, which is erroneously called, "Once saved, and always saved." Baptist teaching recognizes that the believer might stumble. However, the indwelling Spirit will pick him/her up. Baptists also believe that every believer is able to approach God directly through the intercession of Christ. This is known as the Priesthood of the believer. They also believe that man is born in sin and that his nature is corrupted. In order for him to inherit eternal life, he must repent and be born again through faith in Christ.

Baptists also believe in partaking of the Lord's Supper, something like Communion, but only obedient Christians are qualified to partake. They do not believe that the bread and wine is turned into the body and blood of Jesus (transubstantiation), but are rather memorials of Jesus' last supper with his disciples.

Seventh-day Adventists

Seventh Day Adventists is a Christian denomination, which was founded by Ellen G. White, James White, Joseph Bates and J.N. Andrews. Its name comes from their observance of the Sabbath (the seventh day of the week).

Adventists believe that the soul goes to sleep upon death and is awakened on Judgment Day. The Church also believes that the wicked will not suffer eternal damnation, but will be permanently destroyed. Perhaps the most distinctive Adventist belief is that a divine judgment of professed Christians has been ongoing since 1844.

Pentecostal Church

The Pentecostal Church is composed of various groups. Pentecostals assert that upon repentance (sometimes kneeling at the altar, surrounded by members of the church and asking God for forgiveness through Jesus Christ) one becomes "saved." The next step is sanctification, when the old nature is completely uprooted and replaced by a new God-like one, which precludes the possibility of sinning. The third and final step is the baptism of the Holy Spirit, exhibited by glossolia or speaking in tongues.

The Common Ground

At the outset, I defined the Church as an assembly of persons who accept Jesus as their head. I avoided saying "Jesus' teachings", because some of the assemblies described disagree on what that teaching constitutes. The Roman (Catholic) and (Eastern) Orthodox Churches disagree on administrative practices and with respect to the Holy Spirit as originating from the son. However both recognize Jesus as the only begotten son of the Father and the head of the Church.

Baptists do not share in the 7 sacraments and preach personal access to God without clerical intercession. However, they also accept Jesus as the head of their Church.

Seventh Day Adventists observe the Sabbath and hold the distinctive belief in the unconscious state of the dead. They believe that Jesus is the head of their church.

Pentecostals believe that the highest state of the Christian life is speaking in tongues. They accept Jesus as head of their Church.

I, therefore, conclude that the Church means, what it always meant, the body of believers, who accept Jesus Christ as their Head and Savior. I further conclude that no Church is greater than the other in the eyes of

God and that all churches exist for the sole purpose of bringing man closer to God.

> The Church's one foundation
> Is Jesus Christ her Lord,
> She is His new creation
> By water and the Word.
> From heaven He came and sought her
> To be His holy bride;
> With His own blood He bought her
> And for her life He died.
> She is from every nation,
> Yet one o'er all the earth;
> Her charter of salvation,
> One Lord, one faith, one birth;
> One holy Name she blesses,
> Partakes one holy food,
> And to one hope she presses,
> With every grace endued.

CHAPTER FOUR

Jewish Sects—70 ACE

A sound interpretation of New Testament text and an understanding of the polemics of the various sects and Jesus, require a firm grasp of the history of the period from Alexander the Great to, at least 70 ACE, when the Jewish temple was destroyed.

There were many religious groups in Jesus' day, some political, others religious and others a mixture of religion and politics.

There wasn't an official group that determined what was and what was not authentically or officially Jewish therefore a great diversity was found in Jewish faith, practice and belief. The High Priest and the Sanhedrin were the leaders of the Jewish community. Certain rabbis, such as Gamaliel, were able to exert a great influence over the Jewish people. However, a lack of uniformity among themselves limited their abilities to enforce conformity among all Jewish groups.[94]

Notwithstanding, some of the more popular sects managed to exert some form of influence on the religious .and political communities. The more popular of these were the Herodians, Disciples of John the Baptist, Pharisees, Sadducees, Essenes, Zealots, Samaritans, and Rechabites.

---

[94] "Jewish sects at the time of Christ", Aramaic Herald, July 27, 2010, March 21, 2011.

Short history of Palestine

Alexander the Great

I will begin with Alexandros III Philippou Makedonon (356 BCE-323 BCE) known in the West as Alexander the Great or Alexander III of Macedon, a king of Macedon, a state in the north eastern region of Greece. He was son of Philip II, King of Macedon and Olympias, the princess of neighboring Epirus.

From age 13 through 16, he was tutored by the Greek philosopher Aristotle in n rhetoric, literature and philosophy.

He ruled from 336-323 BCE and had conquered most of the civilized ancient world by age thirty. Palestine was one of his colonies. When he died in 323 BCE, his empire was divided by his generals, the Diadochi (successors). Seleucus became king of the eastern provinces—modern Afghanistan, Iran, Iraq, Syria and Lebanon, with parts of Turkey, Armenia, Turkmenistan, Uzbekistan, and Tajikistan. Ptolemy I Soter took Egypt, creating a powerful Hellenistic state stretching from southern Syria to Cyrene and south to Nubia. He also took Palestine, which his family ruled until they were defeated by the Seleucids in 200 BCE. The Seleucids ruled from 202 BCE until 142 BCE.

Ptolemy 1 Soter("preserver")

Ptolemy 1 Soter was born in Macedon around 367/366 BCE and died around 283/282 BCE at Alexandria, Egypt. He was the founder of the Ptolemaic dynasty, which reigned longer than any other dynasty established on the former Alexandrian empire.

He made Alexandria, Egypt, his capital, where he founded the fabled Library of Alexandria, the most renowned centre for learning in the Ancient World. He wrote a history, now lost, on Alexander the Great's military campaigns. Ptolemy sponsored the great mathematician Euclid, but found Euclid's seminal work, the Elements, too difficult to study. A story is told that he asked if there were an easier way to master it. Euclid replied, "Sire, there is no Royal Road to Geometry."

Although he was more concerned over the affairs of Egypt than those of Palestine, he led several military expeditions there. After the battle of Gaza (312 BCE), he returned to Egypt; but before leaving he destroyed the strongholds of Acre, Joppa, Gaza, Samaria and Jerusalem. Many Jews, including the respected high priest Hezekiah, attached themselves to Ptolemy. Others went willingly to Egypt.

Ptolemy 1 died 283 BCE and one of his sons, Ptolemy 11 Philadelphus succeeded him and ruled until 246 BCE.

Ptolemy 2 Philadelphus

Ptolemy II was born 309 BCE and died 246 BCE. At 18, he was made his father's co-regent in order to guarantee his succession. In 283 BCE, he repudiated his first wife and married his older sister Arsinoe II and made her co-regent in 277 BCE. They celebrated their status as sibling co-rulers by both adopting the epithet "Philadephus", which means "brother/sister loving."

During the reign of Ptolemy 2, Palestine was attacked regularly by Seleucids and Bedouins. He increased the number of military units and built many Greek cities. Many of these were organized as military colonies, where soldiers who married native women were given homes and fields.

Palestine began exporting grain, olive oil, smoked fish, cheese, meat, dried figs, honey and date to Egypt and became an important route for the spice trade.

Ptolemy Philadelphus is credited by later Jewish sources with being a benefactor to the Jews. He sponsored the translation of Torah into Greek. He extended his Hellenizing projects into Palestine by transforming ancient Semitic centers into Greek cities. However, he made no attempt to Hellenize Jerusalem or Judea.[95]

Ptolemy 3 Euergetes 1 (the benefactor)

Ptolemy 3 (146-222 BCE) was the son of Ptolemy 2 and Arsinoe 1. His relations with Palestine were not significant.

---

[95]   Mahlon H. Smith, "Ptolemy II Philadelphus", American Theological Library Association Selected Religion Website, 1999, April 15, 2011.

Ptolemy4 Philopator "Lover of his father"

Ptolemy4 (238-205 BCE) was the eldest son of Euergete whom he succeeded in 222 BCE. "He began his reign by ordering the murder of his mother (Berenice 11, uncle (Lysimachus) and younger brother (Magas). A drunken reveler, Ptolemy regularly depended on advice from incompetent court favorites."[96] From all accounts, he was very anti-Jewish and the Jews in Palestine suffered greatly under his rule. Egypt began to decline under his weakness. He died in 205 BCE.

Ptolemy 5 Epiphanes ("illustrious")

Ptolemy 5 (Ptolemy 4 (204-181 BCE) was the son of Ptolemy 4 and Arsinoe III of Egypt. He became ruler at age 5 and reigned from 204BCE-181 BCE. Because of his age, much of his administration was conducted by his father's advisors, who murdered his mother. He was poisoned at age 30.

The Seleucids (Syrians)

Antiochus 3, the Great, was born in Babylon, Mesopotamia 241 BCE and died in Iran 187 BCE. He was the son of Seleucus II Callinicus and Laodice II. He succeeded to the throne at age 18.

Antiochus 3 conquered Palestine in 201 BCE, but it was not until 198 BCE that it was completely subdued.

> By 198 B.C.E. the Jews of Palestine had become disenchanted with Ptolemaic rule, and they opened the gates of Jerusalem to Antiochus, and assisted in the expulsion of its Egyptian garrison.

> Antiochus rewarded the Jews for their "splendid reception" by restoring those parts of Jerusalem destroyed by the war, freeing

---

[96]   Mahlon H. Smith, "Ptolemy IV Philopator", American Theological Library Association Selected Religion Website, 1999, April 15, 2011.

its citizens from taxes for three years and supplying funds for the Temple, and in general by permitting "members of the nation to have a form of governmnt in accordance with the laws of their country" It was also forbidden to bring to Jerusalem animals forbidden for consumption by Jews (Jos., Ant., 12:129-53).[97]

Antiochus 4

Antiochus 4 was born 215 BCE and died 164 BCE. He was the son of Antiochus 3 and Laodice III. Many consider him the cruelest of the Seleucid rulers of Palestine.

> He outlawed reading of the Jewish law and indeed even the owning of it. He persecuted the Jews to the point of extinction and then erected for himself a statue of Zeus in the Jerusalem Temple and sacrificed a sow on the altar as a sign of his contempt for the Jewish religion. Needless to say, he was reviled by the Jews. His incredible cruelty gave rise to a horrid persecution which saw the birth of the Apocalyptic movement and the writing of the Book of Daniel.[98]

Another commentator says that Antiochus "is undoubtedly one of the greatest prototypes of the Antichrist in all of God's Word."[99]

In 167 BCE, he sent some of his officers to the village of Modein (17 miles north west of Jerusalem) to force the Jews living there to offer sacrifices to the pagan gods. The village priest, named Mattathias, an aged man, was commanded to be the first person to offer a sacrifice. He refused.

Another Jew volunteered to offer the sacrifice. Overcome with rage, Mattathias killed him and the officers of the king. He then tore down

---

[97] "Antiochus", Encyclopaedia Judaica© 2008, the American Cooperative Enterprise, 2010, April 16, 2011

[98] "The History of the Levant from Alexander the Great to Herod the Great", Quartz Hill Schooof Theology, n.d., April 14, 2011

[99] Larry W. Cockerham, "Antiochus IV Epiphanes: The Antichrist of the Old Testament", Prophecy Forum, Prophecy Forum Ministries, 2001, April 15, 2011.

the altar to the pagan gods and ran through the village shouting, "Let everyone who is zealous for the Law and who stands by the covenant follow me!" (I Maccabees 2:27). His 5 sons—John, Simon, Judas, Eleazer, and Jonathan—with a number of followers, fled to the mountains of the Judean wilderness.

They organized themselves into a powerful guerrilla army and raided towns and villages, tore down the pagan altars, killed the officials of Antiochus and executed Jews found worshipping the pagan gods. When Mattathias died in 166 BCE, he chose his son Judas to lead the guerillas.

Antiochus took the guerillas lightly and sent a small force of his less capable generals to quell the rebellion. Although greatly outnumbered, Judas and his men defeated every general that he engaged. Antiochus sent Lysias, the commander of the Seleucid army, along with 60,000 infantrymen and 5000 cavalry to battle Judas.

They met Judas and 7000 rebels in the town of Emmaus, 7 miles from Jerusalem. Judas prayed to God for strength and deliverance (I Maccabees 4:30-33), and God enabled him to defeat the Seleucid army!

Judas and his men set about to drive the enemy out of Jerusalem and cleanse the Temple. On December 25, 165 BCE, the Temple was rededicated to God with rejoicing and sacrifices. The celebration continued for eight days. This is the famous "Feast of Lights", known as Hanukkah.

Antiochus 4 died in 164 BCE and his nine-year old son became king as Antiochus 5 Eupator and ruled until 162 BCE. The rightful heir to the throne was Demetrius, son of Seleucus IV. He was being held hostage by Rome, which refused to release him, preferring to have Syria nominally ruled by a boy and his regent Lysias than the 22 year old Demetrius.

In 163 BCE, Antiochus and Lysias defeated the Jewish army at Beth-Zecharia. The same year, Lysias offered peace terms to Judus, who accepted. It allowed the Jews to worship unmolested, if they would remain loyal to the Seleucid Empire. However, Lysias destroyed the walls of Jerusalem before departing.

In 162 BCE, Demetrius escaped from Rome and was accepted by the Syrians as the rightful king. Antiochus and Lysias were overthrown and put to death.

Shortly afterwards, civil war broke out between the Hellenistic Jews and Judas and his followers. The former sought and received help from the Seleucids. In 160 BCE, Judas and his 800 men were surrounded and almost all of them, including Judas, were killed. His brother Jonathan assumed leadership, but was captured by the Seleucids in 143 BCE and executed the following year. His brother Simon became the rebels' new leader.

In 140 BCE, an assembly of the priests, leaders and elders recognised him as High Priest and Military commander and "ruler of Israel."[100] In 134 BCE, his son-in-law Ptolemy assassinated him and his son John Hyrcanus succeeded him.

Antiochus 7 Sidetes, king of the Seleucids, claimed sovereignty over Palestine. When the Jews resisted, he invaded Judea in 134 BCE, conquered Jerusalem and tore down its walls. He did not attack the Temple or interfered with Jewish observances. In order to gain Jewish allegiance, he granted them religious freedom and confirmed John Hyrcanus as High Priest.

John made political gains by conquering Samaria and destroying their chief holy temple, which was built on Mount Gerizim. He also succeeded in conquering and converting the Idumeans who, in later years, became the most patriotic Jews.

John Hyrcanus died in 105 BCE and his son Aristobulus assumed power; but he died a year later. His brother Alexander Jannaeus succeeded him and reigned until 77 B.CE. His rule was marked by violence, cruelty, and civil war. While enjoying the support of the Sadducees, he was detested by the Pharisees. During the civil war, he crucified 800 of the main Pharisees of Jerusalem, executing their wives and children before their eyes as they hung on crosses.

After his death, his wife Alexandra assumed the throne and reigned from 78 to her death in 69 BCE. Hyrcanus II was her heir, but his younger brother Aristobulus II incited civil war and seized power, which he held until 63 BCE, when the Roman general Pompey conquered Palestine. The brothers appealed to Pompey for arbitration in their quest for power.

Pompey sided with Hyrcanus, reinstalled him as High Priest and took Aristobulus to Rome as a trophy of war. Hyrcanus proved a puppet of his Idumean advisor Antipater, who became procurator of Judea upon Pompey's death. Two of Hyrcanus's sons, Phasael and Herod, were given authority over Jerusalem and Galilee respectively. After Caesar was assassinated in 44 BCE, they gave aid to the forces of Brutus and Cassius, two of the conspirators.

By 42 BCE, Antpater was poisoned and the conspirators were defeated by Octavian and Mark Anthony, who made Phasael and Herod tetrarchs of Judea.

In 34 BCE, Antigonas, a surviving son of Aristobulus, besieged Jerusalem. Phasael committed suicide and, upon capturing Jerusalem,

---

[100]   Maccabees", Wikipedia., last modified April 16, 2011, April 19, 2011.

Antigonas cut off the ears of Hyrcanus (his uncle) so that he would no longer qualify as High Priest. Herod fled to Alexandria and sought the help of Mark Anthony.In 37 BCE, with help from the Romans, he retook Jerusalem, executed Antigonus and controlled Palestine.[101]

Herod the Great

Herod the Great or Herod 1 ruled from 37 BCE to 4 ACE. He was suspicious of the political ambitions of the surviving Maccabeans (Hasmoneans) and had them murdered over a period of time. He did not spare Mariamne, the granddaughter of Hyrcanus II and one of his ten wives. He also murdered Alexander and Aristobulus 4, his sons by Mariamne. He also "slew all the children that were in Bethlehem, and in all the coasts thereof, from two years old and under, according to the time which he had diligently inquired of the wise men." (Matthew. 2:16-18)

Despite his cruelty, Herod was a capable administrator. He built cities, expanded religious sites, developed agricultural projects and created a relatively stable government during a difficult period.

> Herod's most famous project was rebuilding of the Temple of Jerusalem, greatly enlarging it and making it into the most beautiful in its time. Some of his other achievements include: the rebuilding the water supplies for Jerusalem, building his own palace in Jerusalem, refurbishing and constructing fortresses such as Masada and Herodion, supporting the financially troubled Olympic Games, and creating whole new cities such as Caesarea Maritima and Sebaste. He also engaged in substantial relief programs during periods of drought or famine and influenced Rome to protect the rights of Jews in the Diaspora.[102]

When he died in 4 BCE in Jericho, the majority of his kingdom was left to his three sons, Archelaus, Antipas and Philip.

---

[101] David C. Carson, "A BRIEF HISTORY OF THE INTERTESTAMENTAL PERIOD AND BEYOND", David C. Carson, 2006 April 14, 2011.
[102] "Herod the Great", New World Encyclopedia, May 7, 2006, May 14, 2011.

Archelaus ruled (4 BCE-6 ACE) over Idumea, Judea, and Samaria. He was proclaimed king by the army, but did not assume the title until he had submitted his claims to Caesar Augustus, the Roman Emperor. Before leaving for Rome, he quelled sedition of the Pharisees, slaying three thousand members of the sect.

In Rome he was opposed by Antipas and by many of the Jews, who disliked his cruelty. In 4 BCE, Augustus gave him the greater part of the kingdom (Samaria, Judea, and Idumea) with the title of ethnarch ((not king). He held this position until 6 ACE when Judaea province was formed, under direct Roman rule, at the time of the Census of Quirinius.

Philip was made ruler over Gaulanitis, Auranitis, Trachonitis, Batanea, Paneas, and Iturea. He rebuilt the cities of Paneas, which he renamed Caesarea Philippi, the site of Peter's confession of Christ (Matt. 16.16) and Bethsaida, where Jesus healed a blind man (Mark 8:22)).

Philip married Salome, Herodias's daughter, but they had no heir. When he died in 34 ACE, Tiberias annexed his territories to Syria and, when Caligula became emperor (37 ACE), they were given to Agrippa I, Herodias's brother.

Antpas became governor of Galilee and Perea. He is best known for imprisoning and beheading John the Baptist, an itinerant Jewish preacher (Matt. 14.1-12). This incident occurred after he had married Herodias, who was his niece and the wife of his brother Philip. According to Mosaic Law, it was unlawful to marry a brother's wife (Lev. 18.16; 20.21). John's criticism of the marriage caused Antipas to imprison him and later, upon the request of Salome, his wife's daughter, execute him.

In 36 ACE, Aretas IV, the Nabatean king, defeated Antipas in retaliation for Antipas's deserting his daughter to marry Herodias. Rome did not help him. Caligula, the emperor, gave his friend Agrippa I, brother of Herodias as well as nephew of Antipas, the territories of Philip ,who had died in 34 ACE, and granted Lysanius the coveted title of king. Herodias became jealous and urged her husband to visit Rome and seek the title of king for his long, faithful service.

When he and Herodias arrived in Rome in 39 ACE to request the title, Agrippa brought charges against Antipas and, as a result, Caligula banished him to Gaul. Agrippa I obtained his territories.[103]

---

[103]   "Herodian Dynasty", Answers.com, Answers. Com corporation, 2011, April 14, 2011.

Agrippa I was the son of Aristobulus (son of Herod the Great and Mariamne) and Bernice (daughter of Herod's sister, Salome, and Costobarus) and the brother of Herodias. Sometime in 36 ACE, he went to Rome and befriended Gaius (Caligula). After publicly stating that he wished if Caligula were emperor instead of Tiberius, the latter imprisoned him. He was released in 37 ACE upon Tiberius's death and the ascension of Caligula.

Caligula also gave him control of the provinces formerly administered by his uncle, Philip, and other provinces in Syria. He awarded him the title "king", which had not been officially bestowed on any member of his family since the death of Herod the Great.

After Caligula was murdered in 41 ACE, Claudius, the new Emperor, gave him control of the provinces of Judea and Samaria. Thus, for four years the extent of Agrippa's kingdom rivaled the extent of his grandfather's. He died in 44 ACE at Caesarea Maritima while conducting a celebration of the Roman imperial cult. [104]

Agrippa 2

Agrippa 2 (28-100ACE) was the son of Agrippa I and the seventh and last king of the family of Herod the Great. He was the brother of Berenice, Mariamne and Drusilla (second wife of the Roman procurator Antonius Felix).

He was educated in Rome and was a thoroughly Hellenistic Jew. At that time and years afterwards, the language and culture of Rome was Greek. His father died when he was a teenager. However, Emperor Claudius provided him with territorial political responsibilities, including the right to name the important post of High Priest of Jerusalem. After Claudius died in 54 ACE, the new emperor, Nero, also favoured him and increased his territories.

Agrippa's Hellenistic lifestyle and insensitivity to Jewish religious issues made him unpopular with Jews. There were also rumors, never proven, that he was living in an incestuous relationship with his sister Bernice.

---

[104]   Mahlon H. Smith "Perspective on the World of Jesus", American Theological Library Association Selected Religion Website, 1999, April 14, 2011.

When his subjects were preparing to revolt against Rome, he urged restraint and tolerance for the behaviour of the Roman procurator Gessius Florus. In 66 ACE, the Jews expelled him and his sister Bernice from the city. That year, Nero, Emperor of Rome, sent an army under General Vespasian to quell the revolt. Agrippa sent 2,000 men, archers and cavalry, to support Vespasian. He fought alongside the general and was wounded at the siege of Gamala.

By 68 ACE, resistance in the northern part of the province had been eradicated and the Romans turned to the subjugation of Jerusalem. That year, Nero committed suicide. In the resultant chaos, Vespasian was declared Emperor and returned to Rome His son Titus took command in the assault on Jerusalem.

In 70 ACE, Jerusalem was captured, thousands of its citizens were slaughtered, its temple destroyed and its sacred relics taken to Rome as spoils of victory.

After the capture of Jerusalem, Agrippa and Berenice went to Rome, where Agrippa was made King and rewarded with additional territory. He died in 100 ACE.

Jewish Sects

I feel that this general history of Palestine up to, during and after Jesus' lifetime will prove useful in understanding the political and religious events and movements that I will now discuss.

The Herodians

The Herodians was a movement that supported the policies and government of the Herodian dynasty (37 BCE to 92 ACE), especially Herod Antipas, monarch of much of Palestine from 4 BCE through 39 ACE. They are mentioned in Mark (Mark 3:6, 12:13) and Matthew (22:16); but not in Luke or John.

Although we are told that they plotted with the Pharisees to kill Jesus (Mark 3:6), we are not told their clear-cut reason(s). They condoned Roman occupation of their land and Jesus preached loyalty to Caesar. (Mark 12:17)

Disciples of John the Baptist

John the Baptist (Aramaic: Yoḥanan) was was an ascetic, messianic prophet, who spent his early years in the wilderness between Jerusalem and the Dead Sea (Matt. 3:1-12). He led a simple life, clothed only with camel's hair and a leather girdle around his loins, and eating locusts and wild honey (Matt. 3:4).

He was born into a priestly family around 6 BCE and was beheaded 36 ACE. He was a travelling preacher, who led a movement of baptism at the Jordan River, where he also baptized his cousin, Jesus of Nazareth. Flavius Josephus, the renowned Jewish historian says that he

> was a good man, and commanded the Jews to exercise virtue, both as to righteousness towards one another, and piety towards God, and so to come to baptism; for that the washing [with water] would be acceptable to him, if they made use of it, not in order to the putting away [or the remission] of some sins [only], but for the purification of the body; supposing still that the soul was thoroughly purified beforehand by righteousness. Now when [many] others came in crowds about him, for they were very greatly moved [or pleased] by hearing his words, Herod, who feared lest the great influence John had over the people might put it into his power and inclination to raise a rebellion, (for they seemed ready to do anything he should advise,) thought it best, by putting him to death. [105]

Even after Jesus began his ministry, John continued his and was very popular. His movement continued after his death. We read in Acts of a a Jew named Apollos, who "knew only the baptism of John" (Acts 18:25).

> A common scholarly view is that the Jesus movement grew out of a larger John the Baptist Movement. Jesus' movement was the smaller, and the gospels' frequent praise of John can be explained

---

[105] Flavius Josephus, Antiquities of the Jews, XVIII Chapter 5. 2, James D. Tabor, 1998, April 11,2011.

by the early Christian efforts to recruit followers of the Baptist, like Apollos.[106]

The Pharisees

The Pharisees was an important Jewish religious sect during Jesus' lifetime and an active political and social movement in Palestine during the Second Temple Era (536 BCE-70 ACE). After the destruction of the Second Temple (70 ACE), Pharisaic Judaism came to be known as Rabbinic Judaism and later, simply as Judaism. The main direct sources on the Pharisees is Flavius Josephus (37-100 ACE), a renowned Jewish historian and hagiographer and the New Testament.

The term "Pharisee" could derive either from the Aramaic "Perisha" (the singular of "Perishaya"), which means "one who separates himself" or from the Hebrew "perushim", from "parash", meaning "to separate." It could also have derived from Hebrew "parosim", meaning "specifier" and the Pharisees tried to specify the meaning of God's law to the people.

Most Pharisees were persons who separated themselves from impure persons and things in pursuit of levels of holiness. They were mostly laymen, but some of their members were priests and they occupied 5 of the 71 seats in the Great Sanhedrin, the supreme court of ancient Israel. Their leaders were called rabbis and were the intellectuals of their day and stressed strict interpretation and observance of the Mosaic Law in both its oral and written form.

Origin

The sect grew out of the resistance movement of the Maccabean period (around 166-160 BCE). Many scholars consider them as the party of Roman resistance. This probably explains their popularity among the masses. When Herod the Great rose to power (37 BCE), the Pharisees, as an official party, withdrew from politics.

---

[106]   "John the Baptist", New World Encyclopedia, last modified September 18, 2008, April 11, 2011.

Politics

The driving force behind Jewish resistance to Rome in Jesus' time was religion. However, the New Testament is significantly silent on this. Hyam Maccoby states:

> The motive force behind the Jewish Resistance was the Jewish religion. This is a difficult point for the modern reader to grasp because we are not used to thinking of religion as a political, activist, revolutionary force. Also, the picture of the Jewish religion given in the New Testament is that of a rigid Establishment clinging to the status quo . . . . There is no indication in the New Testament of any conflict between Jewish religion and Roman power. In fact, the whole issue of Roman power is played down to such an extent that there is hardly a hint of any opposition to Rome. The aim of the Gospels is to present the revolutionary issue of the day as between Jesus and the Jewish Establishment. The fact that there was a Roman Establishment against which revolutionary forces existed is veiled so that the Establishment against which Jesus rebelled can be represented as entirely Jewish.[107]

According to Maccoby, "From the first to the last, the resistance against Rome came from the Pharisee party."[108] He exaggerates a bit in this, because the Zealots resisted Rome to a greater extent than the Pharisees. However, his point is well understood—The Pharisees, at one point in their history, was a well recognized nationalistic resistance movement and drew the wrath of Archelaus Herod, who suspected them of plotting anti-government acts and he killed three thousand members.

After the Judean civil war, Alexander Jannaeus, who ruled Judea (103 BCE 76 BCE) crucified 800 of the main Pharisees and cut the throats of their wives and children.

Many reasons have been advanced to explain why this aspect of Pharisaic life is omitted in the Gospels. One is that the Gospels wanted to

---

[107] Hyam Maccoby, "Religion and Revolt: The Pharisees", abridged from Revolution in Judea: Jesus and the Jewish Resistance by Hyam Maccoby, n.d., March 7, 2011.

[108] Hyam Maccoby, "Religion and Revolt: The Pharisees

present a picture of Jesus against the Jewish Establishment, which would not have been repulsive to Rome. If they had presented a portrait of Jewish resistance, they should have most likely faced Roman wrath.

Another reason concerns the motif of the Gospels. According to this, the Gospels were primarily concerned with presenting the good news of Jesus' message of salvation. Consequently, they limited their portrait to his religious message within the then contemporary religious context and only described the Pharisees within a religious context.

However, the Pharisees were extremely popular with the masses, because of their resistance to Roman occupation.

Religion

After the rebuilding of the Second Temple (516 BCE), the Pharisees were allied to the new group of scribes and sages and controlled the study of Torah, which was read publicly on market-days. The scribes and sages developed and maintained an oral tradition as a means of interpreting the Torah. The Pharisees interpreted and expanded the Torah to cover every possible occurrence of unfaithfulness to the written law, alongside the Torah. They also accepted the writings of the prophets. It was the Pharisees who brought Synagogue worship with them from their Babylonian captivity and introduced it to Israel.

After the second temple was destroyed in 70 ACE, they formed the Jamnia School at Jamnia, which played an important role in transforming Judaism into Rabbinic Judaism

> The Pharisees are interesting, indeed, from the standpoint of historical study. They are the most characteristic manifestation of Palestinian Judaism in the time of Christ. They alone of the Jewish parties survived the destruction of the temple and the city. Modern Judaism is immensely indebted to Pharisaism. The Pharisees remained, as representing all that was left alive of Judaism . . . . . .
> It is impossible to understand the atmosphere of Christ s earthly life without an adequate knowledge of the Pharisees."[109]

---

[109] A.T. Robertson, "The Pharisees and Jesus, The StoneLectures", VICTORIA UNIVERSITY LIBRARY, TORONTO, ONTARIO, n.d., March 21, 2011.

Pharisee Religious Beliefs

There were, at least, seven types or schools of Pharisees during Jesus' lifetime. The two most important were followers of two great Jewish teachers, Hillel and Shammai.

> These two constituted one of the series of "Pairs" (zugot) who led the Pharisees in the last two centuries before the turn of the era. Both Hillel and Shammai led great "schools" in Jerusalem. They and their disciples, called the Bet Hillel and the Bet Shammai in rabbinic literature, represented two distinct currents in the Jewish approach to Halacha—the conservative and the progressive. Generally speaking, Shammai followed a more stringent and literal interpretation of the law, while Hillel expounded a more flexible application of its demands."[110]

Bet Shammai was the Senior Judge of the Court of the Great Sanhedrin and Hillel was its President. The former was conservative and inflexible. The latter was liberal and flexible. For example, in the matter of divorce, Bet Shamnai taught that the only ground for divorce was infidelity, while Bet Hillel taught that there were additional grounds.

Apart from their emphases on the Law, all Pharisaical schools believed in the immortality of the soul and in heaven and hell (Acts 23:8), the physical resurrection of the dead and a day of judgment to be followed by reward or punishment. They believed that people have free will but that God also has foreknowledge of human destiny. They believed that love of man was the essence of Jewish theology. They also believed in the existence of angels.

Opposition to Jesus

The Gospels present the Pharisees in constant opposition to Jesus. Is this picture accurate?

---

[110] William C. Varner, "Jesus and the Pharisees: A Jewish Perspective", Personal Freedom Outreach, Saint Louis, Missouri , 1996, March 9, 2011.

At the same time, a Jew reading the Gospels is immediately aware of aspects which do not seem authentic; for example, the accounts of Pharisees wanting to kill Jesus because he healed on the Sabbath. The Pharisees never included healing in their list of activities forbidden on the Sabbath; and Jesus's methods of healing did not involve any of the activities that were forbidden. It is unlikely that they would have disapproved, even mildly, of Jesus's Sabbath-healing. Moreover, the picture of bloodthirsty, murderous Pharisees given in the Gospels contradicts everything known about them from Josephus, from their own writings, and from the Judaism, still living today, which they created.[111]

The Sadducees

Origin

The Sadducees was a main religio-political movement between 147 BCE and 70 ACE. It originated during the Hasmonaean (Maccabean) dynasty (147-37 BCE) and disbanded after the temple was destroyed in 70 ACE

The derivation of the name is in dispute. Some scholars believe that the word was derived from "Tsaddîq" ('righteous'). Others believe it derives from "Zadok", who anointed Solomon king during the First Temple era. The Catholic Encyclopedia states:

> The old derivation of the name from tsaddiqim, i.e. the righteous; with assumed reference to the adherence of the Sadducees to the letter of the Law as opposed to the pharasaic attention to the superadded "traditions of the elders", is now generally discredited mainly on philological grounds and the term is associated with the proper name "Sadoc", Sadducee being equivalent to Sadokite.[112]

---

[111]   Hyam Maccoby, "Religion and Revolt: The Pharisees",

[112]   James F Driscoll, "Sadducees", The Catholic Encyclopedia, Vol. 13, New York: Robert Appleton Company, 1912,March 23, 2011

Jona Lendering concedes that,

> It is not possible to choose between the alternatives: the name 'righteous ones' may have been adopted as a retort to the Chasidim (i.e., the early Pharisees), who claimed that they were the only pious ones; the name 'sons of Zadok', on the other hand, may refer to the fact that only the descendants of Zadok were . . . . entitled to perform the priestly service in the Temple."[113]

When Herod the Great became sole ruler in 40 BCE, he chose the high priests, but the Sadducees remained involved in the management of the Temple. They continued in this during the Roman occupation (6-70 ACE), when the Roman governors appointed the High Priest. Most High Priests were Sadducees. At least 20 of the 28 high priests between 37 BCE and 66 ACE were Sadducees.[114]

Information on Sadducees

No Sadducee texts have been found. The Dead Sea Scrolls do not mention them. Information about them derives from sources, mostly unsympathetic to them. For example, Josephus in his Jewish Wars states that "the behavior of the Sadducees one towards another is in some degree wild, and their conversation with those that are of their own party is as barbarous as if they were strangers to them." [115]

In Antiquities, he ridicules them:

> But they are able to do almost nothing of themselves; for when they become magistrates, as they are unwillingly and by force sometimes obliged to be, they addict themselves to the notions of the Pharisees, because the multitude would not otherwise bear them. [116]

---

[113] Jona Lendering, "Sadducees", Livius,2005, April 12, 2011.

[114] Jona Lendering, "Sadducees."

[115] F lavius Josephus, The Wars of the Jews, book 2, , chapter 8, translated William Whiston, the Common Man's Perspective, 1990, April 12, 2011.

[116] Antiquities of the Jews, book 18, chapter1.4, April 12, 2011.

Many historians, even those who do not believe he was a Pharisee, accuse Josephus of knowingly distorting the Pharisees' image.

The canonical gospels are not friendlier. Their portrayal is negative and denies the Sadducees any good qualities. It is unlikely that a group, who upheld the letter of the Law and denied oral traditions, would not have been pious and devout.

Politics

Their politics was conservative and they represented the status quo, accepting Roman occupation of their land. They were also the party of the nobility, power, and wealth. Consequently, the masses hated them.

Sadducees and Religion

Josephus (Antiquites book 2, chapter 8) and the gospels (Matthew 22:23; Mark 12:18; Acts 23:8) state that they denied resurrection, immortality of the soul, the existence of angels and the role of fate in human life. They believed in the sole authority of the Torah, which they accepted literally, and rejected the oral traditions.

They did not deny that "the prophets" and "the historical writings" were divinely inspired. However they refused to accept them as sources of law. They had interpretative traditions of their own, which were written down in a book of jurisprudence known as the Book of Decrees. This book was used for clarifying certain vague Torah passages, but was not held as important as the Torah.

The Essenes

The derivation of the word "Essenes" has not been determined. Nahum N. Glazer states:

> "Essenes" is an English transliteration of the Greek Essenoi. The derivation and meaning of the Greek word have been a mystery since the first century A.D. Philo, our earliest source (ca. A.D. 40), speculated that "Essenes" was derived from the Greek

hosios, meaning "holy." Modern scholars have preferred to go back to Semitic originals. The two most probable etymologies offered to date are from the Aramaic 'asen,' asayya, "healers," and from the East Aramaic hasen, hasayya, "the pious." The first etymology would suggest a link between the Essenes and the Therapeutae (Gr. "healers"), a similar Jewish group flourishing contemporaneously in Egypt. The second etymology would imply a historical relationship between the Essenes and the Hasidim (Hebrew: "pious ones"), the faithful Jews who distinguished themselves during the Maccabean revolt (ca. 167 B.C.). Extant evidence will not allow a firm decision between the two etymologies, though it would seem that the latter currently enjoys more credence. In any case, there is no reason to assume that "Essenes," or Semitic equivalent, was a self designation. It may have been a label applied to the group by outsiders. As such, it would point to the manner in which the Essenes were perceived by their contemporaries.[117]

The Encyclopedia of Religion says:

The Essenes were known in Greek as Essenoi or Essaioi. Numerous suggestions have been made regarding the etymology of the name, among which are derivation from Syriac ḥase' ("pious"), Aramaic asayya' ("healers"), Greek hosios ("holy"), and Hebrew ḥasha'im ("silent ones"). The very fact that so many suggestions as to etymology have been made and that none has carried a scholarly consensus shows that the derivation of the term cannot be established with certainty. No Hebrew cognate appears either in the Dead Sea Scrolls, taken by many scholars to be the writings of this sect, or in rabbinic literature (the Talmuds and midrashim). Only with the Jewish rediscovery of Philo Judaeus (d. 45-50 ce) and Josephus Flavius (d. 100 ce?) in the Renaissance was the Hebrew word issiyyim (Essenes) coined.[118]

---

[117] Nahum N, Glatzer "Essenes", Believe webpage, n.d., March 21, 2011.
[118] Lawrence Schiffman, "Essenes", Encyclopedia of Religion2005, March 23, 201.

The origin of the sect is lost. Some scholars claim that it was founded by a Jewish High Priest whom the Essenes (in the Dead Sea Scrolls, specifically, sections of the "Damascus document") called Teacher of Righteousness. According to this literature, he was a prophet to whom God revealed his secrets. Bible scholars continue to debate his identity.

Jewish legend claims that Enoch was their founder. Incidentally, the word "Enoch" means "founder", "initiator" in Hebrew. According to one legend; the Essenes were originally a closed Mystery School founded by Enoch, the great grandfather of Noah. Another legend states that, after they almost reached a point of extinction many centuries later, Moses guided their remanifestation by training hundreds of initiates.

Interestingly, there are frequent references in the New Testament to the other two sects, the Sadducees and Pharisees, but no reference has been found to the Essenes. Despite this silence, they were well known in Palestine in Jesus' lifetime and are mentioned by Flavius Josephus, Philo and Pliny the Elder. Josephus mentions them in Wars of the Jews book 2, chapter 8 and Antquities book 18, chapter 2.5. Philo's Apology for the Jews (now lost but preserved in part by Eusebius, Praeparatio evangelica 8.2) and Every Good Man Is Free, both written in the first half of the first century ACE mention them. They are also mentioned by Pliny the Elder in Natural History 5:18:73.

By the 2nd century ACE, the Essenes had become the third largest Jewish sect, after the Pharisees and Sadducees. Although they observed the Torah, they withdrew from mainstream Judaism over a dispute about whom was qualified to be a High Priest.

In 140 BCE, an assembly of the priests, leaders and elders recognised Simon Maccabee as High Priest, Military commander and "ruler of Israel. The positions were hereditary. The Essenes argued that the Hasamoneans were not qualified to be priests, because they did not belong to the tribe of Levi, the tribe from which priests were chosen. Consequently, they withdrew from worshipping in the temple.

Some scholars state that the Essenes lived throughout Palestine in their own communities. However, others locate them at Lake Mareotes, in Egypt, where they were called Therapeutae, Healers. It is also believed that a small, enlightened group lived at Qumran, on the north western shore of the Dead Sea, where they remained until the Parthian invasion of 40 BCE when they settled around Jerusalem and returned to Quamran after Herod the Great died in 4 BCE. Most scholars agree that the group in Israel disbanded around 70 ACE.

According to Josephus:

> These last (Essenes) are Jews by birth, and seem to have a greater affection for one another than the other sects have. These Essenes reject pleasures as an evil, but esteem continence and the conquest over our passions, to be virtue. They neglect wedlock, but choose out other person's children, while they are pliable, and fit for learning, and esteem them to be of their kindred, and form them according to their own manners. They do not absolutely deny the fitness of marriage, and the succession of mankind thereby continued; but they guard against the lascivious behavior of women, and are persuaded that none of them preserve their fidelity to one man.[119]

The Essenes were ascetics, who practiced self-denial and held all things in common. All activity was geared towards the common good of the community. When they worked, their salaries were handed over to a common purse. If any were in need, they could take from the common supplies.

Essene Beliefs

The Essenes believed that the human body is corruptible and that it is a prison that holds man's soul captive. This soul is immortal and imperishable and when man dies, it is released and ascends to "heaven." They also believed that a Messiah would come to set up a new and glorious kingdom on earth. By setting themselves apart from society, which they considered evil, and by adhering to the law strictly, they would partake of this kingdom.

Some Essenes were also scribes and prophets, who studied and preserved the Jewish scriptures, the books of their sect and the names of angels. They considered themselves the guardians of Divine Teaching found in the precepts that the Hebrews had rejected at Mount Sinai. Their library contained many ancient manuscripts, some of which were found in 1947 at Qumran

---

[119] Flavius Josephus, "The Jewish Wars", Book 2, Chapter 8.

They worshipped in accordance to the Law. Instruction was given every day except on the Sabbath. Although they did not worship in the temple, they remained faithful Jews and sent offerings to the Temple, but made their sacrifices among themselves.

The sect disappeared from the historical record shortly after 70 ACE, but was rediscovered when the "Dead Sea Scrolls", attributed to them, were found at Khirbet, Quamran, between 1947 and 1956.

The Scrolls are mainly written in Hebrew, with 20 percent in Aramaic and a small portion in Greek. The texts include 23 of the 24 books of the Hebrew Bible (the Protestant Old Testament). The missing book is "Esther." Eight or more copies of several books of the Old Testament were found, including the Pentateuch, Isaiah (the oldest Hebrew text), Twelve Prophets, Psalms and Daniel. The scrolls also include material, which describes the rules, beliefs and practices of the brotherhood/sect and commentaries on biblical texts.

Was Jesus an Essene?

There is no proof that Jesus was an Essene. However, there are hypotheses that he was. I will examine the data to see if conclusions could be made one way or the other.

Some argue that he was, because he never mentioned the Essenes. According to this argument, Essenes were sworn to privacy and, consequently, mentioning them would have violated his oath.

We know from the historical record that the majority of Essenes lived in Judea, where Jesus' ministry was concentrated. They led a virtuous life, the kind of life that Jesus would have admired. If he had commended their piety, he should not be breaking any oath he made. The fact that he did not mention the Essenes is not proof of membership.

Another argument advanced for his being an Essene is in his teaching. The Essenes preached the complete renunciation of wealth, abandonment of family and possessions. Jesus did the same.

> And he (Jesus) said to them all, If any man will come after me, let him deny himself, and take up his cross daily, and follow me." (Luke 9:23) On another occasion, he told the disciples, "So likewise, whosoever he be of you that forsaketh not all that he hath, he cannot be my disciple. (Luke 14:33)

Jesus promised future happiness to those who forsook all and followed him,

> Then Peter began to say unto him, Lo, we have left all, and have followed thee. And Jesus answered and said, Verily I say unto you, There is no man that hath left house, or brethren, or sisters, or father, or mother, or wife, or children, or lands, for my sake, and the gospel's, But he shall receive an hundredfold now in this time, houses, and brethren, and sisters, and mothers, and children, and lands, with persecutions; and in the world to come eternal life." (Mark 10:28-30)

Is the similarity of Jesus' teaching to the Essenes' on self-denial, abandonment of family and worldly goods proof that he was an Essene? I should think not, since many other sects and religions preached these things long before the Essenes.

Since the discovery of the "Dead Sea scrolls", our knowledge of the Essenes has increased dramatically. The following comes from "SCROLLS FROM THE DEAD SEA":

> In 1947, young Bedouin shepherds, searching for a stray goat in the Judean Desert, entered a long-untouched cave and found jars filled with ancient scrolls. That initial discovery by the Bedouins yielded seven scrolls and began a search that lasted nearly a decade and eventually produced thousands of scroll fragments from eleven caves. During those same years, archaeologists searching for a habitation close to the caves that might help identify the people who deposited the scrolls, excavated the Qumran ruin, a complex of structures located on a barren terrace between the cliffs where the caves are found and the Dead Sea. Within a fairly short time after their discovery, historical, paleographic, and linguistic evidence, as well as carbon-14 dating, established that the scrolls and the Qumran ruin dated from the third century B.C.E. to 68 C.E. They were indeed ancient! Coming from the late Second Temple Period, a time when Jesus of Nazareth lived, they are older than any other surviving biblical manuscripts by almost one thousand years.[120]

---

[120] "Dead Sea Scrolls", The Ancient Library of Qumran and Modern Scholarship, an Exhibit at the Library of Congress, Washington, DC, Library of Congress, n.d., April 13, 2011.

Most scholars believe that the Essenes lived at Qumran. The "Damascus Document" and commentaries on portions of the Jewish bible (both attributed to these essences) speak of an interesting figure called Teacher of Righteousness.

Teacher of Righteousness

The Damascus Document (CD) (the Cairo Damascus document),, also called The Document Of The New Covenant In The Land Of Damascus, and Zadokite Fragments, is one of the works found in multiple fragmentary copies in the caves at Qumran, and as such is counted among the Dead Sea Scrolls. Most scholars believe that it was written in stages between 70 ACE, the last known record of Essene settlement at Qumran. At the outset, the document talks about Israel's evil ways and how God hid His face from them and "from His Sanctuary, and gave them over to the sword [121]

The document speaks of its sacred community. It also calls on the community to observe the standards of purity the "Teacher of Righteousness" established and obey his words to receive salvation. The Teacher's words are opposed by the evil teachings of a mysterious Man of Mockery (Lies).

But when He remembered the covenant of the forefathers,
He left a remnant to Israel, and gave them not over to destruction.
5 [And in the period of the wrath three hundred and ninety
    years after He had given them in the hand of
Nebuchadnezzar, the King of Babylon He visited them], and He
    made to spring forth from Israel and Aaron,
A root of His planting to inherit His land,
And to grow fat through the goodness of His earth.

---

[121] "FRAGMENTS OF A ZADOKITE WORK FRAGMENTS OF A ZADOKITE WORK also knewn asThe Damascus Document" translated by R. H Charles, edited Diane Morgan, Wesley Center for Appled Theology, n.d., April 13, 2011.

6 And they had understanding of their iniquity,
And they knew that they were guilty men,
And had like the blind been groping after the way twenty years.
7 And God considered their works; for they sought Him with a
perfect heart
And He raised them up a Teacher of righteousness
To lead them in the way of His heart.
8 And He made known to later generations what He had done [to
a later generation] to a congregation of treacherous men:
Those who turned aside out of the way.
9 This was the time concerning which it was written:
As a stubborn heifer
So hath Israel behaved himself stubbornly:
10 When there arose the scornful man,
Who talked to Israel lying words,
And made them go astray in the wilderness where there was no
way,
[to bring low the pride of the world].
11 So that they should turn aside from the paths of righteousness,
And remove the landmark which the forefathers had set in their
inheritance: [122]

Who was the Teacher of Righteousness

He was sent by God to counsel the Israelites on obeying the Law. If
they obeyed his words, they would receive salvation. Most scholars consider
him the organizer of the group that settled at Qumran. However, he died
prior to their settling there. He claimed to have the correct understanding
of the Torah, because it was though him that God would reveal "the hidden
things in which Israel had gone astray" (CD 3:12-15).

There are many theories about the identity of the Teacher.

Suggestions range from Ezra (so T.H. Gaster, The Dead Sea
Scriptures (1956), vi et passim; C.T. Fritsch, The Qumran
Community (1956), 83ff.) and Nehemiah (so L. Rabinowitz, in

---

[122] "Fragments of a Zadokite Work, 1:4-11.

JBL, 73 (1954), 11ff.) at one end, and Menahem son of Judah
the Galilean (or his kinsman and successor, Eleazar b. Jair) killed
by Eleazar captain of the Temple in 66 C.E. at the other (so C.
Roth, Historical Background of the Dead Sea Scrolls (1958),
12ff.; G.R. Driver, The Judaean Scrolls (1965), 267ff.). A
number of scholars have identified him with Onias III, the last
legitimate high priest of the house of Zadok, assassinated at the
instance of the illegitimate high priest Menelaus in 171 B.C.E.
(so H.H. Rowley, Zadokite Fragments and the Dead Sea Scrolls
(1952), 67ff.; M. Black, The Scrolls and Christian Origins
(1961), 20); others have suggested Onias the rain-maker, killed
by partisans of Hyrcanus II in 63 B.C.E. (so R. Goossens, La
Nouvelle Clio, 1-2 (1949-50), 336ff.; cf. A. Dupont-Sommer,
Essene Writings from Qumran (1961), 359 with notes 2, 3),
or Judah b. Jedidiah, one of the sages massacred by Alexander
Yannai (so W.H. Brownlee, in: BASOR 126 (1952), 10ff.,
where this Judah is further identified with Judah the Essene,
contemporary of Aristobulus I).[123]

Dr. Michael O. Wise, internationally renowned expert on the Dead
Sea Scrolls, offers one in his book, The First Messiah: Investigating the
Savior Before Christ, Wikipedia summarized it:

> The Teacher of Righteousness was the "first messiah", a figure
> predating Jesus by roughly 100 years. This figure—whom Wise
> believes was named Judah—rose to prominence during the reign
> of Alexander Jannaeus, and had been a priest, and confidant to
> the king. However, he became dissatisfied with the religious
> sects in Jerusalem, and in reaction, founded a "crisis cult". While
> amassing a following, the Teacher (and his followers) claimed
> he was the fulfillment of various Biblical prophecies, with an
> emphasis on those found in Isaiah. The Teacher was eventually
> killed by the religious leadership in Jerusalem, and his followers
> hailed him as messianic figure who been exalted to the presence
> of God's throne. They then anticipated that the Teacher would

---

[123]   "Teacher of Righteousness", Encyclopaedia Judaica, the Gale Group, Jewish
Virtual Library, 2008 , April 13, 2011.

return to judge the wicked and lead the righteous into a golden age, and that it would take place within the next forty years. Wise explains that dating of manuscript copies among the Dead Sea Scrolls shows that the Teacher's postmortem following drastically increased in size over several years, but that when the predicted time frame failed to live up to expectations, his following dissipated rapidly.[124]

The significance of the Essenes in bible history is that they throw light on religious views at the advent of Jesus and their books have helped millions of Christians to understand Jesus' teaching in a then contemporary light. They are the most interesting religious sect of the 1st century.

The Zealots

In Jesus' time, there were frequent uprisings against Roman colonization, but not a unified movement. One of the groups fighting for Jewish independence was the Zealots. The term, as used in the 1st Century ACE, referred to a zealous political movement for the expulsion of Rome from Palestine. Around 45 BCE, a Jewish patriot named Ezekias (Hezekiah), from Trachonitis (east of Galilee), led a band of freedom fighters against the Romans and their supporters. The uprising was brutally crushed. He was captured and executed and Judea was officially incorporated into the Roman Empire.

Ezekias' son, Judah, continued to revolt against Rome. The Zealot movement was formed around 6 ACE from remnants of his father's followers and other Jewish resistance groups. It was centered at Gamla, a steep mountainside city northwest of the Sea of Galilee.

In 6 ACE, the Romans ordered a census in Judea and it was carried out by Quirinius, governor of Syria. Judah and his followers opposed it and led a revolt, during which he and most of his followers were killed.

The group reorganized around 10 ACE and led small scale revolts in Galilee. They participated in the unsuccessful Great Uprising in Jerusalem against Rome (66-70 ACE). According to Jewish legend, the Zealots, who

---

[124] "Teacher of Righteousness", Wikipedia, last modified April 11, 2011, retrieved April 13, 2011.

did not perish there, hid in the fortress at Masada. In 73 ACE, the Romans discovered their hiding place and attacked them. They put up a fierce defense. However, they were overpowered and 900 fighters committed mass suicide rather than surrender.

Zealot Belief

> The Zealots adopted a strict code comprised of four main beliefs. First, God alone was to be served. Second, God alone was their ruler. Neither Rome nor Herod Antipas was a legitimate authority. Third, they believed taxes were to be paid only to God. Fourth, from the time of the Maccabees, Zealots taught that all foreign rule over the Jews was unscriptural. Serving Rome, whether by Yahad choice or as a slave, violated God's supreme authority.[125]

The Samaritans

The Samaritans were a people who lived in a part of ancient Israel in the time of Jesus. The Gospels describe their conflicts with the Jews (the people of Judea) and a few of their encounters with Jesus and his disciples (John 4:9; 8:48; Luke 9:51-56).

Who were these people and why do the gospel writers show little sympathy for them? After the dissolution of the unified Kingdom of Israel in 930 BCE, the kingdom was divided into 2 parts—the northern part, usually known as Israel and the southern part known as Judah. Israel contained 10 of the 12 tribes and the 2 other tribes resided in Judah.

In 885 BCE, Omri, the seventh king of Israel, bought a hill in Israel from Shemer for 150 pounds of silver. There he built a city and named it Samaria after its former owner (1 Kings 16-24). Shechem remained the religious capital of Israel; but Samaria became its political capital. The city became known for its idolatry.

---

[125] "Zealots", That the World may know Ministries, Holland, MI., 2007. Retrieved March 8,2011

In 722 B.C., after a siege of three years, Shalmaneser the king of Assyria, conquered Samaria and deported the Israelite elite to Assyria. Shalmaneser's successor, Sargon, "brought people from Babylon, Cuthah, Avva, Hamath and Sepharvaim and settled them in the towns of Samaria to replace the Israelites." (2 Kings 17:24)

Each group newly settled in the region brought with them their own gods.

The end result of all this was mingled race—for the remaining Israelites intermarried with the colonists—purporting belief in the God of Israel and the laws of Torah while worshiping the gods of the foreign settlers with whom they had blended. Neither the race nor the religion was pure."[126]

After returning from their Babylonian exile (515 BCE), the Samaritans built their own temple on Mount Gerizim in Samaria, where they offered sacrifices similar to those offered at the temple in Jerusalem.

Alexander the Great conquered the city of Samaria in 330 BCE and settled Macedonians, who would further intermarry with the already mixed race.

After the Roman general Pompey defeated the Seleucid monarchy in 64 BCE, he annexed the region of Samaria to Syria. In 31 BCE, the Roman commander Octavian gave Samaria to the new king of Judaea, Herod the Great. When Octavian changed his name to Augustus, Herod changed Samaria's name into Sebaste (the Greek form of Augustus). By the birth of Christ, the Jews still called the city by its old name.

After the death of Herod (4 BCE), Sebaste was given to his son Herod Archelaus and when the Romans finally annexed Judaea and organized it as a province (6 CE), the city was one of the centers of the new government. The soldiers were integrated as auxiliary troops in the Roman army.

---

[126] David C. Carson, "Who Were the Samaritans?" David C. Carson, 2006, March 3, 2011.

From now on, the history of Samaria-Sebaste is part of the history of Judaea, but not because either the population of the big city or the rest of the inhabitants of the province wanted it like that. There were religious tensions between the Samaritans and the orthodox Jews, there were economic differences between the urban and peasant economies, and the cosmopolitan city was culturally different from many other towns of Judaea. When the Jewish War broke out in 65-66, the inhabitants of Sebaste saw their city razed to the ground by the Jews. It was rebuilt after the fall of Jerusalem and the destruction of its temple" [127]

Conclusion

I am intrigued with the story of the Jews. How did they endure their long periods of colonization? Who were their leaders? Was Jesus just another Jewish false Messiah or the one foretold by the Law and the Prophets? To what extent was he influenced by contemporary thought? This chapter attempted to provide data, which could help in understanding these questions and probably provide answers.

The Jesus story is incomplete in the form handed down. It is only by comparing him to his contemporaries that one can make reasonable assumptions about the real story of his life and teachings.

---

[127] Jona Lendering, "Samaritans", Jona Lendering © 1995-2010, March 5, 2011.

CHAPTER FIVE

The Life and Teachings of Jesus

Primitive Christianity was therefore right to live wholly in the future with the Christ who was to come, and to preserve of the historic Jesus only detached sayings, a few miracles, his death and resurrection.

. . . . Albert Schweitzer

I will begin with the question: Was Jesus of Nazareth a real person? That is, apart from the biblical record (the foundation of the believer's faith), is there any historical evidence that the Jesus of Christianity existed as a human being? After answering this contentious question, I shall discuss his life and teachings as described by the gospels and historians.

Did Jesus really live?

This question has nothing to do with what the priest says in his homily on Sunday or with what I believe, which, incidentally, is in the historicity of Jesus. It concerns the matter of evidence. Put another way, it is a battle between faith and reason. Faith accepts the biblical record as sufficient evidence. Reason seeks verification from the historical record. Those who assert the non-existence of Jesus advance, as one of their strongest arguments, the absence of reference to him during his lifetime and the scarcity of genuine non-Christian reference to him in the early centuries after his death. Those arguing for a historical Jesus point to comments by Flavius Josephus, Pliny, the Younger and the canonical gospels.

That a man named Jesus, an obscure religious teacher, the basis of this fabulous Christ, lived in Palestine about nineteen hundred years ago, may be true. But of this man we know nothing. His biography has not been written. A Roman and others have attempted to write it, but have failed—have failed because no materials for such a work exist. Contemporary writers have left us not one word concerning him. For generations afterward, outside of a few theological epistles, we find no mention of him.[128]

Here is a short list of writers one would expect to have mentioned Jesus, either because they lived during his lifetime or shortly afterwards:

Philo Judaeus (20 BCE-50 ACE) was a Hellenistic Jewish philosopher, born in Alexandria and was part of its Jewish elite. His works on the Jewish religion and on contemporary Jewish politics are extant. He even spent time in Jerusalem during the period that Jesus was supposed to have lived there. One of his nephews, Marcus, was married to Bernice, daughter of Herod Agrippa, Tetrarch of Galilee in Jesus' time.

Kenneth Humphreys says that,

> Philo was also in the right place to give testimony of a messianic contender. A Jewish aristocrat and leader of the large Jewish community of Alexandria, we know that Philo spent time in Jerusalem (On Providence) where he had intimate connections with the royal house of Judaea. His brother, Alexander the "alabarch" (chief tax official), was one of the richest men in the east, in charge of collecting levies on imports into Roman Egypt. Alexander's great wealth financed the silver and gold sheathing which adorned the doors of the Temple (Josephus, War 5.205). Alexander also loaned a fortune to Herod Agrippa I (Antiquities 18)[129]

---

[128]   John E. Remsberg, The Christ, (Chapter 2), "Silence of Contemporary Writers", Positive Atheism Magazine, n.d., March 8, 2011.

[129]   Kenneth Humphreys, "Witness to Jesus?—1 Philo of Alexandria", Kenneth Humphreys, 2006, March 4, 2011.

Humphreys continues:

> Much as Josephus would, a half century later, Philo wrote
> extensive apologetics on the Jewish religion and commentaries
> on contemporary politics. About thirty manuscripts and at least
> 850,000 words are extant. Philo offers commentary on all the
> major characters of the Pentateuch and, as we might expect,
> mentions Moses more than a thousand times. Yet Philo says not
> a word about Jesus[130]

Seneca, the Younger (4 BCE-ACE 65) was a Roman philosopher, statesman
and dramatist during the time Jesus was supposed to have lived. An argument
against expecting him to mention Jesus is that he was a Roman dramatist and,
therefore, totally removed from the world of Jewish religion. However, he was
tutor and advisor to Emperor Nero, who persecuted the Christians. Nero must
have heard much about the Christians to have persecuted them and, most
likely, would have mentioned Jesus to his teacher.

Plutarch (46 ACE-120 ACE) is the most renowned biographer of the
ancient world, author of Parallel lives of Famous Greeks and Romans, now
known as Plutarch's Lives. He was born approximately 16 years after Jesus
supposed death. Is it unreasonable to expect that a historian/biographer of
his stature would have heard about the Jewish leader, who was well known
in Palestine and whose death must have been known to the Romans? Why
did he not mention Jesus?

Juvenal (55 ACE-120 ACE), a wealthy Roman poet, best known for
his 16 Satires, is another writer whom one would expect to have mentioned
Jesus, but did not.

Explaining non-mention

One reason advanced to explain the absence of contemporary or
near-contemporary mention of Jesus is that he was a lowly carpenter
turned itinerant preacher and not a noteworthy figure to earn the mention
of men of letters. This is not tenable, because it presupposes that men
of letters do not mention minor figures, who had some impact on their

---

[130] Kenneth Humphreys, "Witness to Jesus."

society. Furthermore, the gospels portray Jesus as a popular leader, whose death and resurrection made him legendary. Why did not some Jewish contemporary, like Philo, mention some aspect of his story?

For the sake of argument, let me grant the contention that Jesus was a lowly carpenter turned itinerant preacher and not a noteworthy figure to earn the mention of men of letters. What of the Provincial records? They do not mention him. It would hardly be unreasonable to expect them to mention the death of a man who rocked the Jewish establishment, a fact emphasized by the canonical gospels. Even the High Priest got involved in his trial and the Tetrarch of Judaea sentenced him.

Mention of Jesus

Notwithstanding the scarcity of contemporary and near-contemporary mention, Jesus was mentioned by four first century writers.

Flavius Josephus

Late in the 1st century, Flavius Josephus (37ACE-100ACE), a great Jewish historian, mentioned Jesus in his Jewish Antiquities.

Testimonium Flavianum

The passage quoted below is known as the "Testimonium Flavianum" (Testimony of Flavius Josephus), hereafter known as "Testimonium" or "TF". (The words in bold are my own and are used for emphasis)

> About this time there lived Jesus, a wise man, **if indeed one ought to call him a man. For he was one who performed surprising deeds and was a teacher of such people as accept the truth gladly**. He won over many **Jews and many of the Greeks. He was the Messiah**. And when, upon the accusation of the principal men among us, Pilate had him condemned to a cross, those who had first come to love did not cease. **He appeared to them spending a third day restored to life, for the prophets of God had foretold these and a thousand other marvels about him.**

And the tribe of the Christians, so called after him, has still to this day not disappeared. [131]

The words in bold did not appear in the original version, but appeared in a 4th century one. Opinion on its authenticity varies.

> Louis H. Feldman surveyed the relevant literature from 1937 to 1980 in Josephus and Modern Scholarship. Feldman noted that 4 scholars regarded the Testimonium Flavianum as entirely genuine, 6 as mostly genuine, 20 accept it with some interpolations, 9 with several interpolations and 13 regard it as being totally an interpolation. [132]

Ecclesiastical History of Eusebius of Caesarea (264-c.340 ACE), Bishop and Church historian, is the principal source for the history of Christianity. He quoted the TF in the surviving form in all his manuscripts. Most historians believe that it was he who added the words in bold.

TF not genuine

Ken Olsen argues,

> Josephus either said nothing about Jesus at this point in his text or what he said is so completely overwritten by Eusebius that no authentic Josephan substratum of the "Testimonium" can be recovered. It is the nearly unanimous verdict of modern scholarship that the "Testimonium" is at least partially a Christian interpolation."[133]

---

[131] Flavius Josephus, The Works, "Book XVIII, Chapter 3:3," translated William Whiston, n.d., March 16, 2011. Flavius Josephus, The Works, "Book XVIII,

[132] "Early Christian Writings , Testimonium Flavianum", Peter Kirby, 2001, April 1, 2011.

[133] Olsen,Ken, "Eusebius of Caesarea forged the Testimonium Flavianum ", Mountain Man Graphics, Australia, n.d., March 7, 2011.

Joseph Scaliger (1540-1609 ACE), renowned French classical scholar, was the first person to suspect the authenticity of the "TF", due to its Christian content.[134]

Peter Kirby stated,

> It is impossible that this passage is entirely genuine. It is highly unlikely that Josephus, a believing Jew working under Romans, would have written, "He was the Messiah." This would make him suspect of treason, but nowhere else is there an indication that he was a Christian. Indeed, in Wars of the Jews, Josephus declares that Vespasian fulfilled the messianic oracles. Furthermore, Origen, writing about a century before Eusebius, says twice that Josephus "did not believe in Jesus as the Christ.[135]

Shlomo Pines (1908-1990) was professor in the Department of Jewish Thought and the Department of Philosophy at the Hebrew University of Jerusalem from 1952 until his death in 1990. In 1971, he published a translation of a different version of TF from Kitab al-'Unwan (Book of headings or History).written by Agapius, a 10th century Christian Arab Christian historian and Melkite bishop of Manbij (Mabbug, Hierapolis). Agapius'version of the TF was lost to scholarship until 1971:

> For he says in the treatises that he has written in the governance of the Jews: "At this time there was a wise man who was called Jesus, and his conduct was good, and he was known to be virtuous. And many people from among the Jews and the other nations became his disciples. Pilate condemned him to be crucified and to die. And those who had become his disciples did not abandon their loyalty to him. They reported that he had appeared to them three days after his crucifixion, and that he was alive. Accordingly they believed that he was

---

[134] G J Goldberg, "Josephus' Account of Jesus in the Testimonium Flavianum", Radical Faith Magazine, N.d., March 16, 2011.

[135] "Early Christian Writings , Testimonium Flavianum", Peter Kirby, 2001, April 1, 2011.

the Messiah, concerning whom the Prophets have recounted wonders" [136]

This version differs from Eusebius and proves that there was, at least, a then existing version of the TF without the words in bold.

Professor Pines believed that the Agapius' version was more accurate than the version quoted earlier.

Richard Montague (1577-1641), Bishop of Chichester and Norwich, an eminent 17th Century Church of England theologian, declared that the phrase "He was the Messiah" in the TF is a later Christian addition. [137]

Henry St. John Thackeray (1869-1930), Grinfield lecturer on the Septuagint at Oxford and the prince of Josephan scholars, supported the interpolation theory and credits Josephus' "Greek assistants" for variation in styles throughout the Antiquities. [138]

Partially authentic

Louis Harry Feldman (born 1926), Abraham Wouk Family Professor of Classics and Literature at Yeshiva University, where he has taught since 1956 and the acknowledged living authority on Flavius Josephus , believes that the most probable view seems to be that the text represents substantially what Josephus wrote, but that some alterations were made by a Christian interpolator. [139]

Another scholar states:

> Perhaps the most important factor leading most scholars to accept the partial-authenticity position is that a substantial part of the TF reflects Josephan language and style. Moreover, when the obvious Christian glosses—which are rich in New Testament terms and language not found in the core—are removed or

---

[136] Shlomo PINES, "An Arabic Version of the Testimonium Flavianum", WordIq. com. 2010, March 16, 2011.

[137] G J Goldberg, "Josephus' Account of Jesus in the Testimonium Flavianu."

[138] G J Goldberg, "Josephus' Account of Jesus in the Testimonium Flavianu."

[139] G J Goldberg, "Josephus' Account of Jesus in the Testimonium Flavianu."

restored to their original the remaining core passage is coherent and flows well.

We can be confident that there was a minimal reference to Jesus . . . because once the clearly Christian sections are removed; the rest makes good grammatical and historical sense. The peculiarly Christian words are parenthetically connected to the narrative; hence they are grammatically free and could easily have been inserted by a Christian. These sections also are disruptive, and when they are removed the flow of thought is improved and smoother. (James H. Charlesworth, Jesus within Judaism, pages 93-94).

In conclusion, a substantial amount of the TF is characteristically Josephus and only a few phrases are obviously Christian. Moreover, many of the phrases that are characteristically Josephan are absent from the New Testament and other early Christian literature (such as "wise man" and "leading men"), and/or are phrases or terms that Christians would likely have avoided using (such as "startling deeds," and "received the truth with pleasure"). Add in a phrase that any Christian scribe would have known was erroneous ("he gained a following among many Jews and among many of Gentile origin") and a compelling case exists that the core of the TF is authentic. Cementing the case is that the TF actually is coherent and flows better without the obvious Christian glosses.[140]

Second Josephan mention

Ananus was of this disposition, he thought he had now a proper opportunity [to exercise his authority]. Festus was now dead, and Albinus was but upon the road; so he assembled the sanhedrim of judges, and brought before them the brother of Jesus, who was called Christ, whose name was James, and some

---

[140] Christopher Price, "Did Josephus refer to Jesus? Thorough Review of the Testimonium Flavianum", n.p., n.d., April 1, 2011.

others, [or, some of his companions]; and when he had formed an accusation against them as breakers of the law, he delivered them to be stoned.[141]

Discussion on this passage usually centres on whether or not it is a partial interpolation or genuine. Those who argue for the genuineness of the passage point to the words, "Jesus, who was called Christ." They argue that if a Christian had added the words, he would have stated,"Jesus the Christ" and not " who was called Christ."

However, this argument is invalid, because the same expression occurs in Matthew 1:16, 27:17, 22 and in John 4:25. These books were written by christian writers. Thus, a christian writer could have inserted the sentence " who was called christ."

I believe that this passage, like the TF, was partially authentic and that certain words were inserted afterwards by Christian writers. Consequently, Josephus cannot be evidenced for the historicity of Jesus.

Pliny the Younger

Pliny the Younger (62ACE-113 ACE) was Governor of Bithynia Pontus, a Roman province, and a learned Jew. His correspondence in 106 ACE with the emperor Trajan included a report on proceedings against Christians:

> They asserted, however, that the sum and substance of their fault or error had been that they were accustomed to meet on a fixed day before dawn and sing responsively a hymn to Christ as to a god, and to bind themselves by oath, not to some crime, but not to commit fraud, theft, or adultery, not falsify their trust, nor to refuse to return a trust when called upon to do so. When this was over, it was their custom to depart and to assemble again to partake of food—but ordinary and innocent food. Even this, they affirmed, they had ceased to do after my edict by which, in accordance with your instructions, I had forbidden political associations. Accordingly, I judged it all the more necessary

---

[141] Antiquities of the Jews , book 20, chapter 9.1

to find out what the truth was by torturing two female slaves who were called deaconesses. But I discovered nothing else but depraved, excessive superstition."[142]

Although the letter gives some information about Christian beliefs and attitudes, it cannot be considered evidence for the existence of Jesus. In point of fact, Pliny considered the hymns to Christus (Christ) as a superstition.

Cornelius Tacitus

Cornelius Tacitus (55 ACE-120 ACE) was one of the great Roman historians and, arguably, its most reliable. Although his 2 great works (Annals and Histories) exist in fragments, book 15, chapter 44 of the Annals has been preserved. The passage below is part of an account of the Great Fire of Rome (64 ACE), which Roman Emperor Nero blamed on Jesus' followers:

> Consequently, to get rid of the report, Nero fastened the guilt and inflicted the most exquisite tortures on a class hated for their abominations, called Christians by the populace. Christus, from whom the name had its origin, suffered the extreme penalty during the reign of Tiberius at the hands of one of our procurators, Pontius Pilatus, and a most mischievous superstition, thus checked for the moment, again broke out not only in Judea, the first source of the evil, but even in Rome. Accordingly, an arrest was first made of all who pleaded guilty; then, upon their information, an immense multitude was convicted."[143]

Some scholars consider the passage on Christus(Jesus) as spurious. For example, Messianic Jews were not called Christians at the time referenced by Tacitus. Additionally, there was no "immense multitude" of Christians

---

[142] Pliny the Younger, "Letter to Trajan." Early Christian Writings. Peter Kirby, 2001-2006, March 7, 2011.

[143] Cornelius Tacitus, The Annals, book 15, chapter 44, Alfred John Church, William Jackson Brodribb, Ed., Perseus Digital Library, n.d., March 8, 2011

in Rome at that time. Some have suggested that it could be a later addition by Christian writers.

Unlike the two Josephan references, cited, the genuineness of this passage has not been seriously contested by any scholar. However, Tacitus might have borrowed information about Jesus from Pliny the Younger or other secondary source.

Jesus in the Gospels

I now turn to the Gospel record of Jesus of Nazareth. At the outset, it must be noted that the Gospels bearing the names Matthew, Mark and John were not written by them and Luke's author has not been determined. They could not have been written by the disciples, because they were originally written in Greek and the disciples spoke and wrote Aramaic only.

The Gospel record states that Jesus (Yeshua in Aramaic, the language he spoke) was born in either Jerusalem or Nazareth around either 4 BCE or 7 ACE. It is generally accepted that December 25th is not the actual date of his birth, but was chosen by the Church Fathers in 440ACE. He was born sometime between March and October. I make this conclusion based on Luke 2:8-12, which states that at his birth, "Shepherds were keeping watch over their sheep in the fields." It is unlikely that shepherds would be in the pastures watching their sheep on December 25th, the dead of winter in Palestine. They would most likely be there between March and October.

Jesus was circumcised when he was eight years old, according to Moses' law. Being a Jewish boy, he became Bar Mitzvah (that is, ordered to follow the law) when he was thirteen. Matthew's Gospel records that within weeks of his birth, Herod, King of Judaea, wished to kill him. To avoid this, Joseph escaped with him and his mother Mary to Egypt, where they remained until Herod died. (Matthew 2:13-15)

Luke says, "And the child grew, and waxed strong in spirit; filled with wisdom." (Luke 2:40) However, the only incident he offers as proof of this wisdom appears in his description of Jesus' parents' journey to Jerusalem during Passover:

> And when they had fulfilled the days, as they returned, the child Jesus tarried behind in Jerusalem, and Joseph and his mother knew not of it. And it came to pass that after three days, they found him in the temple, sitting in the midst of the doctors,

both hearing them, and asking questions. And all that heard him
were astonished at his understanding and answers. (Matthew
2:43, 46, 47)

Luke's story begs the question, why did it take Jesus' parents one day
to miss him? I would miss my twelve year-old within minutes. Some critics
doubt that Jesus, at 12, could have discussed the law and prophets with
the elders. However, I think this part of the story is plausible. Throughout
history teenagers have astonished the world with their ability. Here are
three examples. Jackie Cooper (1922-present) is an American actor and
TV director, who was the youngest nominee for Best Actor Oscar at 9
years of age. Frederic Chopin (1810-1849) was a gifted Polish pianist/
composer who, at age 7, had composed 2 Polonaises. Maria Gaetana Agnesi
(1718-1799) was an Italian linguist who, by age 13, had mastered Italian,
French, Greek, Latin, Hebrew, Spanish and German and was called the
"Walking Polyglot."

Jesus was baptized by John the Baptist, his cousin, during John's ministry,
which began about 28/29 ACE and lasted until 32 ACE. According to Luke
(Luke 3:1-2), Jesus' ministry lasted 3 years. He was executed by Pontius
around 36 ACE.

Events surrounding Jesus' birth

I will now examine certain events surrounding Jesus' birth. Most
Christians believe that he was born miraculously of the Virgin Mary.
This belief is an act of faith and serves its purpose. However, the facts in
the Gospels do not support it. For starters, the earliest written canonical
Gospel (Mark) does not even mention Jesus' birth and Paul, whose Epistles
were written before the Gospels, only states that he was born of a woman
according to the flesh, that is, born naturally (Galatians 4:4, Romans 1:3).
The Gospel of John says that he was the son of Joseph (John 1:45) and does
not mention anything miraculous concerning his birth.

Only Matthew and Luke mention Jesus' virgin birth. However, there
are contradictions in their narratives. For example, there is discrepancy in
their description of his genealogy. They agree that he was descended from
Kong David. However, Matthew chronicles 28 generations between Jesus
and David, whereas Luke has 41.

Another contentious point surrounding Jesus' birth concerns the star that was said to have guided the wise men to where the infant Jesus lay (Matthew 2:9). Some scholars regard the story as an invention and similar to other stories in the ancient world, in which heavenly events surrounded the birth of deities. Matthew could have gotten his idea from Isaiah (Isaiah 60:1-9). However, Luke's Gospel does not even mention a star.

Jesus' Crucifixion

A careful reading of the canonical Gospels' account of Jesus' death reveals glaring inconsistencies. Here are a few:

(1) **The Cross**: The Gospels disagree over who carried the cross. Matthew (27:32), Mark (15:21) and Luke (23:26) state that Simon of Cyrene carried Jesus' cross. However, John (19:17) says that Jesus carried his own cross to Golgotha.

(2) **The two thieves**: Ignoring the fact that the Romans did not crucify thieves, the Gospels' narratives are not consistent in telling the story

of the thieves on the cross. Matthew (27:39-44) says that the two thieves, who were crucified with Jesus, taunted him. Luke says that the one who mocked Jesus was rebuked by the other (Luke 23:39-40).

(3) **Vinegar or Wine?** Here again, the Gospel writers are in disagreement. Mark (15:23) describes the drink given to Jesus on the cross as wine mixed with vinegar. Matthew (27:48) and Luke (23:36) say the drink was vinegar. John (19:29) states that Jesus was given vinegar upon hyssop on a sponge. All the Gospel writers, except John, say that Jesus did not drink what was given to him.

(4) **Time of Crucifixion**: This aspect of the crucifixion meets with no general agreement among the Gospel writers. Mark (15:25) states that Jesus was crucified on the third hour. Matthew and Luke do not state a specific time. However, John (19:14-15) says that he was crucified on the sixth hour.

(5) **Final words**: Most of us have been brought up to believe that Jesus' last words on the cross were, "My God, my God, why hast thou forsaken me?" We would be correct according to Mark (15:34) and Matthew (27:45-46). However, Luke (23:46) says that his last words were, "Father, into thy hands I commit my spirit." John (19:30) says they were, "It is finished."

DISCREPANCIES EXPLAINED

The first explanation is the old Islamic one that the person who was crucified was not Jesus, but another person put there by God.

The second explanation is that the accounts were not written by eyewitnesses, but others who wrote years after Jesus' death and from oral traditions.

Symbol of the Crucifixion

According to the canonical gospels, Jesus of Nazareth was crucified. Why did it take eight centuries before that Crucifixion was symbolized with a man on the cross? During the first eight centuries of Christianity, a lamb on the cross was the symbol of the crucifixion. It was Pope Adrian 1 (?-795 ACE) who, at the close of the eighth century, ordered that the figure of a man should replace that of the lamb on the cross.

JESUS' RESURRECTION

The basis of Christian faith is that Jesus rose again from the dead. In St. Paul's words, "And if Christ be not risen, then is our preaching vain, and your faith is also vain (1 Corinthians 15:14). I will discuss certain inconsistencies in the Gospels' narrative and a few skeptical observations about the event.

Another Risen Savior?

Skeptics argue that Jesus' resurrection was patterned after other resurrected deities. If that were so, it should be considered sensible. Early Christian writers were writing against a backdrop of Greco-Roman and other literature which described risen god-men. If the aim of the gospel writers was to acclaim their Savior as equal or superior to those deities, they should have had to present him with their "risen" quality, a sign of divinity.

Was this the case? The World's Sixteen Crucified Saviors (chapter 19), by Kersey Graves, the controversially brilliant 19th Century American writer, is a good starting point. He states:

> Quexalcote of Mexico, Chris of Chaldea, Quirinus of Rome, Prometheus of Caucasus, Osiris of Egypt, Atys of Phrygia, and "Mithra the Mediator" of Persia, according to their respective histories, rose from the dead after three days' burial. He also mentions an account more than three thousand years old of the Hindu crucified Savior Krishna, three days after his interment, forsaking "the silent bourn, from where no traveler ever returns," and laying aside the moldy cerements of the dead, again walking forth to mortal life, to be again seen, recognized, admired, and adored by his pious, devout and awe-stricken followers, and thus present to the gaze of a hoping yet doubting world "the first fruits of the resurrection . . . . the ancients had both the crucifixion and resurrection of a God symbolically and astronomically represented among the plants. "Their foundation," says Clement of Alexandria "was the fictitious death and resurrection of the sun, the soul of the world, the principle of life and motion. Jesus' resurrection was one among many."[144]

---

[144] Kersey Graves, The World's Sixteen Crucified Saviors, , Chapter 19, A Witness to Yahweh website, n.d., March 16, 2011.

Many of Graves' examples withstand the scrutiny of history. However, they are not sufficient proof that Jesus' resurrection was patterned after other deities. I agree that a degree of probability exists. However, it could be equally probable that the resurrection of the deities mentioned were patterned after deities preceding them.

Resurrection Inconsistencies

There are glaring inconsistencies in the resurrection narrative with respect to whom visited Jesus' tomb, when the visit occurred and what happened when Jesus appeared before his disciples.

Visiting the tomb: Matthew states that Mary Magdalene and the other Mary (no surname was given) visited the tomb "at the end of the Sabbath as it began to dawn" (Matthew 28:10). Mark adds Salome to the visiting party (Mark 16:1). Luke says that the women who visited the tomb were Mary Magdalene, Joanna and Mary, the mother of James and other women." (Luke 24:10). John locates only Mary at the tomb (John 20:1).

Jesus' appearance: Luke says that the disciples were frightened when Jesus appeared before them (Luke 24:36). John reports that they were happy (John 20:20). Some apologists explain this discrepancy by saying that Luke omitted the disciples' happiness, because he was more concerned with their initial reaction, whereas John omitted the initial fright, because he was more interested in the disciples' reaction after they were convinced that it was indeed Jesus.

THE VISION OF GABRIEL

Was Jesus' life patterned after a Jewish leader who lived in the late century BCE? Such and other related questions become relevant in light of the discovery of The Vision of Gabriel, a 30x90 cm tablet written in Hebrew from the first century BCE. It describes the death of a leader of the Jews who will be resurrected in three days.

An article by Ethan Bronner, published in the New York Times: July 6, 2008 on the subject, "Ancient Tablet Ignites Debate on Messiah and Resurrection" is quoted here:

A three-foot-tall tablet with 87 lines of Hebrew that scholars believe dates from the decades just before the birth of Jesus is causing a quiet stir in biblical and archaeological circles, especially because it may speak of a messiah who will rise from the dead after three days.

If such a messianic description really is there, it will contribute to a developing re-evaluation of both popular and scholarly views of Jesus, since it suggests that the story of his death and resurrection was not unique but part of a recognized Jewish tradition at the time . . . . . Still, its authenticity has so far faced no challenge, so its role in helping to understand the roots of Christianity in the devastating political crisis faced by the Jews of the time seems likely to increase."[145]

Jewish Apocalyptic literature at the close of the 1st century BCE and decades after, mentions persons who would rise after 3 days and redeem Israel. The Vision Of Gabriel could belong to this genre. The fact that it might mention a Messiah cannot reduce the believer's claim that Jesus was the Messiah.

The Missing Years of Jesus

One of the more intriguing mysteries of the New Testament, indeed of Christianity generally, concerns a lack of information on Jesus' life from 13 through 30. The Gospels are deafeningly silent and historians, who lived during and shortly after Jesus' lifetime, provide no account. However, a large body of scholarly conjecture exists. I will describe some of it.

---

[145] Ethan Bronner, "Ancient Tablet Ignites Debate on Messiah and Resurrection", New York Times, July 6, 2008, March 3, 2011.

JESUS IN INDIA

In Jesus' time, Buddhist missionaries travelled to Asia Minor and Egypt. There is a suggestion that Jesus was so impressed with their teaching that he went to India sometime during the years not mentioned in the Bible. This speculation is based on travelers to India who were shown proof that he had spent time there.

Nicolai Notovich, a Russian scholar and Orientalist, was the first to suggest that Jesus visited India. In 1887, he visited Kashmir during one of several journeys to the Far East. He was a guest at a Buddhist monastery in Ladakh, located somewhere in the Zoji—La mountain in the western section of the Himalayan mountain range. One of its monks told him of the bhodisattva saint called "Issa". Notovich was stunned by the remarkable parallels of Issa's teachings and martyrdom with that of Christ's life, teachings and crucifixion.[146]

Holger Kerstein says:

> There is also much historical truth in the towns and villages of Northern India to prove that Jesus and his mother Mary spent time in the area. For instance, at the border of a small town called Mari (or Murri), there is nearby a mountain called Pindi Point, upon which is an old tomb called Mai Mari da Asthan or "The final resting place of Mary". The tomb is said to be very old and local Muslims venerate it as the grave of Issa's (ie Christ's) Mother. The tomb itself is oriented East-West consistent with the Jewish tradition, despite the fact it is within a Muslim area. Assuming its antiquity, such a tomb could not be Hindu either since the Hindus contemporary to Christ cremated their dead or scattered their ashes as do Hindus today." [147]

The Persian scholar F. Mohammed, in his "Jami-ut-tuwarik," mentions Jesus' arrival in the kingdom of Nisibis, (now known as Nusaybin in Turkey) by royal invitation. This is reiterated in the Imam Abu Jafar Muhammed's "Tafsi-Ibn-i-Jamir at-tubri." Holger Kersten, in "Jesus lived in India",

---

146   Dr Ramesh Manocha and Anna Potts, "Synopsis of 'Jesus Lived In India' by Holger Kersten." Knowledge of Reality Magazine, 1996-2006, March 1, 2011.

147   Dr Ramesh Manocha and Anna Potts, "Synopsis of 'Jesus Lived In India'

found that in both Turkey and Persia there are ancient stories of a saint called "Yuz Asaf" ("Leader of the Healed"), whose behavior, miracles and teachings were similar to those of Jesus.[148]

Jesus' Philosophy

Jesus' philosophy is found in the Synoptic Gospels, bearing the names "Mark", "Matthew" and "Luke", and the Gospel bearing the name "John." Some of it is also contained in the Gospel bearing the name Thomas. The Jewish Encyclopedia states that the synoptic gospels, " are interdependent, corresponding to the various forms of contemporary Baraitot, while the fourth, the Gospel of John, is what the Germans call a "Tendenz-Roman," practically a work of religious imagination intended to modify opinion in a certain direction. The supernatural claims made on behalf of Jesus are based almost exclusively on statements of the fourth Gospel."[149]

Repentance

Animal sacrifice was the means of repentance in Judaism up to 70 ACE, when the temple was destroyed. The sacrifice of an animal, usually a lamb, sheep or goat, was performed in the Temple as prescribed by the Law. After the temple was destroyed the practice was discontinued, because the prescribed place for sacrifice no longer existed. Animal sacrifice involved eating the bodies of the sacrificed animals, to which one's sins were transferred, as a peace offering to God.

"In those days came John the Baptist, preaching in the wilderness of Judaea, and saying, Repent ye: for the kingdom of heaven is at hand."(Matthew 3:1-2) He told his listeners to repent and be baptized for the forgiveness of sins. His message would have sounded strange to his listeners, who were accustomed to repentance by animal sacrifice.

---

[148]   Dr Ramesh Manocha and Anna Potts, "Synopsis of 'Jesus Lived In India'
[149]   Joseph Jacobs,Kaufmann Kohler, Richard Gottheil, Samuel Krauss, "Jesus of Nazareth." JewishEncyclopedia.com, 2002,. March 6, 2011.

Jesus preached John's message of repentance without his call to baptism. Instead of John's command, "Repent and be baptized", his command was "Repent and believe the gospel (good news)."

Did Jesus baptize?

John's Gospel describes him as baptizing: "After these things came Jesus and his disciples into the land of Judaea; and there he tarried with them, and baptized." (John 3:22)

However, another passage contradicts this:

> When therefore the Lord knew how the Pharisees had heard that Jesus made and baptized more disciples than John, (Though Jesus himself baptized not, but his disciples)" (John 4:1-3)

Kingdom of God

Matthew tells us, "And Jesus went about all Galilee, teaching in their synagogues, and preaching the gospel of the kingdom." (Matthew 4:23) The kingdom, also called "kingdom of God" or "kingdom of Heaven" is the central theme of Jesus' philosophy and is found 69 times in the New Testament. When he sent his 12 closest disciples and seventy others to preach his gospel, he told them to preach about this kingdom (Luke 9:1-2; 10:1, 9).

I will describe a few meanings of this phrase as used by Jesus. Since he spoke in Aramaic, he would have used the phrase "malkûta' dî 'elaha." His audiences understood the phrase to mean the restoration of the Kingdom of Israel. After years of colonization, the Jews of Jesus' time were expecting a Messiah, who would destroy Rome, their most recent colonizer, and make Judea an independent nation again—a nation of righteousness and glory.

When Jesus appeared to the assembled disciples after his resurrection, they asked him "Lord, wilt thou at this time restore the kingdom of Israel?"(Acts 1:6) He did not tell them that they misunderstood the meaning of the phrase. Rather, he said, "It is not the time for you to know the times or the seasons, which the Father hath put in his own power." (Acts 1:7) He was saying that God will restore the kingdom of Israel, but at a time of his choosing.

Being a Jew, Jesus might have preferred preaching to an independent Israel and, like the rest of his countrymen, might have longed for its deliverance from colonialism. This is the reason he did not chide the disciples, when they asked him when the kingdom of Israel would be restored.

This sense of the phrase is reinforced by Luke. He states that 3 days after Jesus' crucifixion, 2 of his disciples went to the town of Emmaus, 7 miles from Jerusalem. As they discussed recent happenings, Jesus joined them, but they did not recognize him. He asked them why they were sad and they told him how Jesus of Nazareth had been crucified. "But we trusted that it had been he which should have redeemed Israel."(Luke 24:21) That is, restored the kingdom of God (Israel).

Judas' betrayal of Jesus could be understood in this sense. He believed that Jesus came to restore the kingdom of Israel and that if Jesus were pushed to the limit; he should have called upon the army of God and defeat the Romans. He fully expected Jesus to prove that he was the Messiah, when he "betrayed" him to the authorities.

However, Jesus was more concerned with a spiritual kingdom. He taught that the "kingdom of God" is a spiritual kingdom within us. Luke reports him saying, "Neither shall they say, Lo here! or, lo there! for, behold, the kingdom of God is within you." (Matthew 17:21).

In this sense, the kingdom is regeneration from within. In "Gospel of Thomas", Jesus makes the point clearer,

> If those who lead you say to you, 'look, the Kingdom is in the sky,' then the birds will get there first. If they say 'it's in the ocean,' then the fish will get there first. But the Kingdom of God is within you and outside of you:."[150]

The Jesus of Thomas' Gospel is speaking of the Kingdom of God as gnosis, direct spiritual, experiential knowledge and an oneness with God, who is within the individual. Additionally, Thomas's Jesus describes the Kingdom of God as outside us.

His (Jesus) disciples said to him, "When will the kingdom come?"

---

[150] Gospel of Thomas online text, 3.1-3, Peter Kirby, Early Christian writings, February 2006, March 4, 2011.

"It will not come by watching for it. It will not be said, 'Look, here!' or 'Look, there!' Rather, the Father's kingdom is spread out upon the earth, and people don't see it."[151]

The "outside" to which Jesus referred is not material space, but the many enlightened individuals, who exist in finite time. The Kingdom of God is spread out upon the earth now. Those who are enlightened have a divine light within, which enables them to see the Kingdom of God upon the earth.

Self Denial

Jesus also taught a philosophy of self-denial:

And he said to them all, If any man will come after me, let him deny himself, and take up his cross daily, and follow me"(Luke 9:23) "So likewise, whosoever he be of you that forsaketh not all that he hath, he cannot be my disciple." (Luke 14:33)

Here was this itinerant Rabbi, telling his followers, most of whom were poor and outcast, to give all their possessions away and follow him. It was a most radical message, I daresay.

He was not saying to get rid of all money, all houses and all businesses. These are necessary possessions. He was warning against over attachment to these things, because such over-attachment brings disappointment and suffering. This point is illustrated in the story of the rich man, who asked Jesus what he must do to inherit eternal life? Jesus asked him,

Thou knowest the commandments, Do not commit adultery, Do not kill, Do not steal, Do not bear false witness, Defraud not, Honour thy father and mother.

And he answered and said unto him, Master, all these have I observed from my youth.

---

[151] Gospel of Thomas 1. 13

Then Jesus beholding him loved him, and said unto him, One thing thou lackest: go thy way, sell whatsoever thou hast, and give to the poor, and thou shalt have treasure in heaven: and come, take up the cross, and follow me.

And he was sad at that saying, and went away grieved: for he had great possessions.

And Jesus looked round about, and saith unto his disciples, how hardly shall they that have riches enter into the kingdom of God! (Mark 10:10-25)

The man had kept the commandments and Jesus respected him for this and he instructed him to deny himself and follow him. He was sad and did not, because he was too attached to his possessions.

Jesus' message was about over-attachment to earthy possessions. He used the rich as an example. However, the poor are as guilty. The poor have little, but could become over attached to that little.

The Law

Jesus was born and died a Jew and the Torah and the Prophets were his religious frames of reference. Luke tells us, "And he(Jesus) came to Nazareth, where he had been brought up; and, as his custom was, he went into the synagogue on the Sabbath day, and stood up to read. And there was delivered unto him the scroll of the prophet Isaiah."(Luke 4:16-17).

The Law (also called the Torah, the first five books of the Jewish bible) was the preeminent section of the Jewish religious scrolls and most Jews believed they were the only words that came directly from Yahweh. Jesus had no intention of changing anything in it, "Think not that I am come to destroy the Law or the Prophets; I am not come to destroy but to fulfill." (Matthew 5:17)

Jesus preached observance of the Law: "For verily I say unto you, till heaven and earth pass, one jot or one title shall in no wise pass from the Law, till all be fulfilled." (Matthew 5:18)

On another occasion, he said,

The scribes and Pharisees sit in Moses' seat. Therefore whatsoever they bid you, you observe; that observe and do. Whosoever therefore shall break one of these least commandments, and shall teach men so, he shall be called the least in the kingdom of heaven: but whosoever shall do and teach [them], the same shall be called great in the kingdom of heaven.""(Matthew 23:2-3)

Jesus was telling his listeners that their duty was to observe the Law of Moses. In verse 17 of Matthew 5, he says, "Think not that I am come to destroy the Law or the Prophets, I am not come to destroy but to fulfill."

His statement is complex. The Jews of his time believed that the Law of Moses was God's covenant with them and it was fulfilled as it was. Jesus' statement, therefore, was not according to Jewish teaching. Christians believe that the new covenant began with Jesus' death and resurrection and that he was the fulfillment of the Law.

The "Gospel according to Saint Matthew" used the Greek word "pieroo" which is translated in KJV as "fulfill." Among other meanings, "pieroo" means "to cause God's will (as made known in the law) to be obeyed as it should be." If the meaning "to end" or "to complete" were to be used, it should not make sense for Jesus to say that he did not come to abolish the Law. Therefore, I have concluded that he taught that the Law is paramount and should be observed. He also suggested that his mission was to provide a more enlightened interpretation of that Law.

Did Jesus claim to be God?

Did Jesus claim to be God? Some Christians are positive that he did. Others are not quite sure. The question is not the same as if Jesus is God. Whether he is or is not is a question of faith. This question concerns whether he ever made a statement claiming divinity.

I have searched the synoptic Gospels and find no such claim by Jesus. In John's Gospel, he is reported to have said, "I and my Father are one." (John 10:30) These words are usually interpreted as claims to divinity. However, Jesus was merely saying that he was in harmony with God's will towards him. He could not have claimed to be God, because he prayed to God on the cross, "My God, my God, why hast thou forsaken me?"(Matthew 27:48) Additionally, why was this claim not reported by the other gospels?

Jesus was a Jew and must have recited the Shema, "Sh'ma Yis'ra'eil Adonai Eloheinu Adonai echad" (Hear, Israel, the Lord is our God, the

Lord is One). (Duetornomy 6:4) This is a statement that God is not 2 or 3 persons in 1, but 1 indivisible unit.

"Mark's Gospel" describes an encounter between Jesus and a scribe. The scribe asked him which was the greatest commandment. "Yeshua (Jesus) answered, 'The greatest is, 'Hear, Yisra'el, the Lord our God, the Lord is one.'" (Mark 12:29). Rather than denouncing or criticicizing or amending the Shema, he quoted it in full and declared it to be the greatest commandment.

On an occasion while he was preaching, certain persons brought one sick with palsy to him. After he healed the man, he said "Son, thy sins be forgiven thee." (Mark 2:5) If only God can forgive sins, this statement could be taken as Jesus equating himself with God. However, the remark must be interpreted in context. When the pastor, priest, minister etc prays for a sick person and the person is healed, the praise and credit goes to God. What Jesus was saying in the remark aforementioned is that the man's faith healed him and his sins would also be forgiven by God as a result of his faith.

The canonical gospels do not portray Jesus as God and mention no statement by him to the effect. Within the Judaic context, Jesus would have been understood to say that he was a messenger, a teacher of the truth of God. After the Triune God concept was accepted by the Church, Jesus became the second person of the Godhead, truly God. Jesus, the "son of man" also came to mean that the man Jesus was both human and divine. That was not Jesus' teaching.

It was Paul who elevated Jesus to the position of equality with God. He says, "Who (Jesus), being in the form of God, thought it not robbery to be equal with God." (Philippians 2:6) On what words of Jesus was this Pauline view based? In truth, Jesus would have thought it blasphemous to consider himself "equal with God."

Conclusion

I have raised questions and described answers relating to the life and teachings of Jesus. In this task I worked with an incomplete body of information. No firsthand account exists of his life and teachings. The principal mention of him is in the gospels. However, many consider the Jesus they describe, however fascinatingly inspiring, a product of faith and the writers' imaginations. They do not offer sufficient evidence for his existence, probably because they are not firsthand accounts and are not supported by then contemporary non-biblical sources. Nothing is known about these writers, where they derived their information and to what extent the copies of their copies are reliable.

> When we do critique the NT texts further we find that there were many "layers" of tradition and story piled atop the historical Jesus. This dynamic process obscures the historical Jesus from the later Christology. Today we disagree as to who this obscured historical Jesus really was, but we do agree that the post-Easter Christ which is taught today is far different from the real wandering rabbi and Jewish peasant of first-century Palestine.[152]

The secular writers cited are equally unreliable in providing sufficient evidence of Jesus' existence. With respect to Josephus, most scholars regard most of his comments on Jesus as later additions by Christian writers. The references of Pliny the Younger were hearsay and were not concerned with the question of Jesus' existence. Tacitus's reference to Jesus has largely been discounted as spurious.

Historical proof of Jesus' existence requires then contemporary mention of it and not heresy or second-hand sources. In the final analysis, each reader must decide what importance to attach to whatever is contained herein. Those who seek scientific proof will doubtlessly consider Jesus an invention of the imaginary genius of the artist. No more or less. Those, like me, to whom "Faith is the substance of things hoped for, the evidence of things not seen", will accept that Jesus lived, was crucified, buried and rose again, according to the scriptures and will come again in all his glory and his kingdom shall have no end.

---

[152] James Still, "Critique of New Testament Reliability and "Bias" in NT Development", Internet Infidels, 1995, March 16, 2011..

CHAPTER SIX

JUDAISM AND CHRISTIANITY

Judaism and Christianity are two closely related Abrahamic religions that are in some ways parallel to each other and in other ways fundamentally divergent in theology and practice.

_____Christianity Knowledge Base

In this chapter I will discuss the origin and belief systems of these two great religions.

Nature of Judaism

Judaism does not characterize itself as a religion (although one can speak of the Jewish religion and religious Jews). The subject of the Tanakh (Hebrew Bible) is the history of the Children of Israel (also called Hebrews), especially in terms of their relationship with God. Thus, Judaism has also been characterized as a culture or as a civilization.[153]

Jewish peoplehood is closely tied to their relationship with God, and thus has a strong theological element. This relationship is incorporated in the notion that Jews are a chosen people. This means that they choose to obey a certain set of laws found in Torah and halakha as an expression

---

[153] "Judaism and Christianity", important.ca, 2005, April 5, 2011.

of their covenant with God.[154] To the extent that this discussion regards Judaism as a religion, it is understood to be national.

Nature of Christianity

Unlike Judaism, Christianity is universal. Christians believe that Jesus, the head of their faith, was the fulfillment of the Law and the prophets. They believe that one cannot enter the kingdom of Heaven unless one follows the teachings of Jesus. Thus, Christians will evangelize others. Judaism does not.

Origin of Judaism

Judaism is the religion of the Hebrew people and their descendants and began when God made his covenant with Abraham, born Abram. This description is one of convenience, since, strictly speaking, the Abrahamic religion did not become Judaism until Mount Sinai.

Abraham

Abraham was born around 1800 BCE in Ur of the Chaldees, the modern Tell Muqayyar in Southern Mesopotamia. The Jewish bible states that, at age 3, he questioned his nation's practice of worshipping many gods (Polytheism). His father, Terah, was a manufacturer of idols. Abraham destroyed his idols and proclaimed Yahweh the one true God. Consequently, Yahweh told him to leave his country and go to a land (Canaan), which he would show him and promised him a legacy of ancestors (Genesis 12:1-4).

According to Jewish tradition, the Israelites dwelt in the Sinai desert after they left Egypt for 40 years. While there, they received the Torah at Mount Sinai from YHWH, by the hand of Moses. Most Jewish scholars regard this as the beginning of normative Judaism.

---

[154] "Judaism and Christianity."

Origin of Christianity

The commonly held view is that Christianity was founded by Jesus Christ and his disciples. Others have argued that it evolved from Judaism. A great number state that it evolved from Mithraism. There are others who state very firmly that it started with Paul.

Jesus (Yeshua in Aramaic, his native language) and his disciples were not the founders of any religion. They were observant Jews, whose teachings did not constitute a break from Judaism; but rather a call for reform of some of its institutions and practices. Christianity did not evolve from Judaism, since some of its basic beliefs are incompatible with Judaism. There are similarities between Mithraism and Christianity; but Christianity did not evolve from Mithraism. To the extent that some of its more pronounced theology differs from Jesus', one could argue that Christianity started with Paul's teaching.

According to Acts, The word "Christian" was first used in applying to Paul's Gentile converts at Antioch (Acts 11:26). As such, Christianity began with Gentile converts of Paul at Antioch and spread to Greece, Asia and Rome. It became a recognized religion during the Constantinus dynasty (305 ACE-363 ACE) and Emperor Theodosius made it the state religion in 380 ACE.

G-d in Judaism

There are many names for G-d in Judaism. The first one used in Jewish scripture (Genesis 1:1) is Elohim. This Name is used to emphasize G-d's might, creative power, and his justice and rulership. Variations on this name include El, Eloha, Elohai (my G-d) and Elohaynu (our God). El Shaddai is

another Name for G-d and is translated "God Almighty." Another Name
of God is YHVH Tzva'ot, "Lord of Hosts", signifying G-d's leadership and
sovereignty.

The most important of God's Names is YHVH (Yod-Hei-Vav-Hei),
which is referred to as the Ineffable, Unutterable or Distinctive Name.
It is used when discussing G-d's relation with human beings, and when
emphasizing his qualities of lovingkindness and mercy.

> Nothing in the Torah prohibits a person from pronouncing
> the Name of God. Indeed, it is evident from scripture that
> God's Name was pronounced routinely . . . . The Name was
> pronounced as part of daily services in the Temple . . . . However,
> by the time of the Talmud, it was the custom to use substitute
> Names for God.[155]

Although Judaism does not prohibit writing the Name of G-d, observant
Jews substitute letters or syllables, such as G-d for God.

Walter Reinhold Warttig Mattfeld y de la Torre begins his brilliant
article, "Yahweh-Elohim's Historical Evolution" by stating that it is
his understanding that, "Yahweh is an amalgam, a conflation or fusion
of various and sundry earlier gods and goddesses, having absorbed their
functions, epithets and achievements." [156]

His discussion of the evolution of Israel's concept of Yahweh is directly
related to Israel's absorption of the attributes of earlier deities from those
cultures with whom she came into contact. He asserts:

> . . . . as the political fortunes of Israel "waxed" and she triumphed
> over the Canaanites, their gods' and goddesses' powers, epithets
> and feats were ascribed to Yahweh . . . . I understand that Yahweh

---

[155]   Tracy R. Rich, "Judaism 101: The name of G-d", Tracey R Rich , 1995-2000,
        March 7, 2011.
[156]   Walter Reinhold Warttig Mattfeld y de la Torre, "Yahweh-Elohim's Historical
        Evolution (Pre-Biblical)", Walter Reinhold Warttig Mattfeld y de la Torre,
        n.d., March 9, 2011.

is an amalgam of MANY gods and goddesses, Mesopotamian, Hittite, Syrian, Phoenician, Egyptian, and Canaanite."[157] [158]

Some of the gods fused into Yahweh's persona are the Sumerian Enki (Akkadian/Babylonian Ea), Enlil (Ellil), An (Anu), Utu (Shamash), and the Egyptian Hyksos' god Baal Saphon (Baal Hadad) as well as Seth (Seth/Set being assimilated to Baal Saphon) and Sopdu of Egypt. As long as the attributes were attributed, and the rites enacted, to Yahweh, the Israelite felt justified in their absorption.

At some point in their history, prior to the formation of their own kingdom, the Israelites lived among the Canaanites and Yahweh existed within the Canaanite pantheon. Texts found at Ugarit (an ancient city of Western Syria) describe mythical battles between Yahweh and various other Canaanite gods. Yahweh was victorious in most of these battles.

Yahweh was a God of and for the Jewish people. When the Israeli monarchy was established, He became the patron God of the kingdom, and when the kingdom was divided into two kingdoms (Judah and Samaria) He remained the patron God of each. He continued as the God of Israel until the destruction of the temple in 70 ACE.

GOD IN CHRISTIANITY

The Christian supreme deity is named God. I do not conceive of the term as synonymous with YHVH. As I will show later in this chapter, their monotheistic quality aside, they have very little in common.

---

[157]   Walter Reinhold Warttig Mattfeld y de la Torre, "Yahweh-Elohim's Historical Evolution

[158]   "Yahweh-Elohim's Historical Evolution (Pre-Biblical)"

Notwithstanding, the Christian concept of God was influenced by the Jewish concept of YHVH. Jesus, the Christian Saviour, and his followers worshipped YHVH. Throughout his ministry, Jesus claimed to be the son of God and truly man. After his death, first Paul and then the Early Church Fathers made him God alongside God, the Father and the Holy Spirit of God.

DIFFERENCES

I will now discuss differences between Judaism and Christianity with respect to God, Satan, original sin, salvation and Jesus.

YWVW and God

The major difference between Judaism and Christianity is in their conception of the Supreme Being. Firstly, the Jewish deity is one and indivisible; whereas the Christian deity is a Trinity-three equal parts of the Godhead—Father, Son and Holy Spirit. (Christian denominations that do not assent to the Trinity idea are Jehovah's Witnesses, Mormons and Unitarians.) This fundamental doctrine of the Christian Church does not appear in the Bible and Jesus never preached it. It was coined in the 2nd century ACE by Tertullian, a Latin theologian and made an official doctrine of the Church in 325ACE at the First Council of Nicaea.

The Christian concept of a Triune God is at variance with the Jewish concept of their G-d as a one and indivisible entity. The idea is found in Deuteronomy 6:1, "Hear, O Israel: the Lord our God, the Lord is one." Known as the Shema (Shema Y'israel or Sh'ma Yisrael), this verse is recited at Jewish morning and evening services.

Another essential difference between the two deities is in their functions. As I stated earlier, The Jews conceived of their God as a national God-the God of Israel. "Yahweh" is really a contraction of His longer name, "Yahweh Sabaoth", meaning "he musters (commands) armies."

The name identifies this god as the military commander of Israel: "The LORD is a man of war: the LORD is his name." (Exodus 15:3)

He is not the God of the heathen: "The heathen raged, the kingdoms were moved. He uttered his voice, the earth melted. The LORD of hosts (YHVH Tzva'ot) is with us; the God of Jacob is our refuge." (Psalms

46:6-7) In this passage, the Psalmist identifies Yahweh as the God of one of the founders of the Jewish nation and by extension, the Jewish nation, who destroys the armies of the heathen.

Unlike Yahweh, the Christian God is a universal entity. John's Gospel says,

> And as Moses lifted up the serpent in the wilderness, even so must the Son of man be lifted up: That whosoever believeth in him, should not perish, but have eternal life For God so loved the world that he gave his only begotten Son, that whosoever believeth in him should not perish, but have everlasting life. (John 3:14-16)

The God described in these words is different to the Jewish God in that He is Jesus, whom the Jewish religious establishment regarded as another false Messiah. Additionally, he gives eternal life to any person who believes in him. Not only did the Jews not believe in Jesus as God, their God was not in the business of begetting. They found such a concept totally blasphemous.

Christianity and ORIGINAL SIN

This Christian doctrine is not found in Judaism, but originated in St. Paul's teaching. Put simply, the doctrine of original sin asserts that when Adam and Eve disobeyed God, theirs was original (the first) sin. All mankind is born with the stain of their sin, which could only be removed through Jesus' intercession to God, the Father, and by repentance and baptism.

"The Book of Genesis" describes Adam's disobedience as the reason for his and Eve's suffering. However, it does not describe it as hereditary. The curses were directed towards Adam and Eve Genesis (3:13-19). However, apologists for this doctrine point to Romans 5:12: "Through one man sin entered into the world (and through sin death), and so passed into all men, in whom all have sinned" and 1 Corinthians 15:22: "For as in Adam all die, even so in Christ shall all be made alive." This view was held by the Early Church Fathers and ratified by the 16th Council of Carthage, paragraph 2 of which reads:

> Likewise it has been decided that whoever says that infants fresh from their mothers' wombs ought not to be baptized, or says

that they are indeed baptized unto the remission of sins, but
that they draw nothing of the original sin from Adam, which
is expiated in the bath of regeneration, whence it follows that
in regard to them the form of baptism "unto the remission of
sins" is understood as not true, but as false, let him be anathema.
Since what the Apostle says: "Through one man sin entered
into the world (and through sin death), and so passed into all
men, in whom all have sinned" [cf. Rom. 5:12], must not to
be understood otherwise than as the Catholic Church spread
everywhere has always understood it. For on account of this rule
of faith even infants, who in themselves thus far have not been
able to commit any sin, are therefore truly baptized unto the
remission of sins, so that that which they have contracted from
generation may be cleansed in them by regeneration.[159]

I do not wish to be misunderstood on this point. I assent to the doctrine
of original sin as church doctrine, based on St. Paul's teaching. However, I
find no proof that Jesus or his disciples preached it.

Judaism and ORIGINAL SIN

Judaism rejects this doctrine in favor of the idea of free will. It believes
that humans were formed in the image of God, that is, with ability to
reason and, consequently, make choices. It teaches that humans have 2
impulses—the Yetzer tov" and the "Yetzer ra." The former is one's moral
conscience that continually reminds one of God's Laws with respect to
an action or choice. The latter is one's selfishness to satisfy one's desires.
Significantly, Judaism accepts that the Yetzer ra was created by the Supreme
entity and, therefore, is natural. However, it could lead us to make wrong
choices (sin) if not controlled by the Yetzer Tov.

---

[159]   Roman Texts Approving and Defining Augustinian Soteriology, Pope St.
Zosimus—From the Council of Carthage XVI, 418—"Original Sin and
Grace", paragraph 2, April 27, 2011.

SATAN

Christianity believes that Satan is a fallen angel, who disguised as a serpent in the Garden of Eden and tempted Adam and Eve to sin. He is also identified as the arch-enemy of God, bent on disrupting God's plan for fallen mankind. By contrast, Judaism conceives him as an ally of God. In ancient Hebrew, the word "Satan" derives from a word meaning "the accuser." In Judaism, Satan is man's evil inclination.

Throughout the Torah, Satan challenges God to test the true loyalty of his followers, including Adam, Eve, Abraham and Job. "The Book of Job" relates that the angels of God came before God one day and Satan was with them. God did not ask Satan: "What are you doing here with my angels?" (Observe that "Get thee behind me Satan" and other references to Satan as God's adversary occur only in the New Testament.) He asked him if he had observed Job, who was the most righteous man on earth. Satan pointed out to Him that Job only served him because of the bounty he had received from Him. He said that it would be different if it were removed. God told him to do anything to Job, but spare his life. Despite losing everything, Job remained faithful to God.

This poem demonstrates Satan's function as an angel that reports to God as a servant not as an adversary.

HELL

In Christianity, Hell is a place of torment with fire prepared for the devil, his angels and the unrighteous. The New Testament (Matthew 8:12, 24:41 and Revelation 14:10-12) is very clear about what Hell is. However Christian churches differ in their beliefs with respect to Hell. Some teach that it is eternal. Others believe that it is temporary and that the souls that go there are destroyed after serving their time. Others believe that, after serving their time in Hell, souls are reconciled to God and admitted to heaven. The Roman Catholic Church, the largest Christian denomination, views Hell as a state of separation from God resulting from dying in sin.

Judaism has no concept of hell and its Bible makes no direct reference to a place that fits the Christian concept of hell as a place of punishment.

The Talmud speaks of a place where the souls of persons who did not lead exemplary lives on earth go. The Hebrew word for this place is geihinnom, which derives from the Biblical place known both as gei-hinnom, [the] Valley of Hinnom (e.g. Neh 11:30) and (gei ven-hinnom), [the] Valley of the Son of Hinnom (e.g., Jer 19:6). This is a valley located south of Jerusalem, where the fire god Moloch was worshipped (by the sacrifice of children) by the Ammonites. During the times when the Temples stood in Jerusalem, the same place served as a garbage dump where the carcasses of animals offered as sacrifices at the Temple were burned.

The prevalent opinion within traditional Judaism is that all but the souls of the most righteous spend some period in geihinnom. This could last up to, but not exceed,12 months. The place can be likened to a spiritual forge where the souls of the decadent are cleansed of the stains from the sins for which they did not repent prior to dying. Once all sins have been purged from it, the purified soul ascends to the "world to come". The only exceptions to this are the most righteous and the profoundly wicked. The souls of the most righteous are said to ascend directly to the "world to come". According to some, the souls of the profoundly wicked are destroyed after 12-months in geihinnom, or they continue to exist, but remain in a constant state of remorse.

SALVATION IN CHRISTIANITY

The word "Salvation" derives from a Latin word "salus," meaning well being. In religion, it refers to either the stages through which this state is achieved or the state itself.

The Christian concept of salvation refers to Jesus saving mankind from an eternal life in hell. Fundamentalist and Evangelical Christians believe that salvation comes by repentance and turning away from sin and trusting Jesus Christ as lord and Saviour. The central act of salvation is justification by Faith in God: "And by him all that believe are justified from all things, from which ye could not be justified by the Law of Moses."(Acts 13:39)

The Roman Church believes that salvation comes from observing the sacraments. For example, infants are saved when baptized; but they lose that salvation when they sin as mature persons. However, it can be regained through participating in Church Sacraments.

SALVATION IN JUDAISM

To the extent that a salvation concept exists in Judaism, it refers to observance of the Law of Moses and of Halakhah, which are a set of rules and practices from the Torah, from laws instituted by the rabbis and from long-standing customs. Halakhah from any of these sources can be referred to as a mitzvah

The Jewish concept of salvation is also tied to that of restoration for Israel. The Jews were in constant battle with other nations, some of whom held them as captives. Therefore, their idea of salvation was one in which they would be secure and live in peace and when the Temple would be restored.

Since Judaism has no concept of original sin, it has no idea that man is naturally evil needing salvation.

JESUS

The crucial difference between Christianity and Judaism is found in the person of Jesus. Judaism considers Jesus another of many Jewish teachers that flood their history. He was not the Messiach. The term means "the anointed one" and refers to the ancient Jewish practice of anointing a person when he becomes king. The Messiach will be anointed king after he sets up his kingdom in the Olam Ha-Ba, the world to come. This individual is not a savior, who will save the Jews from their sins, because no such concept exists in Judaism. He will establish a government in Israel that will be the center of all world government, both for Jews and gentiles (Isaiah 2:2-4; 11:10; 42:1). He will restore the religious court system of Israel and establish Jewish law as the law of the land (Jeremiah 33:15). The world will recognize the Jewish G-d as the one and only G-d and the Jewish religion as the only true religion (Isaiah 2:3; 11:10; Micah 4:2-3; Zechariah 14:9). These things did not happen in Jesus' lifetime. Consequently, the Jews rejected him as the Messiach.

The English word Messiah refers to an individual who will save people from their sins. Jesus is the Christian Messiah. The writer of Matthew's Gospel tells us that the angels announced Jesus' birth saying, "And she (Mary) shall bring forth a son and thou shalt call his name Jesus, for he shall save his people from their sins." (Matthew 1"21) Although the angels' statement specifically referred to the Jews, Christians have extended it to refer to all people.

Jews and Christians differ with respect to Jesus' divinity. I will not elaborate on this point, since I treat it extensively in my chapter on "The Life and Teachings of Jesus" and in this chapter under the heading of "God."

Conclusion

Christianity and Judaism are similar in some respects. Christianity uses Jewish scriptures, worships the Abrahamic God, recognizes the Jewish prophets and incorporates the Jewish bible into theirs However; they are dissimilar in other respects. Christianity believes in a Trinity, whereas Judaism believes in a one and indivisible God. Christianity believes in original sin and salvation. Judaism does not. Christianity believes in hell as a place of punishment. No such concept exists in Judaism. Christianity conceives of Satan as the enemy of God. Judaism sees him as God's agent. Their differences so far outnumber their similarities that one can reasonably consider them two distinct religions.

CHAPTER SEVEN

Bible Stories—Myth or History?

Every religion is true.when understood metaphorically.
—Joseph Campbell

The word Myth derives from the Greek "mythos", meaning a story. It is usually a story about a people's origins, their Gods and Goddesses, their ancestors and heroes. Like the Egyptians, Babylonians, Greeks and Romans, the Israelites developed their myths as a means to promote national pride and, in many cases, to demonstrate that their God was superior to their neighbors'. In many instances, they took other nations' ancient legends and fashioned them to suit their social, national and spiritual legacy. The stories of Moses and how he led his people out of Egypt, Joshua's conquest of Canaan, Noah's Ark, the Great Flood and the tower of Babel are some that I will discuss. I was brought up to believe that these stories were true and that they were supported by historical and scientific evidence. When I investigated the available data, my childhood acceptance turned to a mellow recognition that they were products of the Israelite imaginative genius.

The Biblical Moses

Moses (Moshe Rabbenu in Hebrew) is arguably Judaism's most significant figure. His story is found in four books of the Torah—Exodus, Leviticus, Numbers and Deuteronomy. According to their accounts, he was born during Israel's captivity in Egypt, when the Israelites' population was more and mightier than the Egyptians. The King (the word Pharaoh was first used in 335 BCE by a visiting Chinese envoy to Egypt), whose name is not mentioned, worried that this might pose a threat to Egypt, since the Israelites might lend support to Egypt's enemies.[160] Consequently he ordered the killing of all newborn Israelite' boys.

When Moses was born, his mother feared for his life and hid him for 3 months. After she could hide him no longer, she placed him in a papyrus basket and hid it among the bushes on one of the banks of the Nile River. The basket containing the child was found by the King's daughter, who took the child to the palace and cared for him as her own.

One day, an adult Moses saw an Israelite slave being mistreated by an Egyptian. He killed the Egyptian and fled to Midian, where he lived in the house of a Midian priest named Jethro. He married Zipporah, the priest's daughter, who bore him a son.

Years later, God appeared to him in a burning bush and sent him back to Egypt with his brother, Aaron, to demand the Israelites' release. When the King refused, God sent plagues on Egypt, the Hebrews escaped and the pursuing Egyptian army drowned in the Red Sea. A wilderness sojourn followed, in which God, through Moses, made a covenant with the Israelites and laid out rites of worship and laws of communal and personal behavior. At age 120, Moses died by God's decree, shortly before his people entered the land known in recent centuries as Palestine.

Moses in history

Does historical or scientific evidence support the existence of Moses? Let me begin with Justin Martyr, an early Christian apologist, born around 100 ACE and suffered martyrdom 165 ACE. In his "Discourse to the Greeks", he cited ancient Greek writers who mentioned Moses.[161]

One of these was Polemon, head of the Platonic Academy from 314-269 BCE. In his "Hellenics book1", he mentions Moses as the leader and ruler of the Jewish nation.

Apion, in the 4th book of his Egyptica (all 5 volumes are now lost, but preserved in some writings of Flavius Josephus), recounted that during the reign of Inachus (mythical King of Argos, whose reign began 1856 BCE),

---

[160] Exodus 1:8-11

[161] Justin Martyr, "DISCOURSE TO THE GREEKS", chapter 9, translated REV M. DODS, M.A., The Forerunner Forum. n.d., March 22, 2011.

the Jews, led by Moses, revolted against Amases, the Egyptian King. He states, "I have heard of the men of Egypt, that Moses was of Heliopolis and that he thought himself obliged to follow the customs of his forefathers."

Justin Martyr also mentioned Diodorus Siculus, a prominent Greek historian of the first century ACE, who states, in the History of Antiquity, that he learned from Egyptian priests that Moses was an ancient lawgiver.

Flavius Josephus (37 ACE-100 ACE), a renowned Jewish historian, mentioned Moses as a historical person. In his Antiquities of the Jews, he mentions that Moses led a military campaign of Egyptians and Israelites against Cush (Ethiopia. After conquering the Ethiopians, he married one of their princesses named Tharbis.(Numbers 12:1 seems to agree with this) According to Josephus, this was Moses' first marriage; only later did he travel to Midian and marry Zipporah. Josephus also states that Moses led the Israelites out of Egypt and gave them their laws.[162]

A Historical Moses?

For starters, there is no historical or archaeological evidence to support the existence of the biblical Moses. The ancient Egyptians, who chronicled their history meticulously, make no mention of a large number of Israelites held captive in Egypt or of Moses and no archaeological find establishes his existence.

Archaeologists have found cuneiform tablets dating to 1000 BCE describing the story of Sargon the Great, a Babylonian King, who lived around 3000 BCE. He was saved as a baby when his mother made a basket out of rushes, sealed it with tar and placed it in a river. The basket containing the baby was later found by a princess who raised him in the palace. Israelites, who were enslaved in Babylon, might have been familiar with the story and later adopted it.

Those who propose that Moses was a historical person lack sustentative corroboration. Hypotheses are assumptions that must be verified by observation or experiment to rise to the level of proof. The Moses' apologists base their assumptions on hearsay reports. For example, Diodorus said that he learned his information from Egyptian priests, who in turn, were

---

[162] Josephus, Antiquities, Book 2, chapters 10 and 11, History Wokshop, n.d., March 22, 2011.

knowledgeable of the Jewish legends. Apion wrote 1,300 years after the "Exodus" and also derived his information from hearsay. In "Against Apion" 1.1, Josephus admits that his facts were derived from the Talmud, Midrish and other sacred books, not by independent investigation.

Apart from the Judeo-Christian and Islamic scriptures, there is no direct historical or scientific evidence that the biblical Moses existed. The writer or writers of the Torah might have used Moses as alesson to teach the Israelites' about God's relationship to them as His chosen people.

The Israeli Exodus

According to Exodus (chapters 12-114), the Egyptian king released the Israelites, who had been captives in Egypt. However, God hardened his heart, and he changed his mind and pursued them. Yahweh, the Jewish God, instructed Moses, the Israelite leader, to lead the people by way of the Red Sea (Sea of Reeds) instead of by the land of the Philistines. God separated the sea and the Israelites crossed over to dry land. The Egyptians who, led by their King, pursued them were drowned.

> And the waters returned, and covered the chariots and the horsemen, and all the armies of Pharaoh that came into the sea after them, not so much as one of them remained . . . . "So the LORD saved Israel that day out of the hand of the Egyptians, and Israel saw the Egyptians dead on the seashore." (Exodus 14:28, 30)

There are many questions concerning the story of an exodus from Egypt by a people known as Israelites. From 1675-1552 BCE, Lower Egypt was ruled by Hykos, Asiatic people, who had migrated from Phoenicia. Eventually, 18th Dynasty Pharaoh Ah-mose, Egyptian King of Upper Egypt (never ruled by the Hyksos) expelled them and his soldiers chased them through the Sinai desert and Canaan, which had once been under Egyptian rule. He reasserted that rule.

By the time Jewish history was written (a thousand years later), the story seems to have been transformed to Moses leading the Israelites out of Egypt.

There is no Egyptian record of a large exodus of persons from Egypt. The total number, including women, children and soldiers of the Israelites would have amounted to half the Egyptian population. If such an exodus occurred, the Egyptian or other contemporary record would have mentioned it.

A cumiform tablet from 14th Century BCE Egypt mentions that a Habiru people, nomads living like gypsies and living in various parts of the Middle East, lived in Egypt. There is absolutely no ancient source for the opinion that these Habiru were the Israelites.

I am prepared to accept that a small number of Israelites from Canaan (ruled by Egypt) could have lived in Egypt, but not in large numbers or as slaves and there was no large scale exodus from Egypt.

Lee I. Levine, a professor at the Hebrew University in Jerusalem, writes,

> There is no reference in Egyptian sources to Israel's sojourn in that country and the evidence that does exist is negligible and indirect. The few indirect pieces of evidence, like the use of Egyptian names, are far from adequate to corroborate the historicity of the biblical account.[163]

Even if there was no Egyptian Exodus from Egypt, the story is a powerful motivation to Jews to free themselves:

The Exodus myth is the foundation of the notion of "liberation" within Judaism. It's not like the personal (individual) concept within Buddhism or Christianity, but a collective, political concept as "national liberation" struggle against an external oppressor.[164]

Mount Sinai and the Ten Commandments

If Moses did not exist, the story of his Mount Sinai encounter with God and his bringing the Commandments down from the mountain should be false. Where did the bible account originate?

---

[163]   Michael Massing, "New Torah for modern minds", New York Times, March 9, 2002, March 22, 2011.

[164]   Peter Myers, "The Exodus & the Expulsion of the Hyksos", Neither Aryan or Jew Website, Canberra, Australia, June 3, 2004, last updated March 30, 2010, March 3, 2011.

Before proceeding, here is a brief description of the events surrounding the Ten Commandments. Yahweh, The God of the Israelites, called Moses to the top of Mount Sinai and gave him a set of 2 stone tablets containing a list of instructions to give to the Israelites. When Moses came down from the mountain, he saw his people worshipping a golden calf, which they had made. Annoyed at this "ungodly" act, he broke the tablets into pieces. Yahweh dictated a second set of instructions (the Book of the Covenant, Exodus 21-23), which he took to the people.

This is the Israelite story about how their laws originated. However, the writer(s) of Exodus might have been acquainted with other ancient laws that predated theirs. Some examples are: Code of Ur-Nammu, king of Ur (ca. 2050 BCE), the Laws of Eshnunna (ca. 1930 BCE), the codex of Lipit-Ishtar of Isin (ca. 1870 BCE) and the Babylonian Code of Hammurabi (1750 BCE).

The first mentioned law formed the basis for all other ancient codes of law. With respect to the Ten Commandments (700-500 BCE), its model seems to be the Hammurabi Code. Let us examine the facts.

Yahweh versus Anu and Bel

According to "Exodus", Yahweh chose Moses to write His commandments and deliver to the Israelites. He told them that if they "obey my voice indeed, and keep my covenant, then ye shall be a peculiar treasure unto me above all people: for all the earth [is] mine" (Exodus 19:4)

In the preface to the Code of Hammurabi, King Hammurabi (ruled around 1796 BC-1750 BC) said he was chosen by the gods to deliver the law to his people. He states,

> When Anu the Sublime, King of the Anunaki, and Bel, thelord of Heaven and Earth, who decreed the fate of theland, assigned to Marduk, the over-ruling son of Ea, God of righteousness, dominion over earthly man, and made him great among the Igigi, they called Babylon by his illustrious name, made it great on earth, and founded an everlasting kingdom in it, whose foundations are laid so solidly as those of heaven and earth; then Anu and Bel called by name me, Hammurabi, the exalted prince, who feared God, to bring about the rule of righteousness in the land, to destroy the wicked and the evil-doers; so that the

strong should not harm the weak; so that I should rule over the black-headed people like Shamash, and enlighten the land, to further the well-being of mankind.[165]

Joshua's "long day"

"Then Joshua spoke to the Lord in the day when the LORD delivered up the Amorites before the children of Israel, and he said in the sight of Israel: "Sun, stand still over Gibeon; And Moon, in the Valley of Aijalon and the sun stood still, and the moon stayed, until the people had avenged themselves upon their enemies. (Joshua 20:12-13.

The present-day view of the earth's movement is that the earth rotates around the sun and night and day are caused by this rotation. In bible times, the view was that the sun revolved around the earth and day and night were caused by the sun's movement. This explains why Joshua commanded the sun and not the earth to stand still. At any rate, the earth stood still for daylight to continue. Douglas E. Cox, noted Astronomer and writer on biblical astronomy, observes that such action "violates the principle of conservation of angular momentum of rotating bodies, a fundamental law. The kinetic energy of a rotating body like the earth cannot just disappear; it must continue to exist; the energy needed somewhere to go. The moon, also, cannot simply stop in its orbit; it would fall towards the earth."[166]

The same writer continues,

The ocean waters have momentum, and if the earth's crust beneath them suddenly stopped, the waters of the oceans would overflow the eastern coasts of the continents, in mighty tidal waves traveling hundreds of km per hour. This would be a catastrophe probably greater in scale than even the world wide flood of Noah's time! Similar flooding on the western coasts would likely occur when rotation resumed. But geologic evidence for such events has not been found.

---

[165] The Code of Hammurabi, Translated L.W.King, Internet Ancient History Sourcebook, Paul Halsall , March 199 8, March 22, 2011.

[166] Douglas E. Cox, "Did Earth's Rotation Stop on Joshua's Long Day?" Douglas E. Cox 1998, March 4, 2011.

The atmosphere has momentum, and if the earth's crust suddenly stopped, winds of hundreds of km per hour would cause devastation around the earth, but such drastic events do not appear to have happened.

If the earth's rotation was halted in Joshua's time, why would it not be mentioned in, say, the faith chapter, Hebrews 11? Either the writer of Hebrews did not know about it, or perhaps he considered the story to be untrue.

There is no mention of this tale in the Psalms, either. Surely in Psalm 136, where some of the mighty works of God are listed, the stopping of the sun (or the earth's rotation) by Joshua would be mentioned, if it were true. But it is not there. The creation of the earth's crust on the second day is mentioned, the making of the great lights on the fourth day is mentioned, the Exodus is mentioned, the dividing of the Red Sea is mentioned, the victories of the Israelites are mentioned, but not the story of Joshua commanding the sun and moon to stand still! [167]

Of course, those who believe that Joshua's long day actually happened would argue that with God all things are possible. He who created the heavens and the earth could make the earth stop rotating for 12 hours. I cannot disagree with such faith. It is only faith, not fact. I view the story as a powerful symbol of God's power and his mediation in the affairs of his children.

Noah's Ark and the Great Flood

The "Book of Genesis" (chapters 6-9) describes how the fallen angels succeeded in corrupting the inhabitants of the earth to such an extent that God regretted making man and decided to destroy mankind by a flood. However, one man found favour with God. His name was Noah and he was the most upright man on earth (The world population numbered

---

[167]   Douglas E. Cox, "Did Earth's Rotation Stop on Joshua's Long Day?"

several billions)[168] and God gave him the specifications to build a huge ship to save himself, his family and animals.

> For yet seven days, and I will cause it to rain upon the earth forty days and forty nights; and every living substance that I have made will I destroy from off the face of the earth."(Genesis 7:4)

Science and the flood

Was this flood global? Scientists who study floods and those studying sedimentary layers of the earth have not found evidence for a universal flood. For example, a severe universal flood would have severely damaged the fossil sedimentary record, mixing fossils from all time periods. There is no evidence of such mixing. Scientists have not found the universal layer of mud from such a flood and no rabbit fossils in the pre-Cambrian, or any layers with both dinosaurs and humans.[169]

Another argument usually advanced against Noah's flood being universal is the historical record of then contemporary civilizations. Noah's flood is said to have occurred around 2345 BCE at which period many civilizations existed. Historical records and archaeological evidence show that most of these, including Egypt and Babylon, have an uninterrupted history.

A local flood?

Noah's flood was local. The Hebrew word "erets", especially as used in the Book of Genesis, is translated "earth" 665 times, "land" 1581 times, "country" 44 times, "ground" 119 times, "lands" 57 times and "countries", 15 times. "Adama" is another Hebrew word for "land" or "ground" and, like erets, is frequently used in Genesis.

Dr. Hochner argues that, "If we view the flood as global, then we must (if we are consistent) apply that same usage in other places were the same

---

[168]   Lambert Dolphin, "World Population since creation", Lambert Dolphin, last updated July 31, 2007, March 23, 2011.

[169]   Robert T. Carroll, "Noah's Ark", Robert Todd Carroll, 1998, last updated November 13, 1998, March 23, 2011.

words and phrases are used." [170] He lists some examples with "the face of the earth/land/ground" with Hebrew words, erets or adamah during Noah's days:

> Gen. 5:29 And he called his name Noah, saying, This same shall comfort us concerning our work and toil of our hands, because of the ground [adamah] which the LORD hath cursed.

> Gen. 6:1 And it came to pass, when men began to multiply on the face of the earth [adamah], and daughters were born unto them,

> Gen. 6:7 And the LORD said, I will destroy man whom I have created from the face of the earth[adamah]; both man, and beast, and the creeping thing, and the fowls of the air; for it repenteth me that I have made them.

> Gen. 7:3—Of fowls also of the air by sevens, the male and the female; to keep seed alive upon the face of the earth [erets].

> Gen. 7:4—For yet seven days, and I will cause it to rain upon the earth [erets] forty days and forty nights; and every living substance that I have made will I destroy from off face of the earth [adamah].

> Gen. 7:23 And every living substance was destroyed which was upon the face of the ground[adamah], both man, and cattle, and the creeping things, and the fowl of the heaven; and they were destroyed from the earth [erets]: and Noah only remained alive, and they that were with him in the ark.

> Gen. 8:9—But the dove found no rest for the sole of her foot, and she returned unto him into the ark, for the waters [were] on the face of the whole earth [erets]: then he put forth his hand, and took her, and pulled her in unto him into the ark.

---

[170]   Donald Hochner. "Noah's Flood: Global or Local?", Donald Hochmer, n.d., March 23, 2011.

Gen. 8:13 And it came to pass in the six hundredth and first year, in the first month, the first day of the month, the waters were dried up from off the earth [erets]: and Noah removed the covering of the ark, and looked , and, behold, the face of the ground [adamah] was dry.

Gen. 8:21 And the LORD smelled a sweet savour; and the LORD said in his heart, I will not again curse the ground [adamah] any more for man's sake; for the imagination of man's heart is evil from his youth; neither will I again smite any more everything living, as I have done. [171]

Here is my final quote from Dr. Hochner:

After the Israelites were delivered from Egypt and settled in Canaan, the scripture says they "covered the face of the earth" (erets, Numbers 22:5,11) Not even fundamentalists would say that Israelites covered every square foot of the planet . . . This is simply a way of stating that they occupied the land in which they were dwelling.[172]

The reader must decide whether Noah' flood was one of the many flood myths found in most cultures and whether it was a global or a local flood. Based on the available data, I conclude that it could have been a local flood or another of the many flood myths found around the world. The Israelite writer(s) used this tale to show God's intolerance of wickedness and his love for righteousness.

Conclusion

The stories discussed in this chapter are generally accepted as myth by most Christians, with the possible exception of fundamentalists, who believe in the literal reading of the bible. Why were they placed in the Holy

---

[171] Donald Hochner. "Noah's Flood: Global or Local?"

[172] Donald Hochner, "Noah's Flood: Global or Local?"

Scriptures? My only answer is that they suited the needs of the Israelites for whom they were written.

They were not addressed to Gentiles. The writers did not intend them to be incorporated into our culture or religion. The myths work for the Jews. It fires their imagination to think that they are the chosen of God, that their heroes did great things and that the people of the earth sprang from one of their great families. We, who are not Jews, have a different responsibility—to recognize the difference between myth and history.

The Christian must go beyond this and recognize the meaning of the myth. He/She must decide whether sufficient evidence is more important than faith in increasing reverence for God, who is no respecter of persons.

CHAPTER EIGHT

John the Baptist's Question

"Verily I say unto you, Among them that are born of women there hath not risen a greater than John the Baptist: notwithstanding he that is least in the kingdom of heaven is greater than he."

—Matthew 11:11

According to tradition, John the Baptist was born 6-2 BCE and died around 36 ACE. He was the cousin of Jesus by his mother Mary, who was the sister of Elizabeth, John's mother.

John was an itinerant preacher, who called upon his fellow Israelites to "Repent for the kingdom of God is at hand." (Matthew 3:2) He baptized to repentance in the Jordan River, where he also baptized Jesus.

John the Baptist preaching

Herod the tetrarch imprisoned John, because he had reproved him for marrying Herodias, his brothers' wife "and for all the evil things that Herod had done." (Luke 3:19-20) Herod wished to kill him, but did not; because the people considered John a prophet and such an act would have sparked an uprising.

At a royal reception celebrating Herod's birthday, Herodias' daughter danced and it pleased Herod to such an extent that he promised to give her whatever she wished. Goaded by her mother, she asked for the Baptist's head. It was given to her on a platter. (Matthew 14:5-12)

While imprisoned, John was told about the works of Jesus and he sent two of his disciples to ask Jesus, "Art thou he that should come, or do we look for another?" (Matthew 11: 2-3) This is a rather strange question coming from John, who had baptized Jesus and told the crowd, "There cometh one mightier than I after me, the latchet of whose shoes I am not worthy to stoop down and unloose." (Mark 1:7) Let us examine the reasoning behind his question and Jesus' answer.

JOHN'S MESSAGE

John's preaching was that God would shortly descend to judge the world, eradicate evil and set up His Kingdom. The Synoptic Gospels describe him as a preacher of repentance to avoid imminent judgment. He subscribed to the Jewish view of repentance as a turning from sin to obedience of the Law. Those who repented would be baptized by immersion as an outward sign of their commitment. (Mark 1:4-5 Luke 3:23 and Matthew 3:2, 6)

Jewish Messianic Concept

One of the basic concepts of Judaism is the coming of the mashiach (messiah). The term means "the anointed one" and refers to the ancient Jewish practice of anointing kings with oil; upon their ascendancy to office. The Messiah of the Jews is not the same as the Messiah of Christianity. The Christian messiah is a "saviour", one who will sacrifice himself for the salvation of mankind. The Jewish messiah will come from the line of King David and be appointed king in the End of Days.

Some Jewish scholars contend that the Mashiach will be a political leader, who will effect the political independence of the Jewish people by returning them to Israel and restoring Jerusalem (Isaiah 11:11-12; Jeremiah 23:8; 30:3; Hosea 3:4-5). Other scholars assert that the mashiach will be a religious leader, who will restore the religious court system of Israel and establish Jewish law as the law of the land (Jeremiah 33:15).

John's question

Some bible scholars use the term "doubt" to describe John's question to Jesus. For my part, it was not doubt, but uncertainty. Why was John uncertain about Jesus being the Jewish Messiah? As a member of, or greatly influenced by, the Qumran Community of the Essenes, John would have believed in the Meshach as a religious leader. His preaching consisted mainly of attacking the Jewish hierarchy, the temple practices and the waywardness of the Jews. He had proclaimed Jesus as the Meshach. However, Jesus' teaching and overall behavior confused him.

Jesus' Preaching

When Jesus heard that John had been imprisoned, he left Nazareth and went to Galilee. "From that time Jesus began to preach, and say, Repent for the kingdom of heaven (God) is at hand." (Matt 4:17) His message of repentance was similar to John's. However, his ministry differed from John's with respect to baptism. Although he was baptized by John, there is no evidence that he baptized anyone. It is only the writer of John's gospel who mentions him baptizing. In John 3:22 he states that Jesus baptized. However, in John 4:2, he says that his disciples, but not Jesus, baptized. John the Baptist believed that baptism was the testimony of repentance and was baffled by the Meshach not baptizing. He was also baffled by Jesus not stressing imminent judgment. Indeed, John thought that it would come in his lifetime with the appearance of Jesus.

Jesus' Actions

According to the synoptic gospels, Jesus was John's immediate cousin. John had baptized him and believed he was the man he said he was. However, Jesus' actions puzzled John. He never visited him in prison, as John would reasonably have expected.I have never heard a sermon on this aspect of Jesus' relationship with John. Was he afraid that he would be considered a disciple of John and imprisoned? Was he distancing himself from the eccentric but powerful baptizer? The gospels are silent.

JESUS' ANSWER

Jesus did not give a direct answer to John's disciples. "Jesus answered and said unto them, go and show John again those things which ye do hear and see." (John 11:4) The problem with this answer is that it could not convince John one way or the other. A question deserves an answer. Are you the Messiah or do we wait for another? Jesus should have said "Yes, I mm." or "No, I am not." The gospels do not tell us John's reaction.

CONCLUSION

John the Baptist's question must be viewed within the context of Jewish expectations of the Messiah. Since John and Jesus were Jews, it is altogether proper to do this. From what I have discussed, Jesus could not have been accepted by the Jews as the Maschiach, because he did not fulfill the minimum requirements of their Messiah. As the Christian Messiah, it is a different discussion. We are awaiting his return, when he might be regarded as the Maschiach.

PART TWO

CHAPTER NINE

THE QUESTION OF EVIL

In many cases, it is very hard to fix the bounds of Good and Evil, because
these part, as Day and Night, which are separated by Twilight . . .
—BENJAMIN WHICHCOTE

I believe that God is omnibenevolent and personally involved in the
affairs of earth and its inhabitants. However, looking around, I see or hear
of, murders, earthquakes, famine, tyranny, oppression, racial and gender
discrimination, wickedness in high places, suffering of those who worship
God with all their heart and cruelty to infants. I ask, what is evil? Where
did it originate? Is it the twin of good?

MEANING OF EVIL

Evil is anything which prevents the happiness of a being or deprives a
being of any good; anything which causes suffering of any kind to sentient
beings; injury; mischief; harm. The subject can be discussed within the
frameworks of various disciplines, including philosophy, psychology,
metaphysics and religion. My discussion focuses on religion, specifically,
Judaism and Christianity.

The Christian concept of evil is derived from the Old and New
Testaments of the bible and the word occurs 683 times in the King
James Version. In Judaism evil is related to the forsaking of God's laws as
written in the Torah, the rituals and laws in the Mishmash and Talmud. In
Christianity it is disobedience to God's laws as expressed in the Old and
New Testaments.

Types of Evil

There are two kinds of evil: moral and natural. Moral evil results from an act, or failure to act, of an individual that causes harm, pain and suffering, among other things. Bodily injury, such as murder and ills resulting from imperfect social organizations, such as oppression, slavery, racial discrimination and poverty are examples of moral evil. In order for the action or inaction to be moral evil, the agent must know that the act will produce the pain, suffering, oppression and so on.

Natural evil springs from nature and is beyond human control. Examples of natural evil are earthquakes, tornados, hurricanes, floods.

ORIGIN OF MORAL EVIL

Christian theology accepts that man is endowed with free-will and his actions arise from this free-will. I choose to murder, steal and do harm. According to this interpretation of my actions, no one or circumstance forces me to commit the aforementioned.

Let us assume provisionally that sin results from free-will and that it existed before the creation of man to cause man to choose between it and something better, what is its origin?

Some believe that evil (sin) originated in the heart of Lucifer when he thought of rebelling against God.[173] According to them, Isaiah's description (Isaiah 14:12) refers to Lucifer's expulsion from heaven for rebelling against God: "How art thou fallen from heaven, O Lucifer, son of the morning! How art thou cast down to the ground, which didst weaken the nations!" (Incidentally, this is the only reference to Lucifer in the bible.)

Isaiah (Isaiah 14:12-20) used a popular Canaanite story to make his point concerning Lucifer. In that story, the Morning Star tried to rise above the clouds to establish a position on the same mountain where the gods gathered. He was cast down into the underworld, because of his aspiration. The prophet used this story to refer to the king of Babylon, an all-powerful

---

[173] Dean Saunders, "The Great Controversy, Lucifer's Rebellion", The Bible Study Collection, McDonald Road Seventh-day Adventist Church, November 3, 2006, March 8, 2011.

ruler, who had refused to allow the Jews to return to their homeland and was brought down to "sheol" (the underground) for his refusal.

For the sake of argument, I will accept as true the proposition evil originated in heaven with Lucifer's rebellion. According to this interpretation, Lucifer (Satan's name before he was cast out of heaven, Revelation 12:9) was God's favorite and most powerful angel. Since God is perfect, and since all that He creates is perfect, how did Lucifer become imperfect? With some, this is not a question at all. They argue that God created Lucifer and his followers with free will, giving them the ability to act as they chose. However, placing the blame on free-will does not get the job done. Firstly, what is free-will? Simply put, it is the ability to make decisions without external pressure. In the case of Lucifer, according to free-will apologists, he had the ability to rebel without pressure from God.

These apologists will agree that everything that God created was perfect. Since God created Lucifer, Lucifer was perfect. Therefore, he could not have committed an imperfect act, since it would not be part of his makeup. One can't have it both ways. One can't argue that everything God created is perfect and, at the same time, argue that Lucifer, a God-creation, committed an imperfect act, making him imperfect.

To those who believe that evil originated with Lucifer, the matter ends there with respect to the origin of evil. Some, who disagree that it originated in heaven, have to locate it somewhere else. Is that somewhere the Garden of Eden? At least, it is a convenient starting point. The Book of Genesis says that God created Adam and Eve "in his image and likeness." (Genesis 1:27) , that is, perfect, since He is perfect.

How could this perfect being sin if sin was not a part of his makeup? Of course, the fable tries to reconcile the position by creating Satan as the villain who made Adam sin. This does not explain how Adam, a perfect being, succumbed to Satan's temptation.

Some scholars argue that God created Adam and Eve with free-will, the ability to make decisions without pressure from Him. If one accepts this premise, Adam's sin is easily explained - he chose to sin. I would still ask why would an Omniscient, Benevolent God waste his time to create a being who would sin? Notice I say "would sin", because God would have had pre-knowledge to the effect. The question of the origin of evil is not answered by locating it with Adam and Eve. They committed evil by disobeying God. However, the thought to disobey would have preceded the act. Where did the thought originate?

Might sin have been in Adam's makeup, so that the external pressure from Satan merely caused him to make a choice as to obeying or not the law that God laid down. In other words, did evil originate with God? Even to consider this is a great leap for many. However, analyze the data.

On one hand, the bible says that God created evil and on the other hand, it says He did not: "I form the light, and create darkness. I make peace and CREATE EVIL. I the Lord do all these things." (Isaiah 45:7) Here God is saying quite unambiguously that he created evil. "Shall a trumpet be blown in the city, and the people be not afraid? Shall there be evil in a city, and the Lord hath not done it?" (Amos 3:6) In unmistakably clear words, God is saying that any evil appearing in a city is done by Him. By extension, He does all evil. "Out of the mouth of the Most High proceeded not evil and good?" (Lamentation 3:38).

Notwithstanding, the same bible says that God does not create evil. "For thou art not a God that hath pleasure in wickedness; neither will evil dwell with thee." (Psalms 5:4) Here the Psalmist is stating his conviction that God and evil are separate and apart. "Therefore hearken unto me ye men of understanding, far is it from God that he should do wickedness." (Job 34; 10)

God does evil. God does not do evil. These are mutually exclusive propositions. However, there are those who seek to reconcile them. A case in point is Tony Warren, who states:

> Some people read verses such as this (Isaiah 45:7) and claim that it means God creates sin. But their problem is in their knowledge and understanding of the word evil. They erroneously surmise that evil always means sin, but that is not the case. The word translated evil in scripture does not "necessarily" mean evil in the same sense that we understand evil in our day. We use the word evil today as a synonym for sin or wickedness, but that is not the case in scripture. The word translated evil is the Hebrew word [ra'], meaning something that is "not good." It is from a root word meaning to be spoiled and by implication something that is not good. i.e. bad. It does not mean evil in the sense that we might think of the word today, but more correctly understood as bad or anything that is "not good" to us. [174]

---

[174]   Tony Warren "What Does God mean, I create Evil", Tony Warren, 2001, Last Modified 1/19/01, March 9, 2011.

This kind of argument does not solve the problem. It only throws light on the word "evil." Even if I grant that "evil" in the Isaiah and the other quoted contexts mean "bad", I am left with the fact that God creates "bad". How can this be, since He is all-Good?

Another writer translates "evil" in the Isaiah context as "calamity" and argues that,

> . . . . the context of the verse is dealing with who God is, that it is God who speaks of natural phenomena (sun, light, dark), and it is God who is able to cause "well-being" as well as "calamity." Contextually, this verse is dealing with natural disasters, and human comfort issues. It is not speaking of moral evil; rather, it is dealing with calamity, distress, etc.[175]

This argument, like the preceding, misses the mark by presenting God as both creator of "well being" (goodness) and "calamity" (bad).

The aforementioned arguments and many similar ones wrongly translate the word "ra" in Isaiah 45:7 as anything but "evil." However, most scholars render it as "evil."

If we accept the passage as stating that God created "evil", the question of the origin of evil is settled. This clears up the mystery of how Adam sinned and where the temptation came from. It would follow that Good and Evil existed within him. When Genesis 1 says that God looked at his work and saw that it was good, it made no distinction between "good" and "evil". They were the same.

Natural Evil

Natural evil arises from so-called "natural" events, such as earthquakes, tsunamis, tornadoes, disease. We have no control over these events and assume that there is a cause or principle operating their occurrences. The

---

"Does God create evil?" Christian Apologetics and Research Ministry © Matthew J. Slick, 1995—2010, March 23, 2011.

[175] "Does God create evil?", Christian Apologetics and Research Ministry, © Matthew J. Slick, 1995 - 2010, May 4, 2011.

Christian identifies God as the primal mover, who directs the universe, including all events that occur within it.

This begs the question: Since God created the world and He is omnibenovlent (all good) and omnipotent (all powerful) why does natural evil exist? This question has engaged the most brilliant minds throughout intellectual history. One of the best attempts at solving the problem was made by Gottfried Wilhelm Leibniz (1646-1716), the great German philosopher, mathematician, logician and linguist and last universal genius. In his book Theodicy, he agrees that God is omnibenovolent and omnipotent, and since He chose our world out of all possibilities, this world must be good—in fact, it is the best of all possible worlds and everything works out for man's good.

> Now this supreme wisdom, united to a goodness that is no less infinite, cannot but have chosen the best . . . . if there were not the best (optimum) among all possible worlds, God would not have produced any . . . . that there is an infinitude of possible worlds among which God must needs have chosen the best, since he does nothing without acting in accordance with supreme reason.[176]

To the argument that the world could have been without sin and suffering, Leibniz denies that such would have made it better.

> Therein God has ordered all things beforehand once for all, having foreseen prayers, good and bad actions, and all the rest; and each thing as an idea has contributed, before its existence, to the resolution that has been made upon the existence of all things; so that nothing can be changed in the universe (any more than in a number) save its essence or, if you will, save its numerical individuality. Thus, if the smallest evil [129] that comes to pass in the world were missing in it, it would no longer be this world;

---

[176]   W. Leibniz, Theodicy, Edited with an Introduction by Austin Farrer, Fellow of Trinity College,Oxford, translated E.M. Huggard, Project Guttenberg, November 24, 2005, "ESSAYS ON THE JUSTICE OF GOD AND THE FREEDOM OF MAN IN THE ORIGIN OF EVIL", Part 1, paragraph 8, April 7, 2011.

which, with nothing omitted and all allowance made, was found the best by the Creator who chose it.[177]

Leibniz's argument with respect to natural evil is not convincing. If he argues that God is all-Good and all-Powerful, He cannot be responsible for natural evil. If He is, as mentioned, He could have produced a world without natural evil.

These contradictions were not lost on François-Marie Arouet (Voltaire 1694-1778), arguably the greatest French wit and philosopher. His objection to Leibniz's philosophy of optimism is expressed in his "Poem on the Lisbon earthquake."

On November 1, 1755, an earthquake followed by fires and a tsunami hit Lisbon, Portugal. Lisbon and adjoining areas were devastated. In Lisbon alone 10,000 to 100,000 persons perished. Voltaire was one of the Enlightenment thinkers, who discussed the event. He used it to question Leibniz's belief that "This is the best of all possible worlds."

After the earthquake, he wrote, "Poem on the Lisbon Disaster, or: An Examination of that Axiom 'All Is Well,'"

> Oh, miserable mortals! Oh wretched earth!
> Oh, dreadful assembly of all mankind!
> Eternal sermon of useless sufferings!
> Deluded philosophers who cry, "All is well,"
> Hasten, contemplate these frightful ruins,
> This wreck, these shreds, these wretched ashes of the dead;
> These women and children heaped on one another,
> These scattered members under broken marble;
> One-hundred thousand unfortunates devoured by the earth
> Who, bleeding, lacerated, and still alive,
> Buried under their roofs without aid in their anguish,
> End their sad days!
> In answer to the half-formed cries of their dying voices,
> At the frightful sight of their smoking ashes,
> Will you say: "This is result of eternal laws
> Directing the acts of a free and good God!"
> Will you say, in seeing this mass of victims:

---

[177] Theodicy, paragraph 9.

"God is revenged, their death is the price for their crimes?"
What crime, what error did these children,
Crushed and bloody on their mothers' breasts, commit?
Did Lisbon, which is no more, have more vices
Than London and Paris immersed in their pleasures?
Lisbon is destroyed, and they dance in Paris![178]

On August 18, 1756, Jean Jacques Rousseau, the great Genevan writer, philosopher and composer, replied to Voltaire:

You reproach Leibnitz with belittling our misfortunes by affirming that all is well . . . .

This optimism which you find so cruel consoles me still in the same woes that you force on me as unbearable. "Have patience, man," Leibnitz tell me, "your woes are a necessary effect of your nature and of the constitution of the universe. The eternal and beneficent Being who governs the universe wished to protect you. Of all the possible plans, he chose that combining the minimum evil and the maximum good. If it is necessary to say the same thing more bluntly, God has done no better for mankind because (He) can do no better."

I have suffered too much in this life not to look forward to another. No metaphysical subtleties cause me to doubt a time of immortality for the soul and a beneficent providence. I sense it, I believe it, I wish it, I hope for it, I will uphold it until my last gasp . . . .

I am, with respect, Monsieur,
Jean-Jacques Rousseau.[179]

After Adam and Eve were expelled from Eden, God sent a second Adam (Jesus Christ) to redeem mankind. Why did he not remake the natural world perfect after Noah's flood? Natural evil continues.

---

[178] Voltaire, "poem on the Lisbon disaster", Online Library of Liberty, 2011, April8, 2011.
[179] Voltaire, "Poem on the Lisbon Disaster", Online Library of Liberty, 2011, April8, 2011

However, there is another Christian answer: At the end of times, this natural world would be abolished and will be replaced by a new and perfect one (revelation 21, 22).

The final answer is evil is an integral part of creation. When God looked upon his creation and said it was perfect, natural evil was created with natural goodness. Earthquakes, tornados, tsunamis, among many other natural evils, do not result from man's actions. The argument goes: Since nothing happens without God's knowledge and control, they are part of his plan. We cannot understand the mind of God. Therefore, natural evil must have a reason, which we cannot understand.

Conclusion

I believe that God is perfect and that nothing exists without his permission and that includes evil. The concept of Satan is a convenient way to explain the existence of evil, but it misses the point. Satan works for God as a tempter and tester. In Jesus prayer he said, "And lead us not into temptation." He recognized that God, through Satan, tempts us to test our faith. As a student of logic, I believe in the validity of conclusions based on consistent premises. If the apologists for Satan as the creator of evil base their conclusion on consistent premises, their conclusion is valid. If those who argue that evil comes from God do the same, their conclusion is valid. I do not recognize benefits in natural evil, but I believe that God has a reason for allowing it. I do not accept that He abandoned the world after creating it , leaving its workings to certain immutable laws he created at the beginning. As Hamlet observed, "There are many things, Horatio, than are dwelt of in your philosophy."

Think on these things.

CHAPTER TEN

The Fruit of the Spirit

There is therefore now no condemnation to them which are in
Christ Jesus, who walk not after the flesh, but after the Spirit
—Romans 8:1

The "Fruit of the Spirit" is a biblical term used by St. Paul (Galatians
5:22-23) to sum up the nine visible attributes of a true Christian life. His
native language was Greek and he described it as agape(love), chara ((joy,);
eirene (peace); makrothumia; (patience) chrestotes (kindness); agathosune
(goodness); pistis; (faithfulness), prautes (gentleness) and egkrateia
(self-control). These are not individual fruits (attributes), but one ninefold
"fruit." Galatians 5:22-23

Love

"Agape (αγάπη in Greek) is one of several Greek words translated
into English as love. Plato and other ancient authors used forms of the
word to denote love of a spouse or family, affection for a particular activity
(different from philia ; which means an affection that could denote either
brotherhood or generally non-sexual affection) and eros, an affection of a
sexual nature, usually between two unequal partners. St.Paul uses "agape"
to denote the unconditional love of God for man through Jesus and man's
reciprocation by his love towards Him and his neighbor.

Christian love towards God

A Christian believes that God so loved the world that He gave his only begotten son to be crucified for his salvation. He is so thankful to God for this that he uses every opportunity to demonstrate his love towards Him and his neighbour.

Thanks and Praise

The Christian thanks and praises God continually. The Psalmist admonishes believers to "enter His gates with thanksgiving, and into His courts with praise: thanking Him and blessing His name."(Psalm 100:4)

Praise

Praising God is different to giving Him thanks. The latter describes our attitude for what He has done for us. The former is an attitude towards Him for whom He is. St. Paul advises us that, "Through Jesus, therefore, let us continually offer to God a sacrifice of praise—the fruit of lips that confess his name."(Hebrews 13:15)

What do I mean by "an attitude towards God for whom He is?" Put simply, who is God that I should praise Him? Among the many attributes of God are: He is most Merciful and Just, "For His merciful kindness is great toward us: and the truth of the LORD endureth for ever. Praise ye the LORD." (Psalms 117:2) , "He is the Rock, His work is perfect; for all His ways are justice, a God of truth and without injustice; righteous and upright is He." (Deuteronomy 32:4) Almighty God is also faithful: "Faithful is he that calleth you, who also will do it." (1 Thessalonians 5:24) "God is faithful, by whom ye were called unto the fellowship of his Son Jesus Christ our Lord." (1 Corinthians 1:9)

> And the LORD passed by before him, and proclaimed, The LORD, The LORD God, merciful and gracious, longsuffering, and abundant in goodness and truth,

Keeping mercy for thousands, forgiving iniquity and transgression
and sin (Exodus 34:6, 7)

The Psalmist says, "I will extol the LORD at all times; his praise will
always be on my lips." (Psalm 34:1) God is worthy of praise all the time.

Thanksgiving

The fruit of the Spirit will be exhibited through Christian thanksgiving.
I thank God continually for what He has done and will continue to do
for me. It is altogether fitting and proper to thank God for material and
intellectual successes and good health.

I thank God for the beautiful rainbow that reminds me of the dreams
of my youth, the clear day when I can see forever, the moon that reminds
me of the love that is my companion and the stars that sing the glory of
God However, beyond these,

> my heart is glad, and my glory rejoiceth: my flesh also shall rest
> in hope.

> For thou wilt not leave my soul in hell; neither wilt thou suffer
> thine Holy One to see corruption.

> [Thou wilt shew me the path of life: in thy presence is fullness of joy;
> at thy right hand there are pleasures for evermore. (Psalm 16:9-11)

Love of God also involves love of one's neighbor, being charitable, not
envious, not behaving arrogant or vain, of a good report, not self-centered
and not provoked easily. (1 Corinthians3:4-8) One day Jesus told his
disciples about the end times,

> When the Son of man shall come in his glory, and all the holy
> angels with him, then shall he sit upon the throne of his glory:"
> All the nations of the earth shall be gathered before him and he
> "shall separate them one from another, as a shepherd divideth
> his sheep from the goats. And he shall set the sheep on his right
> hand, but the goats on the left.

Then shall the King say unto them on his right hand, Come, ye blessed of my Father, inherit the kingdom prepared for you from the foundation of the world. For I was an hungred, and ye gave me meat: I was thirsty, and ye gave me drink: I was a stranger, and ye took me in: " Naked, and ye clothed me: I was sick, and ye visited me: I was in prison, and ye came unto me." (Matthew 25:31-36)

The righteous (the sheep) will be perplexed, knowing that the King (God) never faced these situations. Jesus' disciples, knowing that the parable was directed to them, asked Jesus to explain his sayings. Jesus said that the King shall answer, "Verily I say unto you, Inasmuch as ye have done it unto one of the least of these my brethren, ye have done it unto me."(Matthew 25:40)

Dear reader, the acts of kindness done to your neighbor is a powerful demonstration of your love towards God. One day during the 2010 Christmas season, Noel Brown, a friend of mine, asked me and others to accompany him to feed the poor. We prepared meals and clothes and took them to a shelter. I cried when I observed the happiness that our gifts of thanksgiving brought to these homeless persons.

Whatever one does to one's neighbor one does to God. Good works to others receive God's favour. Bad works receive his damnation. The indwelling presence of God will help believers to do those things which glorify "our Father who art in heaven."

Joy

St. Paul uses the word "Chairo", meaning "to rejoice" to express Christian joy. Christian joy is a state of happiness that is not affected by circumstances, but is the result of having faith that one will triumph over adverse and trying circumstances.

Our example is Jesus, who endured death on the cross "for the joy that was set before him." (Heb 12:2). I recall the beautiful words of Thomas Shepherd's good, old hymn, "Must Jesus Bear the Cross Alone"

> Must Jesus bear the cross alone,
> and all the world go free?
> No, there's a cross for everyone,
> and there's a cross for me.

The consecrated cross I'll bear
till He shall set me free;
and then go home my crown to wear,
for there's a crown for me.
Upon the crystal pavement, down
at Jesus' pierced feet,
with joy I'll cast my golden crown,
and His dear name repeat.

Each of us bears a cross—of misfortune, broken dreams, ill health and so on daily. However, we should rejoice, knowing that we have "a High Priest, who is touched with the feeling of our infirmities. (Hebrews 4:15) "Weeping may endure for a night, but joy cometh in the morning." (Psalms 30:5)

He who endures to the end will receive a golden crown. I will cast mine down with joy at Jesus' pierced feet and repeat his dear name.

There is also an inexpressible joy to a person who receives forgiveness of sins:"Whom (Jesus) having not seen, ye love; in whom, though now ye see him not, yet believing, ye rejoice with joy unspeakable and ful of glory: Receiving the end of your faith, even the salvation of your souls." (1 Peter 1:8-9)

One is confident "that He who began a good work . . . . will carry it on to completion until the day of Christ Jesus.(Philippians 1:6) One knows that when one stands before the judgment seat of God, one's name will be written in the Book of Life and one shall not be condemned to eternal death, but inherit eternal life.

Godly Peace

St. Paul uses the Greek word "eirene" for peace. Eirene was the Greek goddess of peace and in classical Greek the word meant national tranquility, the absence of war or other hostilities. Later, it was used to refer to inner contentment; serenity: peace of mind. St. Paul uses the word to indicate inner contentment and serenity that comes from the indwelling of the Holy Spirit, "His peace will guard your hearts and minds as you live in Christ Jesus." (Philippians 4:6New Living Version)

Jesus said, "Peace I leave with you, my peace I give unto you: not as the world giveth, give I unto you" John 14: 27) The peace that Jesus was speaking of came because he obeyed his Father's command to die on the cross that whosoever believeth in him shall have everlasting life.(John 3:16) It can only be obtained by believing in him. "Therefore being justified by faith, we have peace with God through our Lord Jesus Christ." (Romans 5:1)

Kindness

The Greek word used in Galatians 5:22 is " chrestotes", a form of "chrestos", meaning useful, fit for use, as well as useful to others , kind, pleasant. The Oxford Concise defines kindness as "the quality of being friendly, generous, and considerate." I will add that a kind person also exhibits a great degree of mercy.

A Christian will exhibit kindness in his dealing with others. In the words of Paul, the children of God must be "kind one to another, tenderhearted, forgiving one another, even as God for Christ's sake hath forgiven you."(Ephesians 4:32) Paul's major premise is that Christian kindness reciprocates God's kindness to us by being kind to one another in the faith. However, it does not end there. It extends to our fellow man.

Christians do not bear malice and condemn others, but are tender hearted. Neither do they hate those who harm them. They forgive, even as God, in his loving kindness, has forgiven them. We did not merit God's love, but he sent his son to redeem us while we were in our sins. Through this act, we, who believe, will spend an eternity of bliss. Knowing this, can we allow the unkindly acts of others to prevent us from living a life of kindness? I am convinced that neither wrong done to me, unwarranted criticism of my acts, discernible envy and jealousy shall prevent me from exhibiting the spirit of kindness. The Spirit that is within me strengthens me in these things.

Patience

St. Paul uses the Greek term "makrothumia", a combination of makro—(long, distant in time or space) and thumos (passion, rage, the emotions of suffering)]. Usually the word connotes having an enduringly-calm temper, longsuffering. It refers to the social virtues relating to our thoughts and actions toward our fellow man and our attitude during trials.

What is patience? It is an attitude that enables us to bear our sufferings. The pre-eminent example of this is Job. He was. "perfect and upright and one that feared God and eschewed evil. "(Job 1:1) The New Living Translation renders it as follows, "blameless—a man of complete integrity. He feared God and stayed away from evil."

> And there were born unto him seven sons and three daughters. His substance also was seven thousand sheep, and three thousand camels, and five hundred yoke of oxen, and five hundred she asses, and a very great household; so that this man was the greatest of all the men of the east.(Job 1:2-3)

Job was the richest man in the East, including Asia: the Indian subcontinent, the Far East/Middle East/Near East and Central Asia. He must have been a man, who in ancient fashion, did charity, helped his fellowmen, and gave liberally for the upkeep of God's house. God Almighty himself said that he was a man who loved Him and did no evil, a perfect man. Such a man would be blessed as he was.

Misfortune hit Job, as a result of a deal that God made with Satan (the Accuser). "Now there was a day when the sons of God came to present themselves before the LORD, and Satan came also among them." (Job 1:6) Apparently, Satan used to go around the earth testing the saints of God to see if they would remain steadfast under adversity or trials.

God asked Satan to give him an estimate of Job. Satan acknowledged that Job was all that God said; but that he served Him because of all the blessings he received from God. "But put forth thine hand now, and touch all that he hath, and he will curse thee to thy face."(verse 11) God had confidence in Job that no circumstance would make him curse Him. "And the LORD said unto Satan, Behold, all that he hath is in thy power; only upon himself put not forth thine hand. So Satan went forth from the presence of the LORD." (Verse 12)

Job lost his wealth, his children and he was stricken from head to foot with boils. In all his suffering, he never cursed God or grew anxious. When his friends and wife told him to curse God, he replied, "Though he slay me, yet will I trust in him."(Job 13:15)

He did not know why misfortune and sickness hit him. He knew nothing about the God-Satan pact. What he knew—and knew it with all his being—was that God will never forsake him. He knew that in the end, God will take care of him.

Job is the greatest poem in scripture and one of my regrets in literature is that John Milton did not write an epic of Job.

Shall I know joy and not sadness, plenty and not little? God tests us continually to see what we are made of. The mothers we lose, the little child that cannot speak or is retarded, the sickness that would not go away, are all tests. If you are a child of God, you can be sure of one thing-God does not give us more than we can bear. He knows our limits.

"So the Lord blessed the latter end of Job more than his beginning." (Job 42:12) You might not be as fortunate as Job. You might not get your final blessings on earth However; there is a crown of righteousness laid up for you if you endure to the end.

"Be still and know that I am God." (Psalm 46:10) The psalmist tells us to abandon our usual assumptions about things and accept the will of God. When we stop trusting ourselves, we will experience God's power over us and all around us. Be patient and know that God is in control. Patience is the stuff of which a strong Christian is made.

Goodness

In referring to goodness, St. Paul uses the Greek word agathosune, a noun that is translated "goodness" in most versions of the Christian bible. It is found only 4 times in the New Testament (Rom. 15:14; Gal. 5:22; Eph. 5:9; 2 Thess. 1:11) and is composed of the Greek word "agathos" (good) plus the suffix "sune" which denotes quality.

Thus the word means good quality or goodness. The English word "goodness" means good-natured, helpful and beneficial. It is the quality or state of being morally sound: good, moral, upright, virtuous. In this discourse I will discuss goodness in the sense of uprightness. Donald DeMarco observes that ".uprightness is a manifestation of God's will. The person who is upright presents God to the world."[180]

The same writer states that "Uprightness differs from "righteousness," according to Scripture, more by emphasis than by distinctiveness of meaning. One emphasizes the person who is moral; the other emphasizes

---

180 Donald de Marco, "The Virtue of Uprightness", Catholic Education Resource Centre, 2004, March 4, 2011.

the morality apart from the person."[181] In this sense, an upright person is a morally sound and virtuous person.

This concept is best described as doing what is right (straight). To the Christian, right is what is in accord with Christian teaching based on the bible. The Holy Spirit will direct our shepherds to lead us in the ways of truth. The spirit will also lead us in the right path.

God is good, all the time. In fact, none of us can be good without regeneration. In the words of the Psalmist, "there is none that doeth good, no, not one." (Psalm 14:3) We cannot be good in the sight of God unless we accept salvation through grace and become a new creature. "Not of works, lest any man shall boast.(Ephesians 2:9)

Faithfulness

The Greek word for faithfulness (faith) is "pistis" and refers to loyalty to a person, idea or cause. In this discourse I am discussing it as loyalty to God and the cause of godliness. Whenever I think of faithfulness to God, I recall martyrs of the Christian faith.

St. Polycarp (69-155 ACE), a 2nd Century Bishop of Smyrna, who refused to burn incense to the Emperor and was condemned to death. It is reported that before he was burned at the stake, he said,"Eighty and six years I have served him . . . How then can I blaspheme my King and Savior? Bring forth what thou wilt." [182]

John Hus (1372-1415) was born in Bohemia and was a follower of John Wycliffe. He objected to abuses in the Catholic Church and agreed with Wycliffe that persons should be allowed to read the bible in their own language. At that time the Roman Church threatened anyone possessing a non-Latin bible with death. He was burned at the stake with Wycliffe's bibles used to kindle the fire.His last words were that, "In 100 years, God will raise up a man whose calls for reform cannot be suppressed."[183] In 1517, Martin Luther nailed his famous "95 Theses" to the church door at Wittenberg, which started the Protestant Reformation.

---

[181]   Donald de Marco, "The virtue of uprightness."

[182]   "Polycarp",Biography from Answers.com, "Date of Martyrdom", Answers Corporation, 2011, April 20, 2011.

[183]   "John Hus", Great Site.com, 1997, April 20, 2011.

William Tyndale (1494-1536) was a scholar, translator and a leading figure in the Protestant Reformation. He translated the bible into English from Greek and Hebrew texts. In 1530, he wrote The "Practyse of Prelates", which opposed Henry VIII's Divorce on the ground that it violated scriptural law. In 1535, he was arrested by church authorities and jailed in the castle of Vilvoorde, outside Brussels, for one year. He was later tried for heresy, strangled and burnt at he stake.

These men of faith and countless others counted it worthy to suffer death rather than abandon their Christian principles. Jesus was aware that in the last days many will desert the faith. He asked his disciples, " . . . . when the Son of man cometh, shall he find faith on the earth?" (Luke 18:8)

The writer of "Revelation" gives an example of those who remained faithful to the end:

> After this I beheld, and, lo, a great multitude, which no man could number, of all nations, and kindreds, and people, and tongues, stood before the throne, and before the Lamb, clothed with white robes, and palms in their hands and cried with a loud voice, saying, Salvation to our God which sitteth upon the throne, and unto the Lamb.
>
> And all the angels stood round about the throne, and about the elders and the four beasts, and fell before the throne on their faces, and worshipped God, Saying, Amen: Blessing, and glory, and wisdom, and thanksgiving, and honour, and power, and might, be unto our God forever and ever. Amen. And one of the elders answered, saying unto me, What are these which are arrayed in white robes? and whence came they?: And I said unto him, Sir, thou knowest. And he said to me, These are they which came out of great tribulation, and have washed their robes, and made them white in the blood of the Lamb.
> Therefore are they before the throne of God, and serve him day and night in his temple: and he that sitteth on the throne shall dwell among them." (Revelation 7:9-15)

Those who are faithful to the end shall dwell with God forever. At the end of this life all Christians should be able to say with St. Paul, "I have fought a good fight, I have finished my course, I have kept the faith:

Henceforth there is laid up for me a crown of righteousness, which the Lord, the righteous judge, shall give me at that day: and not to me only, but unto all them also that love his appearing. (2 Timothy 4:7-8)

Gentleness

The Greek term used by Paul is "prautes", which denotes mildness or meekness of spirit, not causing harm. In the sense of meekness, the term gentleness means patience and control when harmed and not causing harm to others.

In Paul's usage gentleness is not weakness or low self-esteem. It is a firm refusal to abandon one's Christian principles. The aforementioned martyrs were meek, but chose death rather than abandon their Christian beliefs.

Self-control

The Free online dictionary defines self-control as "control of one's emotions, desires, or actions by one's own will:" The wise writer of Proverbs says, "³He that is slow to anger is better than the mighty; and he that ruleth his spirit than he that taketh a city." (Proverbs 16:32)

Remez Sasson wrote a very instructive article on self-control or self-discipline. In it, he states,

> Self-control is the ability to control impulses and reactions, and is another name for self-discipline.
>
> It keeps in check self-destructive, addictive, obsessive and compulsive behavior.
>
> It gives one a sense of personal mastery over one's life and bring balance into one's life.It helps to keep over-emotional responses in check. It enables one to control moods and reject negative feelings and thoughts.[184]

---

[184]   Remez Sasson, "Self Control", Success Consciousness.com, 2001, April 5, 2011.

The sinful, corrupt nature of man prevents him from controlling himself completely. One can only develop full self-control by the help of God's indwelling Holy Spirit.

These Fruit of the Spirit is a bright, shining light that persons see and glorify our Father God.

CHAPTER ELEVEN

JUSTIFICATION

This doctrine [justification by faith] is the head and the cornerstone. It alone begets, nourishes, builds, preserves, and defends the church of God; and without it the church of God cannot exist for one hour.

—Martin Luther

Justification is one of the most contentious Christian doctrines. Every theologian accepts that it is an act in which God declares a sinner "just", that is, acquits him of his inherited and actual sin. However, there is disagreement on the means by which the sinner becomes just. Some assert that it is by faith alone; others state that it is by faith plus works and a great, but greatly misunderstood, British monk stirred not a little controversy when he contended that man did not even need justification, because Adam's sin was not inherited and man never lost his free-will. This chapter will trace the history of the concept of justification from St. James to modern times.

St. James

The teaching of justification by faith plus works affirms that a person is saved by the grace of God through both his faith and his good works. St. James, the brother of Jesus, is generally cited as the main proponent of this concept. In the book bearing his name, he says:

How foolish! Can't you see that faith without good deeds is useless?

Don't you remember that our ancestor Abraham was shown to be right with God by his actions when he offered his son Isaac on the altar? You see his faith and his actions worked together. His actions made his faith complete. And so it happened just as the Scriptures say: "Abraham believed God, and God counted him as righteous because of his faith." He was even called the friend of God. So you see, we are shown to be right with God by what we do, not by faith alone. Just as the body is dead without breath, so also faith is dead without good works. (James 2: 20-24, 26)

James' use of Abraham's actions to make his point is interesting, because it is one of the best examples of works and faith leading to righteousness.

God commanded Abraham to go to the city of Moab and offer his only son Isaac as a burnt offering on a mountain that He will show him. In those days, the Israelites were required (Leviticus 1-7) to make burnt offerings of animals, usually sheep or goats, to their God for the forgiveness of sins. The offerings were usually done on an altar.

Abraham did not question God. He obeyed and went to the city aforementioned with Isaac, 2 menservants, wood and fire. On our way to Moab, most of us would have questioned why God would ask us to do something so cruel. Not Abraham. He trusted that God would do what was right.

Isaac said to his father, "Behold the fire and the wood: but where is the lamb for a burnt offering? And Abraham said, My son, God will provide himself a lamb for a burnt offering." (Genesis 22:7-8)

Abraham placed his son on the altar, which he built. As he lifted his hand to kill his son, the angel of the Lord shouted to him to lay down his knife. At that instant, he saw a ram caught in the bushes. He took it and offered it to God in place of his son. (Genesis 22:1-13)

Abraham's works was exhibited in his obedience to God in doing what God told him. His faith was shown in his believing that God would provide a lamb as the substitute for his son. James is saying that because Abraham trusted in God, he was willing to do whatever God commanded. Paul reinforces the point when he states, "It was by faith that Abraham offered Isaac as a sacrifice when God was testing him." (Hebrews 11:16 NLV)

"Abraham, who had received God's promises, was ready to sacrifice his only son, Isaac, even though God had told him, "Isaac is the son through whom your descendants will be counted."(Hebrews 11:16-18 New Living Translation)

"You see his faith and his actions worked together. His actions made his faith complete." (James 2:22) "We are shown to be right with God by what we do, not by faith alone. Just as the body is dead without breath, so also faith is dead without good works."(Verses 24, 26)

St. Paul

St. Paul taught that justification was by faith. However, he did not state whether it was by itself or combined with works. I will examine 2 passages:

(1) Therefore being justified by faith, we have peace with God through our Lord Jesus Christ. (Romans 5:1).
(2) Therefore we conclude that a man is justified by Faith without the deeds of the law. (Romans 3:28).

The first passage states that a person is justified by faith (in Jesus) and the second says that this is done without the deeds prescribed by the Law. Neither passage includes the word "alone". Therefore, I cannot conclude that Paul means "faith alone"

The Jewish Law laid out certain deeds that had to be performed by Jews. Performing those deeds, among other things, guaranteed a person success in this life and a good life in the hereafter. Paul was saying that such deeds do not make a person righteous (justified). Righteousness could only be attained through faith in Jesus.

He used the word faith more than 200 times but never combined it with the word "alone" or any of its synonyms. One would expect such mention if that was what he meant by using the word "faith." Therefore, I conclude that he means what he says—that justification comes by faith in Jesus Christ.

St. Paul and the need for justification

Wherefore, as by one man sin entered into the world, and death by sin; and so death passed upon all men, for that all have sinned

But not as the offence, so also is the free gift. For if through the offence of one many be dead, much more the grace of God, and the gift by grace, which is by one man, Jesus Christ, hath abounded unto many.

> For as by one man's disobedience many were made sinners, so by the obedience of one shall many be made righteous" (Romans 5:12,15,19)

In verse 12, Paul speaks of Adam's sin leading to his death and the judgment of death upon all his descendants (original sin). The death referred to is not physical death, but spiritual separation from God. This eternal separation passed also to those who had not sinned: "Nevertheless death reigned from Adam to Moses, even over them that had not sinned after the similitude of Adam's transgression" Romans 5:14).

Many question this doctrine of original sin. How, they ask, can a just God damn them unless they have sinned? Adam and Eve were justly damned for their sins. A just God will not transfer their sins to them. God will treat each case on its own merit. They argue that this transference of sin from Adam to the human race is not supported by any pronouncement of God, but completely Pauline.

In verse 15, Paul asserts that the gift of God's grace through Jesus Christ is extended to all those who believe in Jesus Christ.

In verse 19, he raises the stakes. Adam's disobedience (sin) made the human race sinners. However, Jesus' obedience to God by dying on the cross made those who believe in him partakers of his righteousness. According to Paul, it is only because a person shares in Christ's righteousness that he can become just.

St Augustine

St. Augustine (364-430 ACE) was Bishop of Hippo and one of the most brilliant thinkers (theological and philosophical) in Western thought. His "Confessions" remains a masterpiece. On justification, the great and profound thinker states:

> That one sin, however, committed in a setting of such great happiness, was itself so great that by it, in one man, the whole human race was originally and, so to say, radically condemned. It cannot be pardoned and washed away except through "the one mediator between God and men, the man Christ Jesus," who alone could be born in such a way as not to need to be reborn.

> Now it is clear that the one sin originally inherited, even if it were the only one involved, makes men liable to condemnation.

> Yet grace justifies a man for many offenses, both the sin which he originally inherited in common with all the others and also the multitude of sins which he has committed on his own."[185]

St. Augustine followed Paul's teaching on original sin. However, he used a word that Paul did not use—"condemned." This word connotes a judicial setting. Augustine saw God as a judge who, as a result of Adam's sin, passed the sentence of death on the human race.

This sentence could be pardoned and erased from the record by God's grace through Jesus Christ. Grace also pardons the sins humans commit and justifies those thus pardoned.

> Yet grace justifies a man for many offenses, both the sin which he originally inherited in common with all the others and also the multitude of sins which he has committed on his own."[186]

While Saint Augustine does place major emphasis on the atonement of Christ, he believed that faith alone is not sufficient to save. Baptism and partaking of the Lord's Supper must be added to the atoning work of Christ.

> The Christians of Carthage have an excellent name for the sacraments, when they say that baptism is nothing else than "salvation" and the sacrament of the body of Christ nothing else than "life." For wherein does their opinion, who designate baptism by the term salvation, differ from what is written: "He saved us by the washing of regeneration?" or from Peter's statement: "The like figure where-unto even baptism doth also now save us?" . . . If, therefore, as so many and such divine witnesses agree, neither salvation nor eternal life can be hoped for by any man without baptism and the Lord's body and blood."[187]

---

[185] St. Augustine, Enchiridion: On Faith, Hope, and Love, Chapters 1-23; 24-53 54-77; Chapters 78-96; 97-122.translated by Pofessor J.F. Shaw, Londonderry,Leadership University, updated July 13,2002, March 1, 2011.

[186] St. Augustine, Enchiridion: On Faith, Hope, and Love, 18.50.

[187] Nicene and Post-Nicene Fathers, Vol. 5.book1, chapter 34,Sacred Texts, n.d., retrieved March 16, 2011.

This teaching would be formally accepted at a church council in 529 ACE

Pelagius

Pelagius (354-420/440 ACE) was the chief opponent of St. Augustine's views, specifically, original sin and salvation. Scholars believe he was a monk born in the British Isles. Little is known of his career up to 380 ACE, when he migrated to Rome and became very famous for his intellect and saintly bearing. Most of his writings are lost and we learn his ideas from the writings of his adversaries, notably Sts. Augustine and Jerome.

Pelagius denied the doctrines of original sin and grace. The gist of his arguments is found in his "Letter to Demetrius" and "Commentarii in epistolas S. Pauli" ("Commentaries on the Epistles of St. Paul"), probably written prior to the destruction of Rome (410 ACE) and known to St. Augustine:

Augustine held that man was born in original sin and, as a result, helpless to attain righteousness. Pelagius disagreed and argued that man was born sinless with unconditional free will and the ability to better himself spiritually without grace.

In his "Letter to Demetrius", he states that man was created in the image of God. However, he was created with free will and capable of choosing either good or evil

> We measure the goodness of human nature in relation to its creator, whom we call God. When he created the world, God declared that everything he had made was good. So if every tree and animal, insect and plant is good, how much better is man himself! God made man in his own image; and so he intends each of us to be like him . . . . But he has given man intelligence and freedom. We alone are able to recognize God as our maker, and thence to understand the goodness of his creation. Thus we have the capacity to distinguish between good and evil, right and wrong. This capacity means that we do not act out of compulsion; nor need we be swayed by our immediate wants and desires, as animals are. Instead we make choices. Day by day, hour by hour, we have to reach decisions; and in each decision, we can choose good or evil. The freedom to choose makes us

like God: if we choose evil, that freedom becomes a curse; if we choose good, it becomes our greatest blessing[188]

Pelagius contended that Adam's sin did not corrupt mankind. Man was born sinless, but became corrupt over the years by continually choosing to sin.

Professor Benjamin B. Warfield noted that the central principle of Pelagius' teaching

> Lies in the assumption of the plenary ability of man; his ability to do all that righteousness can demand,—to work out not only his own salvation, but also his own perfection. This is the core of the whole theory; and all the other postulates not only depend upon it, but arise out of it. Both chronologically and logically this is the root of the system.[189]

St. Thomas Aquinas

St. Thomas Aquinas (1225-1275 ACE) was a Catholic priest of the Dominican Order, Doctor of the Church and the Catholic Church's greatest theologian and philosopher. His views on grace are contained mainly in Summa Theologica, his lengthy theological masterpiece. In it, he argued that "in the state of corrupted nature man cannot fulfill all the Divine commandments without healing grace."[190]

What is this grace to which St. Thomas referred? Prof. Michael Lapierre says that, "Grace, in general, for Aquinas, is a favor of God, the action of God's merciful and gracious disposition towards his creatures created in his own image and likeness." [191]

---

[188]   Pelagius, "Letter of Pelagius to Demetrias A.D. 385", from The Letters of Pelagius, Robert Van de Weyer, ed , n.d., March 11, 2011.

[189]   Professor Benjamin Warfield D.D., "The Origin and Nature of Pelagianism", n.d., March 9, 2011.

[190]   St. Thomas Aquinas, Summa Theologica, "Treatise on Grace", First Part of the Second Part, second and revised edition, 1920, translated by Fathers of the English Dominican Province , online Edition , Kevin Knight 2008, March 2, 2011.

[191]   Rev. Prof. Michael Lapierre "GRACE IN THOMAS AQUINAS", Toronto, Ontario, Canada, September 21, 1994, March 5, 2011.

In the Aquinas' passage, cited earlier, healing grace is grace that cleanses us of the sin with which we were born and heals the wounds caused by sinning. Man is, by nature, corrupt and incapable of fulfilling God's divine commandments. He is also incapable of doing things that will give him everlasting life. In St. Thomas' opinion, it is given to him by grace.

> Hence man, by his natural endowments, cannot produce meritorious works proportionate to everlasting life; and for this a higher force is needed, viz. the force of grace. And thus without grace man cannot merit everlasting life; yet he can perform works conducing to a good which is natural to man, as "to toil in the fields, to drink, to eat, or to have friends," and the like, as Augustine says in his third Reply to the Pelagians.[192]

St. Thomas was clear that man needed grace for salvation when he said that, "man, by his natural endowments, cannot produce meritorious works proportionate to everlasting life." However, in the following passage, he seems to be saying that the sacraments (works) are means by which a person is justified:

> Sacraments are necessary unto man's salvation for three reasons. The first is taken from the condition of human nature which is such that it has to be led by things corporeal and sensible to things spiritual and intelligible . . . . The second reason is taken from the state of man who in sinning subjected himself by his affections to corporeal things . . . . The third reason is taken from the fact that man is prone to direct his activity chiefly towards material things. [193]

On one hand, Aquinas argues that the sacraments are necessary for man's salvation. On the other hand, he states that man is justified by faith in Christ and the sacraments are merely the outward signs of that justification:

> As the ancient Fathers were saved through faith in Christ's future coming, so are we saved through faith in Christ's past birth and

---

[192] St. Thomas Aquinas, Summa Theologica, First Part of Second Part, Treatise on Grace.

[193] Summa Theologica, Third Part, Prologue, "Treatise on the Sacraments."

Passion. Now the sacraments are signs in protestation of the faith whereby man is justified.[194]

The Roman Church

The Roman Church's doctrine of justification is contained in decrees it issued at the 6th session of the Council of Trent (1/13/1947) under Pope Paul 111. Although these decrees were issued in the 20th Century, they describe the Church's traditional views on the crucial doctrine.

Chapter 1 of the decree states:

> It is necessary that each one recognize and confess that since all men had lost innocence in the prevarication of Adam,] having become unclean and, as the Apostle says, by nature children of wrath . . . they were so far the servants of sin and under the power of the devil and of death, that not only the Gentiles by the force of nature, but not even the Jews by the very letter of the law of Moses, were able to be liberated or to rise therefrom, though free will, weakened as it was in its powers and downward bent, was by no means extinguished in them."[195]

This chapter states the traditional doctrine of original sin and argues that neither the strictest observance of the Law or the exercise of freewill could liberate mankind from being a slave of sin.

Chapter 4 defines justification as "being a translation from that state in which man is born a child of the first Adam, to the state of grace and of the adoption of the sons of God through the second Adam, Jesus Christ, our Savior."[196] This is an undeserving grace and a person can choose not to co-operate with it.

---

[194] Summa Theologica, Third Part, Prologue, "Treatise on the Sacraments."
[195] "Council of Trent-6, Decree concerning justification" , Word Television Network, Irondale, AL, n.d., March 3, 2011.
[196] Council of Trent, chapter 4.
[13] Council of Trent, chapter 6.
[14] Council of Trent, chapter 8.
[199] Council of Trent, chapter 7

Chapter 6 states that baptism is the beginning of justification, "finally, when they resolve to receive baptism, to begin a new life and to keep the commandments of God.[197]

Chapter 8 goes further and talks of "the sacrament of baptism, which is the sacrament of faith, without which no man was ever justified finally."[198]

The Roman Church also believes that sanctification is a part of Justification and not, as most evangelicals claim, a separate state.

> This disposition or preparation is followed by justification itself, which is not only a remission of sins but also the sanctification and renewal of the inward man through the voluntary reception of the grace and gifts whereby an unjust man becomes just and from being an enemy becomes a friend, that he may be an heir according to hope of life everlasting.[199]

Additionally, the Roman Church believes in justification by faith plus works.

> For faith, unless hope and charity be added to it neither unites man perfectly with Christ nor makes him a living member of His body. For which reason it is most truly said that faith without works is dead. This faith, conformably to apostolic tradition, catechumens ask of the Church before the sacrament of baptism, when they ask for the faith that gives eternal life, which without hope and charity faith cannot give." [200]

Canon 9 of the Council of Trent decrees that anyone who believes that a person is justified by faith alone will be excommunicated.

---

[200] Council of trent, chapter 6

[201] "Council of Trent, canons concerning justification, canon 9

[197]

[198]

[199]

[200]

> If anyone says that the sinner is justified by faith alone,[114]
> meaning that nothing else is required to cooperate in order to
> obtain the grace of justification, and that it is not in any way
> necessary that he be prepared and disposed by the action of his
> own will, let him be anathema."[201]

The Roman Church believes that persons who have been justified can lose their justification. However, they can regain it through the sacrament of penance.

> Those who through sin have forfeited and received grace of
> justification, can again be justified when, moved by God, they
> exert themselves to obtain through the sacrament of penance the
> recovery, by the merits of Christ, of the grace lost.[202]

The Roman Church's position on Justification can be summarized as: By Adam's sin (original sin) mankind was born with a corrupt nature and separated from God. Nevertheless, he did not lose his will. Neither the strictest observance of the Law of Moses or the exercise of the will can make a person righteous to share the nature of Christ. It is God's grace, through Christ's passion, that justifies a person. This act of justification occurs through faith and works.

Martin Luther

Martin Luther (1483-1546 ACE) was a German theologian and the father of Protestantism. He was once a Catholic monk, but left the church over, among other things, its doctrine of justification. Justification by grace alone (sola gratia) through faith alone (per solam fidem) because of Christ alone (solus Christus) was the basis of his teaching on justification.

He believed that we "are justified before God altogether without works, and obtain forgiveness of sins merely by grace." [203] Elsewhere, he says that

---

201

202   Council of Trent, Chapter 14.

203   Martin Luther, "Of Justification", A Puritans Mind, 1998-2010, March 7,
       2011.

a true Christian is justified and saved only by faith in Christ, without any works or merits of his/her own." [204]

In the "Smalcald Articles", a summary of doctrine written in 1537, Luther asserts that,

> All have sinned and are justified freely, without their own works and merits, by His grace, through the redemption that is in Christ Jesus, in His blood (Romans 3:23-25). Therefore, it is clear and certain that this faith alone justifies us.[205]

John Calvin

John Calvin (1509-1564) was an influential French theologian during the Protestant Reformation. His interpretation of the doctrine of Justification follows Luther's, but differs in some respects.

He defined justification as the act of God deeming a person to be righteous. His magnum opus is Institutes of Christian Religion, published in Latin in 1536 and in French in 1541, with the definitive editions appearing in 1559 (Latin) and in 1560 (French).In the great work, he states:

> . . . . a man will be justified by faith when, excluded from the righteousness of works, he by faith lays hold of the righteousness of Christ, and clothed in it appears in the sight of God not as a sinner, but as righteous. Thus we simply interpret justification, as the acceptance with which God receives us into his favor as if we were righteous; and we say that this justification consists in the forgiveness of sins and the imputation of the righteousness of Christ." [206]

Calvin is saying that justification is an act in which the sinner receives forgiveness of his sins and takes on Christ's righteousness. This justification

---

[204] Martin Luther, "Of Justification 300."

[205] Of Justification 306

[206] John Calvin, "On Righteousness", paragraph 2, from Institutes of the Christian religion, book 3, chapter 11, paragraph 2.

or the imputation of Christ's righteousness is not of works, but the remission
of sins through Christ's intervention:

> .... those whom the Lord has reconciled to himself are estimated
> by works, they will still prove to be in reality sinners, while they
> ought to be pure and free from sin. It is evident therefore, that
> the only way in which those whom God embraces are made
> righteous, is by having their pollutions wiped away by the
> remission of sins, so that this justification may be termed in one
> word the remission of sins."[207]

When Calvin uses the words "the Lord has reconciled to himself", he
is referring to justification.

> But the most satisfactory passage on this subject is that in
> which he(Paul) declares the sum of the Gospel message to be
> reconciliation to God, who is pleased, through Christ, to receive
> us into favor by not imputing our sins, (2 Cor. 5: 18-21.) Let my
> readers carefully weigh the whole context. For Paul shortly after
> adding, by way of explanation, in order to designate the mode
> of reconciliation, that Christ who knew no sin was made sin for
> us, undoubtedly understands by reconciliation nothing else than
> justification.[208]

The justification that Calvin conceives is received by faith:

> I trust I have now sufficiently shown how man's only resource for
> escaping from the curse of the law, and recovering salvation, lies
> in faith; and also what the nature of faith is, what the benefits
> which it confers, and the fruits which it produces. The whole
> may be thus summed up: Christ given to us by the kindness of
> God is apprehended and possessed by faith, by means of which
> we obtain in particular a twofold benefit; first, being reconciled
> by the righteousness of Christ, God becomes, instead of a judge,

---

[207] John Calvin, "On Righteousness", paragraph 21.
[208] Calvin, John, "Of Justification by Faith", paragraph 4, from Institutes of the
Christian religion, Book3:11, A Puritans's Mind, 1999, March 3, 3011.

an indulgent Father; and, secondly, being sanctified by his Spirit, we aspire to integrity and purity of life. [209]

Calvin saw justification as the remission of sins, in which the sinner, now pardoned, is reconciled with God. He saw sanctification as the consecration and dedication of body and soul to God. The pardoned sinner cannot do this by his/her will. Sanctification is the consecration and dedication of both body and soul to God.

Calvin believed that justification and sanctification are distinct, but inseparable. The act of justification is incomplete without sanctification. One cannot have one without the other: However, one cannot do this by one's will. It is God who works the miracle in us:

> . . . . as Christ cannot be divided into parts, so the two things, justification and sanctification, which we perceive to be united together in him, are inseparable . . . . But Scriptures while combining both, classes them separately, that it may the better display the manifold grace of God. [210]

Anglican /Episcopal

Official Anglican belief concerning justification is found in "The 39 Articles of Religion", which was drawn up by the Church in 1563 on the basis of the "42 Articles of 1553" and was largely based on the work of Thomas Cranmer (Archbishop of Canterbury(1533-1556) and his colleagues. There are two editions of the Articles the 1563 Latin edition and the 1571 English edition.

Article 9 discusses original sin:

> Original Sin is not about following the example of Adam, (as the Pelagians wrongly say). It is the fault and corruption of the nature of everyone which is produced in the nature of the descendants of Adam. As a result humans have gone very far from original righteousness, and by their own nature are

---

[209] Of Justification by Faith", paragraph 1.

[210] "Of Justification by Faith", paragraph.6.

inclined to evil, so that the flesh always desires what is contrary to the spirit. Therefore in every person born into this world, this original sin deserves God's wrath and damnation. And this infection of nature remains even in those who are regenerated, so that the lust of the flesh, called in the Greek, phronema sarkos, which some translate as the wisdom, some sensuality, some the affection, some the desire, of the flesh, is not subject to the Law of God. And although there is no condemnation for those who believe and are baptized, yet the Apostle admits that desire and lust has in itself the nature of sin.[211]

Anglican doctrine is that Adam's (original) sin affected the nature of man. Human nature is corrupt and humans have gone very far from original righteousness (the state in which God created Adam) and by their own nature are inclined to evil. Consequently, they deserve God's judgment. The natural desire to lust after the flesh is present even in baptized believers. In this Anglicans differ from Catholics, who believe that baptism removes all sin.

Justification by faith alone

Anglicans believe that we are justified by faith alone:

We are accounted righteous before God, only for the merit of our Lord and Saviour Jesus Christ by Faith, and not for our own works or deservings. Wherefore, that we are justified by Faith only, is a most wholesome Doctrine.[212]

Of Sin after Baptism

Anglicans stress that those who "depart from grace given and fall into sin" may return to their state of grace by repenting.

---

[211] "Articles of Religion", article 9, Anglicans Online Website, n.d.., March 18, 2011.
[212] Articles of "Religion, article h11

Not every deadly sin willingly committed after Baptism is sin against the Holy Ghost, and unpardonable. Wherefore the grant of repentance is not to be denied to such as fall into sin after Baptism. After we have received the Holy Ghost, we may depart from grace given and fall into sin, and by the grace of God we may arise again and amend our lives. And therefore they are to be condemned, which say, they can no more sin as long as they live here, or deny the place of forgiveness to such as truly repent.[213]

John Wesley

John Wesley (1703-1791) was a brilliant 18th Century theologian and the founder of Methodism, which offshoots include Pentecostals, Holiness denominations, Charismatics and General Baptists. He was a marvelous preacher, whose 53 printed sermons are still great points of Christian (Methodist) doctrine. Most of his ideas on Justification occur in Sermon 5, "Justification by Faith."[214]

Wesley believed that man was created in the image and likeness of God and lived happily in paradise.

In the image of God was man made, holy as he that created him is holy; merciful as the Author of all is merciful; perfect as his Father in heaven is perfect. As God is love, so man, dwelling in love, dwelt in God and God in him. God made him to be an "image of his own eternity," an incorruptible picture of the God of glory. He was accordingly pure, as God is pure, from every spot of sin. He knew not evil in any kind or degree, but was inwardly and outwardly sinless and undefiled."[215]

"Such, then, was the state of man in Paradise. By the free, unmerited love of God, he was holy and happy: He knew, loved, enjoyed God, which is, in substance, life everlasting. And in this

---

[213] Articles of Religion, "article 16.
[214] John Wesley, "Sermons—Numeric Index", Global Ministries, United Methodist Church, Evanston, IL., March 9, 2011.
[215] John Wesley, "Sermon 5: 1.1.

life of love, he was to continue forever, if he continued to obey God in all things; but, if he disobeyed him in any, he was to forfeit all. "In that day," said God, 'thou shalt surely die. [216]

Wesley makes an interesting point here. "He knew, loved, enjoyed God, which is, in substance, life everlasting." God's gift to Adam was everlasting life and he was born to live forever. To Wesley, everlasting life was knowing, loving, enjoying and obeying God.

> Man did disobey God. He "ate of the tree, of which God commanded him, saying, Thou shalt not eat of it." And in that day he was condemned by the righteous judgment of God. Then also the sentence whereof he was warned before, began to take place upon him. For the moment he tasted that fruit, he died. His soul died, was separated from God; separate from whom the soul has no more life than the body has when separate from the soul. His body, likewise, became corruptible and mortal; so that death then took hold on this also. And being already dead in spirit, dead to God, dead in sin, he hastened on to death everlasting; to the destruction both of body and soul, in the fire never to be quenched."[217]

When Adam disobeyed God, he was separated from God and his soul and body "hastened on to death everlasting." Wesley, like Luther and Calvin, believed that Adam's (original) sin passed on to the human race. He stated his position very eloquently:

> Thus "by one man sin entered into the world, and death by sin. And so death passed upon all men," as being contained in him who was the common father and representative of us all. Thus, "through the offence of one," all are dead, dead to God, dead in sin, dwelling in a corruptible, mortal body, shortly to be dissolved, and under the sentence of death eternal." [218]

---

[216] John Wesley, 5: 1.4.

[217] John Wesley, 5:1.5.

[218] John Wesley, "Sermon 5", 1.6.

God, in his mercy, sent Jesus to become the representative of mankind, a second Adam. As Adam's sins were transferred to us, our sins were transferred to Jesus.

> He poured out his blood for the transgressors: He "bare our sins in his own body on the tree," that by his stripes we might be healed: And by that one oblation of himself, once offered, he hath redeemed me and all mankind; having thereby "made a full, perfect, and sufficient sacrifice and satisfaction for the sins of the whole world.[219]

Under the old covenant, a sacrifice of an animal had to be offered on the altar for the expatiation of sins. Under the new covenant, Christ became our eternal sacrifice to God for us.

Wesley agreed with Luther and Calvin concerning original sin and Jesus' redemptive sacrifice. However, he disagreed with them on justification and sanctification. Whereas they saw the two as inseparable, he saw them as separate.

> This is "sanctification;" which is, indeed, in some degree, the immediate fruit of justification, but, nevertheless, is a distinct gift of God, and of a totally different nature. The one implies what God does for us through his Son; the other, what he works in us by his Spirit. So that, although some rare instances may be found, wherein the term "justified" or "justification" is used in so wide a sense as to include "sanctification" also; yet, in general use, they are sufficiently distinguished from each other, both by St. Paul and the other inspired writers. So that, although some rare instances may be found, wherein the term "justified" or "justification" is used in so wide a sense as to include "sanctification" also; yet, in general use, they are sufficiently distinguished from each other, both by St. Paul and the other inspired writers.[220]

To Wesley, justification is God's pardon, the forgiveness of sins.

> To him that is justified or forgiven, God "will not impute sin" to his condemnation. He will not condemn him on that account,

---

[219] John Wesley, "Sermon 5",: 1.7.
[220] John Wesley5:2.1

either in this world or in that which is to come. His sins, all his past sins, in thought, word, and deed, are covered, are blotted out, shall not be remembered or mentioned against him, any more than if they had not been.[221]

In this wonderful sermon, John Wesley turned to the question of how a person is justified and concluded that it is by faith alone.

But on what terms, then, is he justified who is altogether "ungodly," and till that time "worketh not?" On one alone; which is faith.[222]

This is Wesley's way of stating that man is justified by faith alone. As he stated later, "I cannot describe the nature of this faith better than in the words of our own Church: "The only instrument of salvation" (whereof justification is one branch) "is faith."[223]

He stated later:

Whatsoever virtues (so called) a man may have,—I speak of those unto whom the gospel is preached; for "what have I to do to judge them that are without?"—whatsoever good works (so accounted) he may do, it profiteth not; he is still a "child of wrath," still under the curse, till he believes in Jesus." [224]

In other words, all our works will not make us righteous unless we have faith in the redemptive power of Jesus' blood

Ellen G. White

Ellen Gould White (1827-1915) was a great American theologian, author, preacher and a founder of the Sabbatarian Adventist movement that led to the rise of the Seventh-day Adventist Church.

---

[221] John Wesley, 5:2.5
[222] John Wesley %:4.1
[223] John Wesley, "Sermon 5",::4:1
[224] John Wesley, 5: 4:4

Mrs. White's main premise concerning justification was that it is by faith alone

> There is not a point that needs to be dwelt upon more earnestly, repeated more frequently, or established more firmly in the minds of all, than the impossibility of fallen man meriting anything by his own best good works. Salvation is through faith in Jesus Christ alone."[225]

Mrs. White is clear and brilliant in her belief that justification cannot be merited, but is the gif of God through grace by faith:

> Let the subject be made distinct and plain that it is not possible to effect anything in our standing before God or in the gift of God to us through creature merit. Should faith and works purchase the gift of salvation for anyone, then the Creator is under obligation to the creature. Salvation, then, is partly of debt, that may be earned as wages. If man cannot, by any of his good works, merit salvation, then it must be wholly of grace, received by man as a sinner because he receives and believes in Jesus. It is wholly a free gift. Justification by faith is placed beyond controversy. And all this controversy is ended, as soon as the matter is settled that the merits of fallen man in his good works can never procure eternal life for him . . . . Justification is wholly of grace and not procured by any works that fallen man can do.[226]

Mrs. White considered justification to be the same as pardon.

> As the penitent sinner, contrite before God, discerns Christ's atonement in hisbehalf and accepts this atonement as his only hope in this life and the future life, his sins are pardoned. This is

---

[225] Ellen G. White, "Justification and Sanctification,. "THIS IS JUSTIFICATION BY FAITH", Adventist Biblical Truths Website, N.d. March 17, 2011.

[226] Ellen G. White, "Through Faith Alone Part 1 A general manuscript", Ellen G. White Estate, 1999, March 9, 2011.

justification by faith . . . . Pardon and justification are one and
the same thing.[227]

The Holiness Movement

The Holiness movement is a fundamentalist religious movement that
arose within 19th century American Protestantism. Its members believe
that justification is the act in which a sinner repents of his/her sins and
is pardoned by God through Jesus Christ. In holiness terminology this
is termed "born again." If he/she does not backslide (fall from grace by
sinning), he/she will go to heaven.

Since a justified person can backslide, Holiness churches, following
the teachings of John Wesley, believe in entire sanctification, a baptism
of the Holy Spirit in an instantaneous act that precludes the possibility of
voluntarily sinning.

The largest Holiness body in these United States is the Church of the
Nazarene, established in 1908 by a merger of the Pentecostal, Nazarene,
and Holiness Churches.

Pentecostals

These churches, the fastest growing Christian churches in North
America, hold the same views on justification as the Holiness churches.
They differ in their emphasis on glussolia (speaking in tongues) as the
second and highest stage of the Christian life.

The Catholic-Lutheran Joint Declaration

"The Catholic-Lutheran Joint Declaration on the doctrine of
justification" was a significant step towards a consensus on the subject. It is
a document created by and agreed to by the *Pontifical Council for Promoting
Christian Unity* and the Lutheran World Federation in 1999.

---

[227] Ellen G. White, Justification and Sanctification. "THIS IS JUSTIFICATION
BY FAITH" , Adventist Biblical Truths Website. N.d. March 17, 2011.

The preamble states that its intention was

> To show that on the basis of their dialogue the subscribing Lutheran churches and the Roman Catholic Church are now able to articulate a common understanding of our justification by God's grace through faith in Christ. It does not cover all that either church teaches about justification; it does encompass a consensus on basic truths of the doctrine of justification and shows that the remaining differences in its explication are no longer the occasion for doctrinal condemnations. [228]

Their shared understanding of justification is:

> In faith we together hold the conviction that justification is the work of the triune God. The Father sent his Son into the world to save sinners. The foundation and presupposition of justification is the incarnation, death, and resurrection of Christ. Justification thus means that Christ himself is our righteousness, in which we share through the Holy Spirit in accord with the will of the Father. Together we confess: By grace alone, in faith in Christ's saving work and not because of any merit on our part, we are accepted by God and receive the Holy Spirit." [229]

The document addressed the historical differences on the doctrine between the 2 churches. Catholics believe that persons "cooperate" in preparing for and accepting justification by consenting to God's justifying action. Lutherans, on the other hand, teach that human beings are incapable of cooperating in their salvation.

Lutherans believe that persons are justified by faith alone, but Catholics believe that they are justified by faith through baptism.

These two incompatible positions have caused many Christians to doubt that any real progress was made to Christian unity by the Declaration, which was adopted by the World Methodist Conference in July 2006.

---

[228] "Joint Declaration on the doctrine of justification", paragraph 5, Evangelical Lutheran Church in America, March 18, 2011.

[229] Joint Declaration on the doctrine of justification , paragraph 15, March 18, 2011.

CONCLUSION

Justification will remain the head and cornerstone of Christian doctrine. However, differences concerning the mechanism by or through which it is achieved will continue. Is the Church weakened by these differences? I think not, because all denominations believe that everlasting death was handed down from Adam to us and that the sentence could only be removed and expunged from the record by justification. Whether it is a combination of faith and works or by faith alone is a theological debate, because the person of faith must do works to the glory of God and works to God's glory could only be done by persons of faith.

CHAPTER TWELVE

Understanding the End Times

But I tell you of a truth, there be some standing here, which shall
not taste of death, till they see the kingdom of God.

—Luke 9:27

If I were asked which religious themes dominate Christian discourse
these days, I should unhesitatingly mention Preterism, millenniumism, the
Rapture and the Last or Final Judgment. The Church has no common
point of view on any of these teachings and some denominations do not
believe in rapture

Preterism

Preterism is a viewpoint that places many or all end times (eschatological)
events in the past, especially during the destruction of Jerusalem in 70
ACE. The term is derived from the Latin word "praeter" meaning "past."
Preterist thought is usually categorized as Full and Partial. The former has
existed from the earliest days of church history; but the latter has only
become well-known during the last forty years.

Full Preterism

Full Preterism is known as "Covenant Eschatology", "Realized
Eschatology" and "Hyper-Preterism." Churches that adhere to Full Preterist

positions include Reformed, Presbyterian, Baptist, United Church of Christ and Non-denominational.

Full Preterists believe that most 'end times" events were fulfilled with the destruction of Jerusalem (70 ACE), including Christ's second coming (parousia), the resurrection of the dead, the Great White Throne Judgment and the new heavens and new earth. They do not believe in a future rapture, antichrist, 7-year tribulation and future millennium.

With respect to Christ's second coming, Full Preterists cite Matthew 16:28 to support their contention that Christ's second coming occurred in 70 ACE:

> Verily I say unto you, There be some standing here, which shall not taste of death, till they see the Son of man coming in his kingdom.

David B. Curtis, pastor of Berean Bible Church, in Chesapeake, Virginia, a Full Preterist , states:

> I strongly believe in the second coming, but I believe it is past not future. To deny the fact of the second coming is to deny the inspiration of scripture . . . . I believe that the time of the second coming is just as clear as the fact of the second coming. I believe that to deny the time statements that the Bible gives of the second coming is also to deny inspiration
>
> Matthew 16:27-28 (NKJV) "For the Son of Man will come in the glory of His Father with His angels, and then He will reward each according to his works.28 "Assuredly, I say to you, there are some standing here who shall not taste death till they see the Son of Man coming in His kingdom."
>
> Verse 27 clearly speaks of the second coming; He comes with the angels to reward every man. So far no problem, but look at the next verse. I say to YOU there are some standing HERE who shall not taste death till they see the Son of Man coning in His kingdom. Who are the "YOU" of this verse? Verse 24 tells us that Jesus is speaking to his disciples. So Jesus is saying to his disciples who were standing there that some of them would still be alive when He returned in the second coming.

Now some say he is talking about the transfiguration of 17:2 but that is only six days later and none of them had died in that six day period. Did he come in the glory of His Father with His angels, and reward each according to his works at the transfiguration? Of course not! How about Pentecost? No, that was only two months later and they were all still alive except Judas. [230]

In the nineteenth century, Dr. J. Stuart Russell (1816-1895), in his classic book The Parousia, argues that Jesus predicted his second coming within the lifetime of some of his disciples. He quotes from Matthew 10:23:"But when they persecute you in this city, flee ye into another: for verily I say unto you, Ye shall not have gone over the cities of Israel, till the Son of man be come."[231]

Dr. Russell argues for the literal meaning of the words and dismisses those scholars who argue for a double meaning.

> Can anything be more specific and definite as to persons, place, time and circumstance, than this prediction of our Lord? It is to the twelve that he speaks; it is the cities of Israel which they are to evangelize. the subject is his own speedy coming; and the time so near, that before their work is complete His coming will take place."[232]

Dr. Russell also cites Matthew 16:27, 28 to prove his point and asserts,

> This remarkable declaration is of the greatest importance in this discussion, and may be regarded as the key to the right interpretation of the New Testament doctrine of the Parousia."[233]

---

[230] David B. Curtis, "Inspiration and the Second Coming of Christ", Sermon April 27, 1997, March 4, 2011.

[231] J. Stuart Russell, The Parousia, p.28, Free Online Books @PreteristArchive. com, n.p. March 8, 2011.

[232] J. Stuart Russell, The Parousia, p.28

[233] J. Stuart Russell, The Parousia.,p. 29

Verily I say unto you, There be some standing here which shall not taste of death till they see' it? The very form of the expression shows that the event spoken of could not be within the space of a few months, or even a few years: it is a mode of speech which suggests that not all present will live to see the event spoken of; that not many will do so; but that some will. It is exactly such a way of speaking as would suit an interval of thirty or forty years, when the majority of the persons then present would have passed away, but some would survive and witness the event referred to.[234]

He concluded that the coming of Christ was declared by Himself to fall within the limits of the then existing generation.

Don K. Preston is another leading advocate of Full Preterism. He was former pastor of Church of Christ, which played an important role in shaping Full Preterism. In "Every Eye Shall See Him", he states:

When attempting to explain that Jesus returned at the fall of the Old World of Judaism in 70 AD, one of the first objections offered is Revelation 1:7, "Behold, he cometh with the clouds and every eye shall see him, and they also that pierced him, and all kindreds of the earth shall wail because of him." One detractor challenged this scribe: "Did every eye see him (Christ) in 70 A.D.? Did your eye see him? I know my eye did not see him in 70 A.D.

It seems to have escaped the notice of those who offer Revelation 1:7 as proof of a yet future coming of Jesus that this verse is taken directly out of the book of Zechariah; and as we shall see Jesus also uses this verse in the great eschatological discourse of Matthew 24. In Zechariah 12:10 the Spirit is speaking of a time which he designated as "in that day." This little term is used extensively by the prophet and is a limiting factor for everything which he discusses.

---

[234] J. Stuart Russell, The Parousia, p.31

Some of the "in that day" statements are confessedly enigmatic; but enough of them are sufficiently specific as to subject or time that there can be no misunderstanding.

1. "In that day" was to be when God would "break my covenant made with all the people" 11:7-11. This is undeniably when the Old Covenant would pass.
2. "In that day" would be "when they shall be in the siege both against Judah and Jerusalem" 12:1.
3. "In that day would be when "there shall be great mourning in Jerusalem," 12:11.
4. "In that day" would be when "there shall be a fountain opened to the house of David . . . for sin and for uncleanness," 13:1.
5. "In that day" would be when God would "cause the prophets and the unclean spirit to pass out of the land," 13:2.
6. "In that day" would be when the shepherd would be smitten and the sheep scattered, 13:6-7.
7. "In that day" would be when only a remnant would be saved, 13:8.
8. "In that day" would be when God would "gather all nations against Jerusalem to battle," 14:2.
9. "In that day" "living waters would go out from Jerusalem," 14:8.
10. "In that day" there would be only one God and one Lord,

Now in the same "in that day" when all the above was to happen we are told "they shall look upon me whom they have pierced, and they shall mourn for him . . . ," 12:10; and this is the very foundation of the citation in Revelation 1:7! Is it not patent that all the above; the betrayal of the shepherd, the fountain for sin, the cessation of miraculous gifts and demonic possession, the coronation of the one Lord; and the siege of Jerusalem all happened in one generation? How then can one divorce the appearance of the Messiah, when they would look on him whom they had pierced, from that same fateful generation?[235]

---

[235] Don K. Preston, "Full Preterism Every eye shall see him", Don K. Preston, Ardmore, Oklahoma , n.p., March 7, 2011.

According to David Curtis, Dr. James Stuart Russell and Don K. Preston, Jesus returned at the fall of the Old World of Judaism in 70 ACE. I disagree with them, because certain events the bible speaks of as accompanying Jesus' second coming did not occur in 70 ACE:

(1) Jesus said:

> When the Son of man shall come in his glory, and all the holy angels with him, then shall he sit upon the throne of his glory: And before him shall be gathered all nations: and he shall separate them one from another as a shepherd divideth his sheep from his goats." (Matthew 25.31-32)

Jerusalem and its temple were destroyed in 70 ACE, but there was no spectacular return of a deity with accompanying angels and the event was limited to Israel. All nations of the earth did not gather at Jerusalem.

(2) Paul wrote to the Thessalonians about "the coming of our Lord Jesus Christ with all his saints." (1 Thessalonians 3.13) There is no historical evidence of any such event occurring in 70 ACE.

(3) In II Thessalonians 1.7-10, Paul speaks of "when the Lord Jesus shall be revealed from heaven with his mighty angels, in flaming fire taking vengeance on them that know not God, and that obey not the gospel of our Lord Jesus Christ." Such an event did not occur in 70 ACE.

Partial Preterists

Partial Preterists believe that prophecies such as the destruction of Jerusalem, the Antichrist, the Great Tribulation and the "judgment-coming" of Christ were fulfilled in 70 ACE, when Titus, the Roman general and future Emperor, sacked Jerusalem and destroyed the Jewish Temple. However, they believe that a future judgment, a resurrection of the dead and a bodily return of Christ will occur in the future.

> Partial Preterists . . . . hypothesize that there are two second comings (for a total of three comings.) The first second coming

they place in 70 AD with the destruction of the Temple as a sign of Christ's judgment. And the second coming they place in the future when Christ will again return and gather the elect and resurrect the dead[236]

In The Last Days according to Jesus, R.C.Sproul (1939-present), theologian and pastor wrote:

> This immediately calls attention to another of Jesus' time-frame references in the Gospels: "For the Son of Man will come in the glory of His Father with His angels, and then He will reward each according to his works. Assuredly, I say to you, there are some standing here who shall not taste death till they see the Son of Man coming in His kingdom." (Matt. 16:27-28)

> Matthew declares that some who were in Christ's immediate presence as he was speaking ("some standing here") would not "taste death" before they would "see the Son of Man coming in His kingdom." The term coming that appears in the Greek text of Matthew 16:28 is not the word parousia. Nevertheless, Jesus does speak of a "coming" of the Son of Man.[237]

According to Dr. Sproul, there will be more than 1 coming of Christ—one referenced in the above Matthew quote and another to occur in the future.

> That events like the transfiguration and resurrection are manifestations of the coming of God's kingdom is hardly in dispute among most New Testament scholars. The only problem with this linkage is the time-frame reference. In this case, however, it is not that the time-frame is too remote or temporally disconnected from the prediction. Rather it is that the time-frame reference is too near. In Mark's Gospel the account of the transfiguration is set in the very next verse,

---

[236] "Particulars of Christianity: 313 Preterism , Part 1: The Basics and Partial Preterism", Biblestudying.net, n.p., March 3, 2011.

[237] R.C. Sproul, The Last Days According to Jesus, pages 53-55 , "The Spiritual Kingdom of God", n.p., March 8, 2011.

and this verse begins with a specific time reference: "After six days . . ." (9:2). If Jesus' prediction to the disciples is fulfilled within one week (or a few weeks, if the prediction refers to the resurrection, ascension, or Pentecost), why would he specify that these events will occur before "some (of them) standing here . . . will . . . taste death" (9:1)?[238]

Like most Partial Preterists, Dr. Sproul asserts that the Olivet Discourse (Matthew 24, Mark 13 and Luke 21.) referred to the destruction of Jerusalem and its temple.

If the Olivet Discourse refers primarily to events surrounding the destruction of Jerusalem and if the word generation refers to a forty-year period, then it is possible, if not probable, that Jesus' reference to his coming in Matthew 16:28 refers to the same events, not to the transfiguration or other close-at-hand events. [239]

In addition to their views on Christ's second coming, Partial Preterists believe the term "last days" refers to the last days of the Mosaic covenant, which God made exclusively with Israel until 70 ACE. They distinguish these days from the "last day," which is considered still future and entails the Second Coming of Jesus, the Resurrection of the dead from the grave in like-manner to Jesus' physical resurrection, the Final judgment and the creation of a literal New Heavens and a New Earth.

Millennialism

The concept of Millennialism (Greek "chiliasm") or a thousand year period of universal peace was first proposed in Zoroastrianism and is found in the "Gathas", the earliest and holiest part of the Avesta, the bible of Zoroastrianism. According to the Gathas, there will be thousand-year periods, each of which will end in a cataclysm of heresy and destruction,

---

[238] R.C. Sproul, The Last Days According to Jesus, pages 53-55
[239] R. C. Sproul. The Last Days According to Jesus, p.55

until the final destruction of evil and of the spirit of evil by a triumphant king of peace at the end of the final millennial age.[240]

The term "Millennial" comes from the Latin "Millennium", which derives from Latin "mille" (thousand) and "annus" (year). The writer of Revelation is credited with being the originator of the Christian concept. In chapter 20 of his Revelation, he describes a thousand year interval period of universal peace on earth, when Christ will be its ruler: The period is an interval, because Satan will be loosed after the thousand years for a season.

> And I saw an angel come down from heaven, having the key of the bottomless pit and a great chain in his hand
>
> And he laid hold on the dragon, that old serpent, which is the Devil, and Satan, and bound him a thousand years,
>
> And cast him into the bottomless pit, and shut him up, and set a seal upon him, that he should deceive the nations no more, till the thousand years should be fulfilled: and after that he must be loosed a little season
>
> And I saw thrones, and they sat upon them, and judgment was given unto them: and I saw the souls of them that were beheaded for the witness of Jesus, and for the word of God, and which had not worshipped the beast, neither his image, neither had received his mark upon their foreheads or in their hands; and they lived and reigned with Christ a thousand years (Revelation 20:1-4)

Most Millennial theories are divided into Premillennialism, Amillennialism and Postmillennialism.

Premillennialism

This is the belief that Jesus will physically return to earth prior to the beginning of his thousand-year reign. It holds that he will return after the tribulation-a period of great trouble and suffering: "For then shall be great

---

[240] "Zoroastrianism", New World Encyclopedia, New World Encyclopedia, 2005, March 9, 2011.

tribulation, such as was not since the beginning of the world to this time, no, nor ever shall be. " (Matthew 24:21)

Robert K. Whalen states that,

> Historically Christian premillennialism has also been referred to as "chiliasm" or "millenarianism". The theological term "premillennialism" did not come into general use until the mid-19th century, the modern period in which premillennialism was revived. Coining the word was "almost entirely the work of British and American Protestants and was prompted by their belief that the French and American Revolutions (the French, especially) realized prophecies made in the books of Daniel and Revelation[241]

The same writer goes on to point out that,

> The concept of a temporary earthly messianic kingdom at the Messiah's coming was not an invention of Christianity. Instead it was a theological interpretation developed within the apocalyptic literature of early Judaism. According to M. Simonetti "Behind Millenarism was the Jewish belief in the future Messianic kingdom understood as political and material rule, and in fact Millenarism spread initially in the Asiatic world, where Christianity was strongly influenced by Judaism and took on a distinctly materialistic colouring."[242]

According to the same writer, there are two forms of premillennialism-historic and dispensational. The former draws no theological distinction between Israel and the Church. It maintains that the Church, believers and Jews, will be caught up (raptured) in the air to meet Jesus after the tribulation and escort him to the earth to begin his thousand year reign.

Dispensational premillennialism sees Israel and the church as two distinct entities. It posits that Christ will return and take up (snatch up)

---

[241] Robert K. Whalen. "Premillennialism , ", MedLibrary.org, n.p., March 21, 2011.

[242] Robert K. Whalen. "Premillennialism ."

his beloved immediately before a seven year worldwide Tribulation. This will be followed by an additional return of Christ with his saints

One of the leading proponents of Christian premillennialism was Charles Haddon Spurgeon (1834-1892), arguably the most brilliant 19th century British preacher. Here is what he said on the subject:

> If I read the word aright, and it is honest to admit that there is much room for difference of opinion here, the day will come, when the Lord Jesus will descend from heaven with a shout, with the trump of the archangel and the voice of God.

> Some think that this descent of the Lord will be postmillennial that is, after the thousand years of his reign. I cannot think so. I conceive that the advent will be pre-millennial that he will come first; and then will come the millennium as the result of his personal reign upon earth. But whether or no, this much is the fact, that Christ will suddenly come, come to reign, and come to judge the earth in righteousness."[243]

Amellennialism

Amelennialism is the belief that there will not be a literal 1000-year reign of Christ. The prefix "a" means not or no. Thus, Amiellinnialists do not believe in a millennium and contend that the 1,000 year mentioned in Revelation 20 is symbolic. They believe that the Millennium has already begun and that Christ is presently sitting on the throne of David and that the present church age is the kingdom over which he reigns.

> Amillennialism holds that while Christ's reign during the millennium is spiritual in nature, at the end of the church age, Christ will return in final judgment and establish a permanent physical reign."[244]

---

[243] C.H. Spurgeon, "Statement on Premillennialism", James Dearmore - Gospel Web, 2009, March 8, 2011.

[244] "Amillennialism", Theopedia Encyclopedia, last updated March 8, 2010, retrieved March 21, 2011

Michael J. Vlach, Associate Professor of Theology at the Master's Seminary in Sun Valley, California, summarizes Amillennialism as follows:

> Christ is now ruling in His kingdom while Satan is bound from deceiving the nations. Tribulation is experienced in the present age even though Christ is ruling. Jesus will return again to earth.

> After Jesus returns there will be a general bodily resurrection of all the righteous people and a general judgment of all unbelievers. The Eternal Kingdom will begin."[245]

Amillennialism is the official position of the Roman Church. The Catechism of the church rejects millennialism as false and a deception by the Antichrist.

> The Antichrist's deception already begins to take shape in the world every time the claim is made to realize within history that messianic hope which can only be realized beyond history through the eschatological judgment. The Church has rejected even modified forms of this falsification of the kingdom to come under the name of millenarianism.[246]

Roman Catholics believe that the thousand years mentioned in Revelation 20 "simply means a long time, just as we might say, "You won't guess this in a thousand years." We are now in the long period between Christ's victory (symbolically expressed by tying up Satan) and his coming in glory. It could last millions of years."[247]

---

[245]　Michael J. Vlach, Ph.D., "What is Amillennialism?", TheologicalStudies. org, n.p.,March 21, 2011."

[246]　"Catechism of the Catholic Church, paragraph 676", Holy See. Archive, March 3, 2011

[247]　Bishop Kenneth E. Untener, " What Catholics Believe About The End of the World", Franciscans and St. Anthony Messenger Press ©1996-2011, March 8, 2011.

Postmillennialism

The term derives from the Latin "post' meaning "after", "mille" (thousand) and "annus" (year). Thus it means "after a thousand years." Some Postmillennialists believe in a literal 1,000 year period, while others hold to a figurative period.

> Among those holding to a non-literal "millennium" it is usually understood to have already begun, which implies a less obvious and less dramatic kind of millennium than that typically envisioned by premillennialists, as well as a more unexpected return of Christ."[248]

Lorraine Boettner, a prominent post-millennialist, seems to articulate both a historic pre-millennialist and an Amillennialist position when she states that the thousand years of peace will occur without Christ' s presence:

> The millennium, the prophesied era of peace, righteousness, and prosperity, will take place without the personal presence of Christ, through the agency of the church, before the visible glorious return of Christ at the end of the age. The nations will be converted and the world Christianized and brought under God's law, through the preaching of the gospel. Christ will return at the end of the millennium, hence a postmillennial return."[249]

She also states that,

> Postmillennialism is that view of the last things which holds that the Kingdom of God is now being extended in the world through the preaching of the Gospel and the saving work of the Holy Spirit, that the world eventually will be Christianized, and that the return of Christ will occur at the close of a long period of righteousness and peace commonly called the Millennium."[250]

---

[248] Wikipedia the free online Encyclopedia. Postmillennialism
[249] Lorraine Boettner.. Taken from "The Millennium" by Lorraine Boettner, p.4
[250] Lorraine Boettner.. Taken from "The Millennium" by Lorraine Boettner, p.4

Each position on the 1,000-year era of world peace has brilliant advocates. Brilliant theologians support the Amillennialist position and as brilliant scholars espouse the postmillennialist argument. I believe in a symbolic 1,000 years of peace. I also believe that at some future time Christ will rule on earth.

Great Tribulation

Four horsemen of the Apocalypse

"Great Tribulation "describes a period of great trouble and suffering on Earth before Christ's second coming. There are 3 main views on this subject: (1) The event has already occurred; (2) We are living in the period and (3) the event will occur in the end-time.

(1) **The event has already occurred**

There are 2 kinds of apologists for this view. The first are those who believe that the event occurred in 70 ACE when Jerusalem and its temple were destroyed by Roman Armies. Luke 21:20 is cited by some as support for the destruction of Jerusalem: "And when ye shall see Jerusalem compassed with armies, then know that the desolation thereof is nigh." Luke 21:5-6 is cited as referring to the destruction of the temple in 70 ACE:

> And as some spake of the temple, how it was adorned with goodly stones and gifts, he (Jesus) said, As for these things which ye behold, the days will come, in the which there shall not be left one stone upon another, that shall not be thrown down.

However, there are those who argue that the Tribulation does not refer to the destruction of Jerusalem in 70 ACE, because the Book of Revelation was written, at least, 20 years after this event. This would be a sound argument if Revelation were our only source of information on the subject. Such is not the case. Jesus stated that, " . . . . then shall be great tribulation, such as was not since the beginning of the world to this time, no, nor ever shall be." (Matthew 24:21) Jesus lived before 70 ACE.

The second believers in a past tribulation are those who assert that the event refers to persecution faced by Christians during the latter part of the first century, an event which Revelation seems to be describing when it states, "And I said unto him, Sir, thou knowest. And he said to me, These are they which came out of great tribulation, and have washed their robes, and made them white in the blood of the Lamb."(Revelation 7:14)

(2) **We are living in this period**

This is the view that much of the Great tribulation is being fulfilled now. In this sense, bible prophecy is being interpreted subjectively. Since contemporary writers are interpreting the tribulation 2000 years after Jesus mentioned the event, their interpretations are greatly influenced by contemporary events. For example, the historical persecution of Christians by Roman emperors could have been seen by persons of the relevant periods as the beginning of the Great Tribulation. Christians who are persecuted in countries where their religion is banned, might see their persecution as part of the Great Tribulation.

(3) **An end-time event**

According to the end-time position, the Great Tribulation is a future event. Some end-timers believe that it will occur before Christ's return (the Second Coming) and the church will be present on earth during the event. The church must endure the tribulation, but not God's wrath. Others believe that the event will occur in the future but the church will have been raptured, a theme I will discuss shortly.

Most believers in a future tribulation state that it will be a seven-year period and connect it with the seventieth week in Daniel 9:24-27. They also believe that the Tribulation and the Great Tribulation are not synonymous terms. The Great Tribulation is the last half of the Tribulation period, three and one-half years in length. The Tribulation refers to the full seven-year period.

It is Jesus who used the phrase "Great Tribulation" with reference to the last half of the Tribulation. He said,

> For then there will be a great tribulation, such as has not occurred since the beginning of the world until now, nor ever shall."(Matthew 24:21)

In this verse, Jesus is referring to the event of Matthew 24:15, which describes the revealing of the abomination of desolation, the man also known as the Antichrist. It also should be noted that in Matthew 24:29-30 Jesus states:

> Immediately after the tribulation of those days, the Son of Man will appear in the sky, and then all the tribes of the earth will mourn, and they will see the Son of Man coming on the clouds of the sky with power and great glory."

Jesus is defining the Great Tribulation (Matthew 24:21) as beginning with the revealing of the abomination of desolation (Matthew 24:15) and ending with Christ's second coming (Matthew 24:30 .30).

A distinction is usually made between the two halves of the seven years. The last half, often called the Great Tribulation, is measured variously as three and a half years (Dan. 9:27), forty-two months (Rev. 11:2, 13:5) 1,260 days (Rev. 11:3, 12:6), or "a time, and times, and half a time" (Rev. 12:14 ▫).with the seventieth week of a prophetic framework taken from Daniel 9:24-27. Distinctive to this view is the teaching that the church will be ruptured at the beginning of the tribulation period.

The Rapture

The term "rapture" is not found in the Bible, but refers to the words "caught up" in 1Thessalonians 4:5-7:

> For this we say unto you by the word of the Lord, that we which are alive and remain unto the coming of the Lord shall not prevent them which are asleep.

> For the Lord himself shall descend from heaven with a shout, with the voice of the archangel, and with the trump of God: and the dead in Christ shall rise first:

> Then we which are alive and remain shall be caught up together with them in the clouds, to meet the Lord in the air: and so shall we ever be with the Lord."

This passage tells us that Jesus will return in the clouds, not to the earth, as he will do at the end of the tribulation. At that time he will "snatch up" ALL believers (the Church, which includes the Old Testament and New Testament saints, both dead and alive, to meet him. Their bodies will be changed to a different form, which will never die or will not require air, food or water.

Catholics, Orthodox, the Anglican Communion, most Protestants (including LCMS Lutherans, United Methodist) do not believe in the Rapture. Most fundamentalists and Evangelicals do.

There are 3 main views on when the rapture will occur in relation to the Great Tribulation: Pre-Tribulation (the rapture occurring prior to the tribulation), mid-tribulation (the rapture occurring at or near the mid-point of the tribulation) and post-tribulation (the rapture occurring at the end of the tribulation).

Pre-Tribulation

Pre-Tribulationism is the belief that the rapture will occur before the great tribulation. Pre-tribulationists distinguish the rapture from Christ's second coming, when he will return to set up his kingdom on earth at the end of the tribulation.

They support their views from Luke 21:36:

"Watch ye therefore, and pray always, that ye may be accounted worthy to escape all these things that shall come to pass, and to stand before the Son of man."

The "things" to which Jesus was referring were those things to which he referred in Matthew 24: 21, "great tribulation, such as was not since the beginning of the world to this time, no, nor ever shall be." According to pre-tribulationists Christians will escape the things to which Jesus referred.

Mid-Tribulationists

According to Mid-Tribulationiststhe, the seven-year tribulation is divided into two halves; the first half is described as the wrath of man, and the last half as the wrath of God. The rapture will take place at the middle of the tribulation period three-and-one-half years.

The Last or Final Judgment

In Christianity, The Last or Final Judgment is the belief that God will judge all persons at some point in the end times. I will examine the differing views among Christian denominations on the subject.

The Roman Church

The Roman Church believes in 2 judgments—a first, or "Particular" Judgment, is what each individual experiences at the time of his or her death. Based on the state of the person's soul, God will decide where the soul will reside until the General or Last Judgment—heaven, purgatory, or hell. The last judgment will occur after the dead are resurrected and the person's soul is reunited with its physical body.

The church teaches that at the time of the last judgment Christ will return, accompanied by angels, and the truth of each man's relationship with God will be revealed in his presence. Every person who has ever lived will be judged according to his deeds. Those already in heaven will remain there; those already in hell will remain in hell; and those in purgatory will be released into heaven. After the last judgment there will be a new heaven and a new earth.

Lutherans

Lutherans believe that all dead persons will be resurrected and at that time their souls will be reunited with the same bodies they had before dying. These bodies will then be changed as will those of the living. After these things, all nations shall gather before Christ, who will separate the righteous from the wicked. He will publicly judge all persons by their works. The works of the righteous will be proof of their belief in him and the works of the wicked will be proof of their unbelief. The righteous will be rewarded with everlasting life of bliss and the wicked sentenced to everlasting damnation.

Seventh-day Adventists

Seventh-day Adventists believe that when a person dies his soul remains in an unconscious state (soul sleep) and that when Christ returns, the righteous dead will be resurrected and, with the living righteous, will be glorified and caught up to meet him.

According to Adventists, the process of determining who is righteous began in 1844,[251] when Jesus entered the holy of holies and began the process of investigative judgment.

> Attended by heavenly angels, our great High Priest enters the holy of holies and there appears in the presence of God to engage in the last acts of His ministration in behalf of man—to perform the work of investigative judgment and to make atonement for all who are shown to be entitled to its benefits.[252]

---

[251] Ellen G. White, The Great Controverary, chapter 28, p. 486
[252] Ellen G. White., chapter 28, page 480.

Seventh-day Adventists assert that the works of persons are written in "books of record", kept in heaven in the Holy of Holies. During the investigative judgment, these books will be opened and the lives of all persons, living and dead, will be examined to determine the nature of their judgment.

At the final Day of Atonement only believers will be judged. The wicked will be judged later.

> So in the great day of final atonement and investigative judgment the only cases considered are those of the professed people of God. The judgment of the wicked is a distinct and separate work, and takes place at a later period. "Judgment must begin at the house of God: and if it first begin at us, what shall the end be of them that obey not the gospel?" 1 Peter 4:17.[253]

After Christ, the Advocate for Believers, presents the cases of each true believer, who has pardon entered against his/her name and whose sins have been blotted out, God will judge that person worthy of eternal life.

> The work of the investigative judgment and the blotting out of sins is to be accomplished before the second advent of the Lord. When Christ returns the second time, he the righteous dead will be resurrected, and together with the righteous living, will be glorified (their bodies changed) and taken to heaven. [254]

Seventh-day Adventists believe that the wicked will be destroyed by fire.[255] The reward of righteousness will be everlasting life, but the reward for wickedness will be death.

Pentecostals

Pentecostals generally believe in a resurrection of all dead persons. Those whose sins have not been pardoned will stand before the Great

---

[253]   Ellen G. White., chapter 28, page 480.
[254]   Ellen G. White, chapter 28, p.485.
[255]   Ellen G. White, chapter 28, p.486

White Throne for judgment, where God will be the judge. The saved will stand before another throne, the Bema Seat, for judgment. This will be presided by Christ. All will be judged according to their deeds on earth. Those who are saved (born again) will inherit eternal life and those who are unrighteous will be doomed to eternal damnation.

PART THREE

CHAPTER THIRTEEN

Best Loved Hymns

Like a Poet hidden In the light of thought, singing hymns
unbidden, Till the world is wrought To sympathy with hopes
and fears it heeded not

.... Percy Bysshe Shelley

The hymns I have selected are some of my favourites and have comforted
me throughout the years. I hope their words and my comments will be a
source of rich blessings to you.

God Leads Us Along

In shady, green pastures, so rich and so sweet,
God leads His dear children along;
Where the water's cool flow bathes the weary one's feet,
God leads His dear children along.

Refrain

Some through the waters, some through the flood,
Some through the fire, but all through the blood;
Some through great sorrow, but God gives a song,
In the night season and all the day long.
Sometimes on the mount where the sun shines so bright,
God leads His dear children along;
Sometimes in the valley, in darkest of night,
God leads His dear children along.

Refrain

Though sorrows befall us and evils oppose,
God leads His dear children along;
Through grace we can conquer, defeat all our foes,
God leads His dear children along.

Refrain

Away from the mire, and away from the clay,
God leads His dear children along;
Away up in glory, eternity's day,
God leads His dear children along.
Lillenas was born on NoRefrain

Haldor Lillenas (born 1885 in Norway and died 1959 in the United States) is regarded by many as the most influential Weslyan/Holiness songwriter and publisher in the 20th century,

His father migrated to the United States in 1986 and the family joined him in 1887 in South Dakota. In 1889, the family moved to Astoria,

Oregon. While living there, a young Haldor was taught English by an elderly Christian woman. She would always sing, God Leads His Dear Children Along, written by C.A. Young.

Years later, Haldor set out to learn something about the hymnist. He learned that the hymnist had passed on; but his spouse lived in a nearby town. He drove there and found her living in a little rundown cottage. She told him that God led her there and had used her to lead many hearts to Christ. Rather than complaing, she was exceedingly happy to serve God however he wished.

Life's circumstances continually teat our faith. The weak fall by the wayside. The strong will stand up for God, knowing that He will be their guide. Although tested by the harshest trials, they are confident that God will lead them to victory. Amen. Can I get a witness?

Guide me, O thou Great Jehovah

The first time I heard this beloved hymn was in the 1956 rerun of the 1939 Best Picture movie, "How Green was my Valley", starring Walter Pidgeon with a young Roddy McDowell and Maureen O'Hara. It was sung in the movie by the then famous Welsh Singers. It was also sung at the funeral of Diana, Princess of Wales, in Westminster Abbey, London, England on September 6, 1997.

Its words were written in Welsh by William Williams, a Welsh hymnist in 1745 and translated into English by Peter Williams in 1771. William Williams had been preparing for a medical career, when he was converted and became a minister in the Church of England. He later left the Church and joined a group of dissenters called "Calvinistic Methodists" They traveled throughout Wales preaching revivals for forty three years.

In 1907, John Hughes wrote the tune to commemorate a music festival held in nearby Capel Rhondda, Hopkintown. It was first performed November 1 that year in Welsh by Ann Griffiths.

Guide me, O Thou great Jehovah,
Pilgrim through this barren land;
I am weak, but Thou art mighty,
Hold me with Thy pow'rful hand.
Bread of heaven, Feed me till I want no more. Bread of heaven,
Feed me till I want no more.

Open now the crystal fountain,
Whence the healing waters doth flow;
Let the fiery cloudy pillar
Lead me all my journey thro;
Strong deliverer, Be Thou still my strength and shield.
Strong deliverer, Be Thou still my strength and shield.

When I tread the verge of Jordan,
Bid my anxious fears subside;
Bear me through the swelling current,
Land me safe on Canaan's side;
Songs of praises,I will ever give to Thee.
Songs of praises,I will ever give to Thee.

The hymn's theme is God's protection of his loved ones and supplying their needs according to his riches in glory. Amen! It uses the experience of the Israelites in their journey through the wilderness after escaping from Egypt (Exodus 12-14) as its symbol. The Israelites were guided by a cloud by day and a fire by night, (Exodus 13:17-22) to their final arrival forty years later in the land of Canaan, (Joshua 3). During this time, their needs were supplied by God.

This world is not my home I'm just passing through
my treasures are laid up somewhere beyond the blue
the angels beckon me from Heaven's open door
and I can't feel at home in this world anymore

The Christian is in, but not of, this world. He longs for the mansions which have been prepared for the children of God: I am waiting for my home far away. My life on earth is, like the Israelites, a journey, a passing through, to Canaan, the hymnist's symbol for heaven.

Life on earth can be a bowl of cherries, a glorious sonata to the blessings of prosperity, fame or wealth. To far too many the song never began. They eke out their existence under the yoke of misery and want. Frustrated by this human tragedy, Matthew Arnold wrote,

for the world, which seems
To lie before us like a land of dreams,
So various, so beautiful, so new,

Hath really neither joy, nor love, nor light,
Nor certitude, nor peace, nor help for pain;
And we are here as on a darkling plain
Swept with confused alarms of struggle and flight,
Where ignorant armies clash by night.

This is the cynic's view of life. However, it is different with the children of God. The great Jehovah will guide them through their earthly journey and provide for them, as he provided manna from heaven for the Israelites.

Jesus knew that his disciples worried about what they shall eat, drink; or wear, and said to them;

Therefore take no thought, saying, What shall we eat? or, What shall we drink? or, Wherewithal shall we be clothed?

(For after all these things do the Gentiles seek:) for your heavenly Father knoweth that ye have need of all these things.

But seek ye first the kingdom of God, and his righteousness; and all these things shall be added unto you. (Matthew 6:31-33)

Our heavenly Father knows what we need and He will supply all our needs according to his wishes in glory.

When my days on earth are ending ("When I tread the verge of Jordan"), I will not be afraid, for Jehovah will "guide me safe on Canaan's side" (Heaven).

Amazing Grace

The composer of this wonderful hymn is John Newton (1726-1807), an Englishman who, until 1748, was a slave trader in West Africa. He had no regard for his captives and was well known for debauchery and blasphemy. One day in 1748, while reading The Imitation of Christ by Thomas A. Kempis, he repented, but continued in the slave trade. In 1755, he abandoned the trade and became a minister in 1760. Among his hymns are "How Sweet the Name of Jesus Sounds" and "Glorious Things of Thee Are Spoken" and his most famous, "Amazing Grace" , possibly one of the hymns written for a weekly service. The origin of the melody is unknown.

However, many believe that it was the tune of one of the slave songs that Newton had heard in West Africa.

> Amazing grace! How sweet the sound,
> That saved a wretch like me!
> I once was lost, but now am found,
> Was blind, but now I see.
> 'Twas grace that taught my heart to fear,
> And grace my fears relieved;
> How precious did that grace appear
> The hour I first believed.
> Thru many dangers, toils and snares,
> I have already come;
> When we've been there ten thousand years,
> Bright shining as the sun,
> We've no less days to sing God's praise
> Then when we'd first begun.

The theme of the piece is grace. In my chapter on "Justification by Faith", I point out that we were born in sin through Adam's disobedience. As such, the sentence of death issued to him passed to us. However, Jesus paid the price for us by his passion.

If we believe in the efficacy of his sacrifice, the grace of God, not our works, will gain us God's pardon and we will no longer be under God's judgment. That is what Newton meant when he penned, "Amazing grace! How sweet the sound, that saved a wretch like me . . . . .Tis grace hath brought me safe thus far, And grace will lead me home."These words express his confidence in the ability of God to perform the work he began, because he would seek his blessings day by day. Jesus told his disciples that, if they obey his words, they will one day live with him in glory.

Count your Blessings

I wish to share with the reader a little quotation I kept on one of the walls of my room when I was a boy: "I was without shoes and I murmured, until I looked through the window and saw a man without feet, and I cried." Every time I am tempted to complain about situations, this quotation strengthens me.

When upon life's billows You are tempest tossed,
When you are discouraged Thinking all is lost,
Count your many blessings Name them one by one,
And it will surprise you What the Lord hath done.

Chorus:

Count your blessings Name them one by one.
Count your blessings See what God hath done.
Count your blessings Name them one by one.
Count your many blessings See what God hath done.
Are you ever burdened With a load of care,
Does the cross seem heavy You are called to bear.
Count your many blessings Every doubt will fly,
And you will be singing As the days go by.
When you look at others With their lands and gold,
Think that Christ has promised You His wealth untold.
Count your many blessings Money cannot buy,
Your reward in heaven Nor your home on high.
So amid the conflict Whether great or small,
Do not be discouraged God is over all.
Count your many blessings Angels will attend,
Help and comfort give you to your journey's end

The hymn "Count your blessings" was written by Johnson Oatman (1856-1922) and the melody was composed by Edwin Excel (1851-1921), both Americans. Oatman was a businessman, who held a preacher's license in the Methodist Church. He wrote more than 5,000 hymns, including: "Higher ground" and "No, not one." However, it is "Count your blessings" that made him famous.

Are you ever burdened With a load of care,
Does the cross seem heavy You are called to bear.
Count your many blessings Every doubt will fly,
And you will be singing As the days go by.

"Are you ever burdened with a load of care?" Caring for your mother who has Alzheimer's or dementia? Facing serious mortgage problems? Is your teenage child beyond bounds? Does the job frustrate you? "Does the cross seem heavy you are called to bear?"

You lift your hand to high heaven and ask, "Why me?" I am true and faithful to God. I attend church regularly, pay my tithes, sing in the choir and teach Sunday school. Why me? Then Omar Khayyám's words tease you:

> And that inverted bowl we call The Sky, where under crawling coop't we live and die, lift not thy hands to It for help—for it rolls impotently on as thou or I.

Perhaps, you ask yourself, might it be that my God is indifferent to, my plight? Might it be that he does not interfere in the affairs of mortals? Is he a clockmaker God?

Then you read the words again, "Count your many blessings Every doubt will fly" and reproach yourself for harbouring doubts about our Omnibenevolent God. You have sight, hearing, speech, loving family and friends and enjoy many other blessings.

The poet is asking you to consider these blessings, however small, and you will believe in God's care for you and "And you will be singing As the days go by."

We face challenges everyday and we think we are losing the battle. We might be ministers, missionaries, social workers and others trying to do deeds to improve the human condition and see no improvement in the state of affairs. We might be sick and see no cure. The poet says that "amid the conflict Whether great or small, Do not be discouraged God is over all."

"His eye is on the sparrow, and I know He watches me"

In the Sweet by and By

They don't compose songs like this anymore. They don't even like to sing them at funerals these days. They say funerals are a "celebration" and that this grand daddy of them all is not celebratory. Dear reader, this hymn is about the steadfast faith that we believers will someday meet God and the eternal celebration will begin.

All background sketches of this hymn give the words of its composer. I shall do likewise:

Mr. Joseph Webster, like many musicians, was of an exceeding nervous and sensitive nature, and subject to periods of depression. I found that I could rouse him by giving him a new song on which to work.

He came into my drug store, walked down to the stove, and turned his back on me without speaking. I was at my desk writing. Turning to him I said, "Webster, what is the matter now?" "It's no matter," he replied, "it will be all right by and by." The idea came to me like a flash of sunlight and I replied, "The Sweet By and By! Why would not that make a good hymn?" "Maybe it would," said he indifferently. Turning to my desk, I penned the words as fast as I could write. I handed the words to Webster. As he read, his eyes kindled, and stepping to the desk, he began writing the notes. Taking his violin, he played the melody and then jotted down the notes of the chorus. It was not over thirty minutes from the time I took my pen to write the words before two friends with Webster and myself were singing the hymn, "The Sweet By and By."

There's a land that is fairer than day,
And by faith we can see it afar;
For the Father waits over the way
To prepare us a dwelling place there.
Refrain:
In the sweet by and by,
We shall meet on that beautiful shore;
In the sweet in the sweet
By and by by and by
We shall meet on that beautiful shore.
We shall sing on that beautiful shore
The melodious songs of the blest,
And our spirits shall sorrow no more
Not a sigh for the blessing of rest.
Refrain:
To our bountiful father above
We will offer our tribute of praise
For the glorious gift of His love
And the blessings that hallow our days.

The first stanza tells believers that upon death they will go to heaven, where Jesus has prepared a room for them in one of his Father's mansions. This heaven, this land fairer than day, can only be seen through faith. In the words of St. Pau; "Faith is the substance of things hoped for, the evidence of things not seen."In that far away place believers will sing the song of the redeemed forever and forever and not be tired and all those ills which afflict mankind will be banished.

The Holy City

Last night I lay a-sleeping
There came a dream so fair,
I stood in old Jerusalem
Beside the temple there.
I heard the children singing,
And ever as they sang
Methought the voice of angels
From heaven in answer rang,
Methought the voice of angels
From heaven in answer rang.
Jerusalem! Jerusalem!
Lift up your gates and sing,
Hosanna in the highest!
Hosanna to your King!
And then methought my dream was changed,
The streets no longer rang.
Hushed were the glad Hosannas
The little children sang.
The sun grew dark with mystery,
The morn was cold and chill,
As the shadow of a cross arose
Upon a lonely hill,
As the shadow of a cross arose
Upon a lonely hill.
Jerusalem! Jerusalem!
Hark! How the angels sing,
Hosanna in the highest!

Hosanna to your King!
And once again the scene was changed,
New earth there seemed to be.
I saw the Holy City
Beside the tideless sea.
The light of God was on its streets,
The gates were open wide,
And all who would might enter,
And no one was denied.
No need of moon or stars by night,
Or sun to shine by day;
It was the new Jerusalem
That would not pass away,
It was the new Jerusalem
That would not pass away.
Jerusalem! Jerusalem!
Sing for the night is o'er!
Hosanna in the highest!
Hosanna forevermore!

I cannot describe my joy whenever I hear this song/hymn, whether by Beniomino Gigli, Enrico Caruso, Richard Tauber, Richard Crooks or John Mc Cormick.

The lyrics were written by Frederick E. Weatherly and the music by Stephen Adams. Frederic Edward Weatherly (1848-1929) was an English Judge, author, lyricist and broadcaster. He wrote approximately 3,000 songs, the most popular being "Danny Boy" set to the tune Londonderry Air, Picardy (popularly known as The Roses of Picardy) and The Holy City, arguably his best loved. James Joyce, the celebrated Welsh writer/poet used it in his brilliant novel, Ulysses. This song/hymn might have been inspired by words in Revelation:

And I saw a new heaven and a new earth: for the first heaven and the first earth were passed away; and there was no more sea.

And I John saw the holy city, New Jerusalem, coming down from God out of heaven, prepared as a bride adorned for her husband. (Revelation 21:1)

The new world will have one King, God, and one central city, called
here Jerusalem. The city of Jerusalem has always been considered the Holy
City in Judeo-Christianity. The poet envisions the destruction of old
Jerusalem, which becomes a symbol of the world. A new, more glorious
one replaces it.

> And I heard a great voice out of heaven saying, Behold, the
> tabernacle of God is with men, and he will dwell with them, and
> they shall be his people, and God himself shall be with them,
> and be their God.

> And God shall wipe away all tears from their eyes; and there shall
> be no more death, neither sorrow, nor crying, neither shall there
> be any more pain: for the former things are passed away.

> And he that sat upon the throne said, Behold, I make all things
> new. And he said unto me, Write: for these words are true and
> faithful

> And he said unto me, It is done. I am Alpha and Omega, the
> beginning and the end. I will give unto him that is athirst of the
> fountain of the water of life freely (Revelation 21:1-6)

I will not offer a literary appreciation of the poem, but give my heartfelt
response to it. Our world is so corrupt that all men of good faith ask, "How
long shall we endure these things?" The writer of "Revelation" says that
these things will end. He saw a new, perfect universe coming from God to
replace the old one, whose ruler will be God.

Weatherly tells us that he was transported to Jerusalem, the holy city
to Judeo-Christianity. There he heard the children (symbol of the purified
ones) singing praises to God, which praises the angels in heaven returned.

The scene was changed to Golgotha, where Jesus died for the sins of
the world and Christians believe that faith in his sacrifice for their sins,
through God's grace, makes them sons and daughters of God.

Then the poet saw, like the writer of Revelation, a new earth, with no
need of seas or sunlight, because God, who is light, will be its King. He
says "All who would might enter and no one was denied." No one could be
refused, because those who were waiting at the gates had had their names
written in the book of life and were children of the King.

My friends, this earth hosts some wonderful, stately occasions—the inauguration of a President, a Royal coronation, a Royal performance at Buckingham Palace to name a few. If you do not have an invitation, you would be turned away. Is it not wonderful to know that all will be welcomed to enter the New Jerusalem? I had rather be with God than with the greatest person on this earth. That is my hope and comfort. It is my joy.

The Christian' Goodnight (Sleep on beloved)

Sleep on, beloved, sleep and take thy rest,
Lay down thy head upon thy Saviour's breast;
We love thee much, but Jesus loves thee best:

Sleep on, belovèd, sleep, and take thy rest;
Lay down thy head upon the Saviour's breast;
We love thee well, but Jesus loves thee best—
Good night! Good night! Good night!
Only "Good night," belovèd—not "farewell!"

A little while, and all His saints shall dwell
In hallowed unison indivisible—
Good night! Good night! Good night!
Until we meet again before His throne,
Clothed in the spotless robe He gives His own,
Until we know even as we are known—
Good night! Good night! Good night!

Dear friend, do not be offended that I include this "death hymn", because death is inevitable. As William Shakespeare sys,

Of all the wonders that I have yet heard,
It seems to me most strange that men should fear,
Seeing that death, a necessary end,
Will come when it come.

The Christian should not fear death, because it transports the soul to its maker and when it shall have been reunited with the body, he/she shall live in eternal bliss. For this reason, John Donne (1570-1631), England's greatest Metaphysical poet, wrote:

Death be not proud, though some have called thee
Mighty and dreadful, for, thou art not so,
For, those, whom thou thinkst, thou dost overthrow,
Die not, poor death, nor yet canst thou kill me.
From rest and sleep, which but thy pictures be,
Much pleasure, then from thee, much more must flow,
And soonest our best men with thee do go,
Rest of their bones, and souls' delivery.

I loved my mother dearly and when my nephew phoned me that she had died, I rushed to the scene. It seemed to me that her countenance was one of serenity. I cried, because she was kind, loving, helpful and my closest friend. To think that she had left me made me sad. However, that sadness did not last long, because I knew that she had gone to be with her heavenly Father and her Saviour, Jesus Christ and all the saints that had gone before. I love her well; but Jesus loved her best.

This hymn was composed by Sarah Doudney, English author and hymnist. Her venture might have been inspired by Psalm 127:2, "For so he giveth his belovesleep" The music was composed by Ira D. Sankey, the incomparable American sweet singer of Methodism and Dwight L. Moody's associate. He sang it at Charles H. Spurgeon's funeral.

"Only "Good night," belovèd—not "farewell!"

God be with you till we meet again;
By His counsels guide, uphold you,
With His sheep securely fold you;
God be with you till we meet again

Tell Mother I'll be there

When I was but a little child how well I recollect
How I would grieve my mother with my folly and neglect;
And now that she has gone to Heav'n I miss her tender care:
O Savior, tell my mother, I'll be there!

Refrain

Tell mother I'll be there, in answer to her prayer;
This message, blessèd Savior, to her bear!
Tell mother I'll be there, Heav'n's joys with her to share;
Yes, tell my darling mother I'll be there.
Though I was often wayward, she was always kind and good;
So patient, gentle, loving when I acted rough and rude;
My childhood griefs and trials she would gladly with me share:
O Savior, tell my mother, I'll be there!

Refrain

When I became a prodigal, and left the old rooftree,
She almost broke her loving heart in mourning after me;
And day and night she prayed to God to keep me in His care:
O Savior, tell my mother, I'll be there!

Refrain

One day a message came to me, it bade me quickly come
If I would see my mother ere the Savior took her home;
I promised her, before she died, for Heaven to prepare:
O Savior, tell my mother, I'll be there!

There's a beautiful story behind this glorious hymn. William McKinley (25th President of the United States 1843-1901) and his mother were very close. When he became president, he had a special telegraph line installed between Washington and her hometown, because she lived a great distance from the capital. In the winter of 1897, she was gravely ill. When word reached the President that she was dying, he wired back, "Tell mother I'll be there." Charles M. Fillmore read this and wrote these wonderful words in 1898"

I love the first refrain:

Tell mother I'll be there, in answer to her prayer;
This message, blessèd Savior, to her bear!
Tell mother I'll be there, Heav'n's joys with her to share;
Yes, tell my darling mother I'll be there.

When I was a little Christian, my mother, bless her soul, was very happy to see this. I heeded Solomon's advice, "Remember now your Creator in the days of your youth, while the evil days come not, nor the years draw near, when you shall say, I have no pleasure in them." (Ecclesiastes 12:1) I asked god to keep me faithful and true. I testified about his blessings and mercy. I led others to Him through his grace.

However, I became a prodigal and walked away from the saints and their wonderful testimonies. I wanted to experience "the world" and its enchantments.

> When I became a prodigal, and left the old rooftree,
> She almost broke her loving heart in mourning after me;
> And day and night she prayed to God to keep me in His care:
> O Savior, tell my mother, I'll be there!

"Where is your son, who was such a great testimony for Christ?" they would ask her at church. She must have answered, "He has become a backslider. I'm praying for him."

Many years have passed. I no longer have questions about the hope that lies in me. I no longer look to Kant, Hegel or Marx to solve the problems within my soul. I have learned that "There are more things in heaven and earth, Horatio, Than are dreamt of in your philosophy." [256]

Let the bells of heaven ring and may He who opens the Book of Life on the final day hear me say,

> Tell mother I'll be there, in answer to her prayer;
> Tell mother I'll be there, Heav'n's joys with her to share;
> Yes, tell my darling mother I'll be there.

---

[256] William Shakespeare, Hamlet, Act 1, scene 5, 167

BIBLIOGRAPHY

A

"Antiochus." *Encyclopaedia Judaica.* American Cooperative Enterprise, 2010. Retrieved April 16, 2011 www.encyclopedia.com/article-1G2-2587501155/antiochus.html

"Antiochus v." *Wikipedia.* Last modified March 29, 2011. Retrieved April19, 2011. en.wikipedia.org/wiki/Antiochus_V

Arendzen, John. "Gnosticism." *The Catholic Encyclopedia.* Vol. 6. New York: Robert Appleton Company, 1909. Retrieved March 3, 2011. www.newadvent.org/cathen/06592a.htm

_____ "Mithraism." *The Catholic Encyclopedia.* Vol. 10. New York: Robert Appleton Company, 1911. Retrieved March, 2011. www.newadvent.org/cathen/10402a.htm.

Alden, Andrew. "Earth's Formation in a Nutshell." *About.com.* Retrieved March 11, 2011. geology.about.com/od/nutshells/a/aa_earthbirth.htm

"Aldhelm Biography." *The Biographicon.* Retrieved March 5, 2011. www.biographicon.com/view/ztbug

"Amillennialism." *Theopedia Encyclopedia.* Last updated March 8, 2010. Retrieved March 21, 2011. www.theopedia.com/Amillennialism

Anderson., Jeff. "Christianity and the Mystery Religions." Jeff Anderson,1999. Retrieved March 15, 2011. faculty.cua.edu/pennington/ChurchHistory220/lectureone/...

"Apostles Creed." Retrieved March 22, 2011. www.ccel.org/creeds/apostles.creed.html

Aquinas, Thomas St. *Summa Theologica.* Second and Revised Edition 1920. Translated by Fathers of the English Dominican Province Online. Kevin Knight 2008. Retrieved March 2, 2011. www.newadvent.org/summa

"Articles of Religion." *Anglicans Online Website.* Retrieved March 18,2011. anglicansonline.org/basics/thirty-nine_articles.html"

"A Short History of the Anglican Church." The Anglican Church of Canada,Christ Church, Rawdon, Quebec. Retrieved April 5, 2011. www.montreal.anglican.org/parish/rawdon/anglican%20

Augustine, Saint. "Confessions." From Augustine: *Confessions & Enchiridion.* Newly Translated and Edited by Albert C. Outler. Institute of Practical Bible Education. Retrieved March 7, 2011. www.iclnet.org/pub/resources/text/ipb-e/epl-ag.html

_____ *On the Merits and Forgiveness of Sins and on the Baptism of Infants.*Book 1, Ch. 34. *Eternal Word Television Network.* Irondale, AL. Retrieved March 1, 2011. www.ewtn.com/library/PATRISTC/PNI5-1.HTM

_____*Enchiridion ; OR ON FAITH, HOPE, AND LOVE.* Chapters 1-23, Chapters 24-53, Chapters 54-77, Chapters 78-96, Chapters 97-122. Translated J.F. Shaw. Londonderry. Leadership University. Updated: Saturday, 13-Jul-2002. www.leaderu.com/cyber/books/augenchiridion/enchiridion

B

Barton, George A., Wilhelm Bacher, Judah David Eisenstein. "Rechabites." *Jewish Encyclopedia.*2002. Retrieved April 11, 2011. www.jewishencyclopedia.com/view.jsp?artid=152&letter=R

Beeke, Joel R. "The Relation of Faith to Justification. Chapter 5. From *Justification by Faith ALONE.* The Highway. Retrieved March 3, 2011. www.thehighway.com/articleJan98.html
Bel and the Dragon. *Early Jewish Writings.* Peter Kirby. Retrieved March 9, 2011. earlyjewishwritings.com

Benedict, David. "History of the Donatists." *The Reformed Reader.* 1999. Retrieved March 3, 2011._www.reformedreader.org/history/benedict/donatists/toc.htm

Benton , J H. *The Book of Common Prayer: Its Origin and Growth.* J.H. Benton. Boston.1910. Last updated October 30, 1998. Retrieved_April 15, 2011. justus.anglican.org/resources/bcp/Benton.htm

"Big Bang Theory—An Overview." *All About Science.* All about science. Colorado Springs. 2002. Retrieved June 2010. www.allaboutscience. org/big-bang-theory.htm

Boettner, Lorraine. "POSTMILLENNIALISM." From *The Millennium.* p.4. The American Presbyterian Church. Retrieved March 3, 2011. www.americanpresbyterianchurch.org/postmillennialism.htm

_____ "Postmillennialism: Introduction." Grace Online Library. 2001. Retrieved March 3, 2011 www.graceonlinelibrary.org/articles/full.asp?id=9|69|846

Bond, Tim. "The Development of Christian Society in Early England." *Britannia Internet Magazine.* 1996. Retrieved March 3, 2011. www.britannia.com/church/bond1.html

Book of Common Prayer. Anglican Resource Collection.. last updated August 30, 2008. Retrieved April 16, 2011. justus.anglican.org/resources/bcp

"BOOK OF ENOCH." Andy McCracken. Modern English Translation with introduction and notes. Exodus 2006. Retrieved March 9, 2011. exodus2006.com/ENOCH.HTM

"Book of Jasher." J.H. Parry and Company. Salt Lake City.1887. Retrieved March 9, 2011.] www.ccel.org/a/anonymous/jasher/1.htm

"Book of Jubilees." Translated R.H. Charles. Society for Promoting Christian Knowledge. London, England. 1917. Retrieved March 3, 2011. www.sacred-texts.com/bib/jub/index.htm

"Book of Susanna." *Searchable Online King James Bible.* Biblical Proportions.2004-5.RetrievedMarch9,2011.www.biblicalproportions. com/modules/ol_bible/King_James

Bowers, Paul. "NUBIAN CHRISTIANITY: THE NEGLECTED HERITAGE." *Africa Journal of Evangelical Theology* iv.1 (1985) pages 3-23. 1985. Retrieved March 3, 2011. www.theoledafrica.org/ OtherMaterials/Files/Nubia

Bronner, Ethan. "Ancient Tablet Ignites Debate on Messiah and Resurrection". *New York Times.* July 6, 2008. Retrieved March 3, 2011. mowbraypublishing.com/files/Ancient_Tablet_Ignites

C

Calvin, John. "Of Justification by Faith." From his *Institutes of the Christian religion.* Book3:11. A Puritans's Mind. 1999. Retrieved March 3, 3011. www.apuritansmind.com/Justification/CalvinJohnJustification.htm

_____ "On Righteousness." III. xi. 2. *Institutes of the Christian Religion.* 21-23. A Puritan's Mind. 1998-2010. Retrieved March 10, 2011. www. apuritansmind.com/Justification/CalvinJohn

"Canons of the seven Ecumenical Councils Table of Contents." Èulogos SPA 2007. Retrieved March 3, 2011. www.intratext.com/ IXT/ENG0835

Carrier, Richard. "The Formation of the New Testament Canon." Internet Infidels.1995-2011. Retrieved March 15, 2011. www.infidels.org/library/modern/richard_carrier/NTcanon.html.

Carroll, Robert Todd. "Noah's Ark." Robert Todd Carroll. 1998. Last updated November 13, 1998. Retrieved March 23, 2011. www.genpaku.org/skepticj/noahsark.html

Carson, David C. "A BRIEF HISTORY OF THE INTERTESTAMENTAL PERIOD AND BEYOND." David C. Carson. 2006. Retrieved April 14, 2011. davcarson.home.mindspring.com/Intertestamental//brief... –

_____ "Who Were the Samaritans?" David C. Carson. 2006. Retrieved March 3, 2011. davcarson.home.mindspring.com/Intertestamental/samaritan.htm

"Catechism of the Catholic Church." *The Holy SeeArchive*. Retrieved March 3, 2011. www.vatican.va/archive/ccc/index.htm

"Cathars. " Net helper. 2011. Retrieved March 7, 2011. nethelper.com/article/Cathars

Chapman, John. "Donatists." *The Catholic Encyclopedia.* Vol. 5. New York: Robert Appleton Company.1909. Mar 22. 2011 www.newadvent.org/cathen/05121a.htm.

_____. "St. Cyprian of Carthage." *The Catholic Encyclopedia.* Vol. 4. New York: Robert Appleton Company, 1908. Retrieved March 22, 2011. www.newadvent.org/cathen/04583b.htm..

_____. "Tertullian." *The Catholic Encyclopedia.* Vol. 14. NewYork: Robert Appleton Company. 1912. Retrieved Mar. 2011 www.newadvent.org/cathen/14520c.htm

"CHICAGO STATEMENT ON BIBLICAL INERRANCY." Southwestern Baptist Theological Seminary. Fort Worth. 2009. Retrieved March 9, 2011. www.swbts.edu/index.cfm?pageid=1723

"Christianity in Africa." *Wikipedia Encyclopedia*. Last modified February 15, 2011. Retrieved March 9, 2011. en.wikipedia.org/wiki/Christianity_in_Africa

"Christianity in Ethiopia." *EthiopiaFamine.com*. Retrieved March 22, 2011. www.fhi.net/fhius/ethiopiafamine/christian.html

Cline, Austin. "Popes of the 10th Century. Part 2: History of the Roman Popes." *About.com guide*. Retrieved March 15, 2011. atheism.about.com/od

Cockerham, Larry W. "Antiochus IV Epiphanes: The Antichrist of the Old Testament." *Prophecy Forum.* Prophecy Forum Ministries. 2001. Retrieved April15, 2011. www.prophecyforum.com/antiochus.html

"Code of Hammurabi." Translated L.W.King. *Internet Ancient History Sourcebook.* Paul Halsall , March 1998. Retrieved March 22, 2011. www.fordham.edu/halsall/ancient/hamcode.html

Corelli, Marie. *Life Everlasting*. " Prologue." WATTPAD. Retrieved March 3, 2011.
www.wattpad.com/8494-the-life-everlasting-a-reality-of

"Council of Nicaea." The Nazarene Way of Essenic Studies. Retrieved March 9, 2011. www.thenazareneway.com/council_of_nicaea_nicea_325.htm

"Council of Trent-6:Decree concerning justification." Eternal Word Television Network. Irondale, AL. Retrieved March 3, 2011. www.ewtn.com/library/COUNCILS/TRENT6.HTM

Cowley, A, Joseph Jacobs, Henry Minor Huxley "SAMARITANS." *Jewish Encyclopedia*. 2002. Retrieved March 4, 2011.www.jewishencyclopedia.com/view.jsp?artid=110&letter=S

Cox, Douglas E. "Did Earth's Rotation Stop on Joshua's Long Day?" Douglas E. Cox. 1998. Retrieved March 4, 2011. www.sentex.net/~tcc/astropro.html

Crabtree, Vexen. "Mithraism and Early Christianity." Vexen Crabtree. Jan 20, 2002. Retrieved March 4, 2011. www.vexen.co.uk/religion/mithraism.html—

Curtis, David B. "Inspiration and the Second Coming of Christ." Sermon April 27, 1997. Retrieved March 4, 2011. www.bereanbiblechurch.org/transcripts/eschatology/...

D

Davies, Paul. *The Fifth Miracle*. Chapter 1. Education Resource Centre, 2004. Retrieved March 4, 2011 www..catholiceducation.org/articles/religion/re0770.html

"Dead Sea Scrolls. The Ancient Library of Qumran and Modern Scholarship, an Exhibit." Library of Congress, Washington, DC. Retrieved April 13, 2011., faculty.ucc.edu/ egh-damerow/dead_sea_scrolls.htm

"Deism." *Wikipedia*. Last modified March 21, 2011. Retrieved April 9, 2011.
en.wikipedia.org/wiki/Deism

Dei Verdum: Dogmatic Constitution on Divine Revelation. CHA PTER III, paragraph 11. "SACRED Scripture" www.aodonline.org/courseresources/DeiVerbumExcerpts.pdf

deLacey,Douglas. "Sadducees." *The Ecole Initiative*. Douglas R. de Lacey, 1995. Retrieved March 4, 2011. www2.evansville.edu/ecoleweb/articles/sadducees.html

DeMarco, Donald. "The Virtue of Uprightness." Catholic Education Resource Centre. Lay Witness 2004. Retrieved March 4, 2011.www.catholiceducation.org/articles/religion/re0770.html

"Development of the Jewish Bible canon." *Wikilpedia Encyclopedia*. Modified March 2, 2011. Retrieved March 9, 2011. n.wikipedia.org/wiki/Development_of_the_Jewish_Bible_canon

Dicks, Tim. "Review of Richard Llewelyn's book *How Green Was My Valley*." American Movie Classics Company. 2011. Retrieved March 3, 2011. www.filmsite.org/howg.html

"Did contemporary historians mention Jesus?" *Forerunner Discussion Group*. phpBB Group .2007. Retrieved March 9, 2011. www.forerunner.com/discussion/viewtopic.php?t=31

"Does God create evil?" *Christian Apologetics and Research*, Matthew J. Slick, 1995-2010. Retrieved March 3, 2011. carm.org/does-god-create-evil

*Dogmatic Constitution on Divine Revelation—(Dei Verbum.)*_Retrieved March 4, 2011. www.christusrex.org/www1/CDHN/v5.html

Dolphin, Lambert. "World Population Since Creation." Lambert Dolphin. Originally written 1987. Last updated July 31, 2007. Retrieved March 23, 2011. www.ldolphin.org/popul.html

Driscoll, James F. "Sadducees." *The Catholic Encyclopedia*. Vol. 13. New York: Robert Appleton Company, 1912. Retrieved March 23, 2011. www.newadvent.org/cathen/13323a.htm.

E

"ECCLESIASTICUS." These Last Days Ministries. Lowell, MI, 1996. Retrieved March 4, 2011. www.tldm.org/bible/Old%20Testament/eccltus.htm

Edgecomb, Kevin P. "SBL Notes, part two." *Biblicalia.* Retrieved March 15, 2011. www.bombaxo.com/blog/?p=451

"English translations of the Bible." *Wikipedia the free Encyclopedia.* Last modified February 12, 2011, Retrieved March 15, 2011. en.wikipedia.org/wiki/

"EPISTLES of JESUS CHRIST and ABGARUS KING of EDESSA." Globusz Publishing.2001-2011. Retrieved March 9, 2011. www.globusz.com/ebooks/ForbiddenGospels/00000018.htm

"Essene Communion: their purpose and meaning." The Nazarene Way of Essenic Studies. Retrieved March 4, 2011. www.thenazareneway.com/comu_essene_communions.htm

Evans, William B. "A layman's historical guide to the inerrancy debate." Alliance of Confessing Evangelicals. 2005. Retrieved March 4, 2011. www.reformation21.org/articles/a-laymans-historical

"Evil." *New World Encyclopedia.* Last revised June 20, 2008. Retrieved April25,2011 http://www.newworldencyclopedia.org/entry/Evil?oldid=7384

"Evolution of the God Concept Among the Hebrews." Urantia Book Fellowship. Retrieved March 9, 2011. urantiabook.org/newbook/papers/p097.htm

"Evolution of Man—Theory Concepts." *All About Science. Org.* All About Science.Colorado Springs. 2002. Retrieved June2010. www.allaboutscience.org/evolution-of-man.htm

F

Finkelstein, Louis. *The Pharisees THE SOCIOLOGICAL BACKGROUND OF THEIR FAITH.*The Jewish Publication Society of America. Philadelphia. 1938. Retrieved March 4, 2011.www.come-and-hear.com/talmud/finkelstein.html

"First Baptist Church in America." *Wikipedia Encyclopedia.* Last modified March 8, 2011. Retrieved March 9, 2011. en.wikipedia.org/wiki/First_Baptist_Church_in_Americ

"First Council of Nicaea." *New World Encyclopedia.* Retrieved March 11, 2011. www.newworldencyclopedia.org/entry/Council_of_Nicea

"First Diet of Speyer." *Wikipedia Encyclopedia.* Last modified February 17, 2011. Retrieved March 9, 2011. en.wikipedia.org/wiki/First_Diet_of_Speyer

"First Vatican Council, Dei Filius (Dogmatic Constitution on the Catholic Faith." April 24, 1870), Session III, Chapter 2, "On revelation." Retrieved March15, 2011. www.shc.edu/theolibrary/resources/vat1rev. htm

Foley, Jim. "Hominid Species." Jim Foley. Retrieved March 4, 2011. www.talkorigins.org/faqs/homs/species.html

Fox, John. *Book of Martyrs.* Edited William Byron Forbush. Retrieved March 4, 2011. www.ccel.org/f/foxe/martyrs/home.html

"FRAGMENTS OF A ZADOKITE WORK" also known as "The Damascus Document."Translated byR. H Charles. Edited Diane Morgan. Wesley Center for Applied Theology, 2000. Retrieved April 13, 2011.
www.pseudepigrapha.com/pseudepigrapha/zadokite.html

"From Jesus to Christ: the story of the Gospel of Thomas." *FRONTLINE.* WGBH educational foundation. April 1998. Retrieved March 4, 2011.
www.pbs.org/.../frontline/shows/religion/story/thomas.html

"Fruit of the Holy Spirit" *Wikpedia the Free Encyclopedia.* last modified February 10, 2011. Retrieved March 22, 2011. en.wikipedia.org/wiki/Fruit_of_the_Holy_Spirit

"Full Preterism." *Wikipedia.* Last modified March 9, 2011. Retrieved March 9, 2011.
en.wikipedia.org/wiki/Full_Preterism

G

Gerstner, John. "History of the Doctrine of Justification." A Puritans Mind. 1998-2010. Retrieved March 4, 2011. www.apuritansmind. com/justification/gerstnerjohn

Glatzer, Nahum N. "Essenes." *Believe webpage.* Retrieved March 21, 2011. mb-soft.com/believe/txo/essene.htm

Goldberg, G.J. "Josephus' Account of Jesus." *Radical Faith Magazine.* Retrieved March 16, 2011. homepages.which.net/~radical.faith/ background

"Gospel of Mary Magdalene." Introduced KAREN L. King. Translated George W. Macrae and R. Mc.L. Wilson. Edited Douglas M. Parrott. The Nazarene Way of Essenic Studies. Retrieved March 7, 2011. www. thenazareneway.com/the_gospel_of_mary_magdalene.htm

"Gospel of Thomas." Online text. Peter Kirby. *Early Christian writings.* February 2006. Retrieved March 4, 2011. www.earlychristianwritings. com/thomas.html

Graves, Kersey. *The World's Sixteen Crucified Saviors.* Chapter 19. *A Witness to Yahweh website.* Retrieved March 16, 2011. www.awitness.org/essays/ bkup/16_crucified_saviors/chap19

Guggenberger, S.J. A General History of the Christian Era. B. HERDER. NY. Retrieved March 4, 2011 www.archive.org/stream/generalhistoryof03gugguoft

H

Hardwick, J. "Deism Defined." J. Hardwick 2004-2010. Retrieved March 4, 2011. www.moderndeism.com/html/deism_defined.html

"Herod the Great." *New World Encyclopedia.* May 7, 2006. May 14, 2011. www.newworldencyclopedia.org/entry/Herod_the_Great

"Herodian Dynasty." *Answers.com.* 2011. April 14, 2011. www.answers. com/topic/herodian-dynasty

Hillar, Marian. "Philo of Alexandria." *Internet Encyclopedia of Philosophy.* Last updated April 21, 2005. Retrieved March 4, 2011. www.iep.utm. edu/philo

" Historical Lilith." AvatarSearch OccultLink Exchange. Retrieved March 9, 2011. www.lilitu.com/lilith/historical.html

" History of Christianity in Egypt Birth and Early Growth." *Tour Egypt.* 2010. Retrieved March 8, 2011. www.touregypt.net/Chiste1.htm

"History of Europe Timeline. Northwest Europe 9th to 12th century A.D." *History World.* Retrieved March 15, 2011. www.historyworld. net/wrldhis/PlainTextHistories.asp?g..

"HISTORY OF FEUDALISM". *History World.* Retrieved March 15,2011. www.historyworld.net/wrldhis/PlainTextHistories.asp?g..

Hochner, Donald. "Noah's Flood: Global or Local?" Donald Hochmer. Retrieved March 23, 2011. www.angelfire.com/ca/DeafPreterist/noah. html

" History of the Levant from Alexander the Great to Herod the Great." Quartz Hill SchoolofTheology. Retrieved April 25, 2011. www.theology.edu/b414.htm.

Holding, J.P. "The Reliability of the Secular References to Jesus." Retrieved March 4, 2011.
www.british-israel.ca/tacitus.htm

Hooker, Richard. "Reformation: Ulrich Zwingli." Richard Hooker, 1996. Updated 6-6-1999. Retrieved March 4, 2011. wsu.edu:8000/~dee/ REFORM/ZWINGLI.HTM

_____. "Reformation: John Calvin." Richard Hooker.1996. Updated 6-6-1999. Retrieved March 4, 2011. www.wsu.edu/~dee/ REFORM/CALVIN.HTM]

"HOW DID CHRISTIANITY SPREAD THROUGHOUT THE WORLD?" Retrieved March 15, 2011. www.suscopts.org/.../ apostolicagechristianity.pdf

Hughes, Philip. *A HISTORY OF THE CHURCH To the Eve of the Reformation.* Ewin.1934. Retrieved March 4, 2011 www.franciscan-sfo. org/ap/hu/00-index.htm

Huie, Bryan T. "Who were the Sadducees and the Pharisees?" Bryan T. Huie. March 16, 1997. Revised: April 8, 2009. Retrieved March 4, 2011. www.herealittletherealittle.net/index.cfm?page_name= . . .

Humphreys, Kenneth. "Witness to Jesus?—1 Philo of Alexandria." Kenneth Humphreys. 2006. Retrieved March 4, 2011. www.jesusneverexisted. com/philo.html

Huntington, William Reed. *A short history of the Book of Common Prayer.* Thomas Whittaker. 1893. Retrieved April 2011. justus.anglican.org/resources/bcp/short_history_ BCP.htm

"John Hus." Great Site.com. 1997. April 20, 2011. www.greatsite.com/ timeline-english-bible-history/john . . .

I

"Inerrancy of the Bible." *Theopedia Encyclopedia of Biblical Christianity.* July 2010. Retrieved March 8, 2011. www.theopedia.com/Inerrancy

Isaak, Mark. "What is Creationism?" *The Talk Origins Archive.* 2000. Retrieved March 4, 2011. www.talkorigins.org/faqs/wic.html

J

Ja cobs,Joseph, Kaufmann Kohler, Richard Gottheil, Samuel Krauss. "Jesus of Nazareth." *JewishEncyclopedia.com.* 2002. Retrieved March 6, 2011. www.jewishencyclopedia.com/view.jsp?artid=254&letter=

Jeffcoat III, John L. "English Bible History and timeline." WWW. GREATSITE.COM, 2002. Retrieved March 15, 2011. www.theologue. org/TimelineOfBibleTranslationHistory.html

"Jewish Sects at the Time of Christ." Aramaic Herald. Tuesday, July 27,2010. Retrieved March 8, 2011. aramaicherald.blogspot.com/2010/07/ jewish-sects-at-time . . .

"John the Baptist." New World Encyclopedia. Retrieved April 25, 2011. www.newworldencyclopedia.org/entry/John_the_Baptist

"Joint Declaration on the Doctrine of Justification ." Evangelical Lutheran Church in America.Retrieved March 18, 2011. www.vatican.va/roman_curia/pontifical_councils/chrstuni/ . . .

"Josephus the Eyewitness ." *All About History.* All About History.org. 2002. Retrieved March 16, 2011. www.allabouthistory.org/josephus.htm

Josephus, Flavius. *Antiquities of the Jews.* Book 2. History Workshop. Retrieved March 22, 2011. rbedrosian.com/Josephus/jan2.htm

_____. *The Works.* "Book XVIII. Chapter 3:3." Translated William Whiston. Retrieved March 16, 2011. www.ccel.org/j/josephus/works/ant-18.htm

_____ "Testimonium Flavianum." Alan Humm. 1995. Retrieved March 16, 2011. jewishchristianlit.com/Topics/JewishJesus/josephus. html

_____*The Jewish Wars.* "Book 2, Chapter 8." Bible Study Tools.com. Retrieved March 21, 2011. ancienthistory.about.com/od/ josephus/l/bl_josephus_JW

"Judaism and Christianity. Comparisons, Similarity." Important.ca. Retrieved April 22, 2011. www.important.ca/judaism_christanity_ comparison.html

Just, Felix. "Jewish Groups at the Time of Jesus." Retrieved April 25, 2011. www.azwalker.com/ . . . /history-of-jewish-sects-and-groups.pdf

K

Kent, William. "Indulgences." *The Catholic Encyclopedia*. Vol. 7. New York: Robert Appleton Company, 1910. Retrieved March 3, 2011. www.newadvent.org/cathen/07783a.htm.

Kahn, Jerome. "Ancient Sacred Works of the Christians, The Jesus Interpollation in Josephuss." Encyclopædia Britannica Inc. 1994-2002. Retrieved April 11, 2011. jeromekahn123.tripod.com/chxbible/id12. html

Kirby, Peter. "Epistle of Barnabas." *Early Christian Writings*. Feb 2, 2006. Retrieved March 14, 2011.2010. www.earlychristianwritings.com/ barnabas.htm

Kirsch, Johann_Peter. "Council of Trent." *The Catholic Encyclopedia.* Vol.15. New York: Robert Appleton Company.1912. Retrieved March 30. 2011 www.newadvent.org/cathen/15030c.htm

Kohler, Kaufmann. "Pharisees." *Jewish Encyclopedia*. 2002. Retrieved March 4,2011. www.jewishencyclopedia.com/view.jsp?artid=252&letter=P&

L

Lapierre, Michael. "Grace IN THOMAS AQUINAS." Toronto, Ontario. September 21, 1994. Retrieved March 5, 2011. catholic-church.org/ grace/western/scholars/lap1.htm

"Last Judgment." *Answers.com*. Answers Corporation. 2011. Retrieved February, 2011. www.answers.com/topic/last-judgment.

Leibniz, G.W. *Theodicy*. Edited with Introduction by Austin Farrer. Translated E.M. Huggard. Project Guttenberg. November 24, 2005. Retrieved April 7, 2011. www.gutenberg.org/files/17147/17147-h/17147-h.htm

HANDEL ANDREWS

Lendering, Jona. "Sadducees." Livius.2005. Retrieved April 12, 2011. www.livius.org/saa-san/sadducees/sadducees.html

_____ "Samaritans." Jona Lendering. 1995-2010. Retrieved March 5, 2011. www.livius.org/saa-san/samaria/samaritans.htm

"Ussher-Lightfoot Calendar—Definition." Word Iq.com 2010. Retrieved March5, 2011. www.wordiq.com/definition/Ussher-Lightfoot_Calendar

"Lost Books of the Bible." *All about Jesus christ.org.* Colorado Springs, Colorado. 2002. Retrieved June 2010. www.allaboutjesuschrist.org/lost-books-of-the-bible-faq.htm

"Lost Books of the New Testament (1)." Windmill Ministries-Christian Apologetics. Retrieved March 9, 2011. www.windmillministries.org/CH13.htm

"Lost Years of Jesus: The Life of Saint Issa." Translated T. Notovitch. The Reluctant Messenger. Retrieved March 7, 2011. reluctant-messenger.com/issa.htm

Luther, Martin. "An Open Letter to the Christian Nobility." Project Wittenberg. Retrieved March 5, 2011. www.iclnet.org/pub/resources/text/wittenberg/luther/web/..

_____ "The Babylonian Captivity of the Church." Walther Library, Concordia Theological Seminary. Ft. Wayne. Retrieved March5, 2011. www.lutherdansk.dk/WebBabylonian%20Captivitate/Martin

_____ "Excerpts from his statement at the Diet of Worms." Translation H.C. Bettenson. Documents of the Christian Church (1903. Retrieved March 6, 2011. www-personal.ksu.edu/~lyman/english233/Luther-Diet_of_Worms

_____ "The Ninety-five theses." *Works of Martin Luther.* Adolph Spaeth, L.D. Reed, Henry Eyster Jacobs, et Al. Trans. & Eds. Philadelphia: A. J. Holman Company, 1915. Vol.1, pp.

29-38. Retrieved March 7, 2011. www.iclnet.org/ . . /wittenberg/luther/ web/ninetyfive.html

_____Of Justification. A Puritans Mind, 1998-2010. RetrievedMarch 7, 2011. www.apuritansmind.com/justification/luthermartin

_____"Smalcald Articles." Translated F. Bente and W. H. T. Dau. St. Louis: Concordia Publishing House. 1921. pp.453-529. Triglot Concordia. Retrieved March 7, 2011. www.iclnet.org/pub/resources/text/wittenberg/concord/web/. . .

M

"Maccabees." *Wikipedia.* Last modified April 16, 2011. Retrieved April 19, 2011. en.wikipedia.org/wiki/Maccabees

Maccoby, Hyam. "Religion and Revolt: The Pharisees." Abridged from *Revolution in Judea: Jesus and the Jewish Resistance.* Lewis Loflin. Retrieved March 7, 2011. www.sullivan-county.com/id3/maccoby1.htm

Manocha, Ramesh Dr and Anna Potts. "Synopsis of Jesus Lived In India by Holger Kersten." *Knowledge of Reality Magazine.* 1996-2006. Retrieved March 1, 2011. www.sol.com.au/kor/7_01.htm

Martyr, JUSTIN. *DISCOURSE TO THE GREEKS.* "Chapter 9." Translated M. DODS. The Forerunner Forum. Retrieved March 22, 2011. www.forerunner.com/churchfathers/ X0031_27._JUSTIN-_DI

Massing, Michael. "New Torah for modern minds." *New York Times.* March 9, 2002. Retrieved March 22, 2011. www.nytimes.com/ . . . /09/books/ new-torah-for-modern-minds.html

Maxey, Al. "THE SILENT CENTURIES The Maccabean Revolt." Retrieved April 14, 2011. www.zianet.com/maxey/Inter3.htm
McHugh, John. "General Judgment." *The Catholic Encyclopedia.* Vol. 8. New York: Robert Appleton Company, 1910. Retrieved Mar. 2011 www.newadvent.org/cathen/08552a.htm.

McKinney, Clay. "Church History Timeline, the Early Church in the Apostolic Period (35-120)." Clay McKinney 1998-2006. Retrieved March 7, 2011. www.churchtimeline.com/ChurchTimeline.pdf

McMahon, Matthew C. *The Patristic Period the beginnings of the Early Church.* A Puritan's Mind 1998-2010. Retrieved March 7, 2011. www.apuritansmind.com/HistoricalTheology/PatristicPeriod.htm

_____ "Dr. John Calvin: Theologian, Pastor, and Social Reformer."A Puritan's Mind.1998-2010. Retrieved March 7, 2011. www.apuritansmind.com/.../mcmahoncalvintheologianpastor.htm

Meeker,Brent. "Cosmology and Cosmogony of Ancient Civilizations." *Muktomona website.*Retrieved March 7, 2011. www.muktomona.com/ . ./Articles/brent_meeker/cosmology.htm

Jastrow, Marcus , S. Mendelsohn. " BET HILLEL AND BET SHAMMAI." *JewishEncyclopedia.com.* 2002. Retrieved March 4, 2011. www.jewishencyclopedia.com/view.jsp?artid=956&letter=B

Meyer, Marvin, Stephen Patterson. The "Scholars' Translation of the Gospel of Thomas ." Retrieved March 7, 2011. www.piney.com/ ApocThomGos.html

Miles, Kathy A., Charles F. Peters II. "The Age of the Earth." Kathy A. Miles and Charles F. Peters11. 2001. Retrieved March 7, 2011. starryskies.com/Artshtml/dln/6-97/earth.age.html

Mizzi, Joe. "St. James on Justification by Works." Joe Mizzi. Retrieved March 4, 2011. www.justforcatholics.org/a85.htm

Morgan, R.W. "Christianity came to Britain when? And those who brought it." *Restitution Of All Things.* Retrieved March 7, 2011. www.keithhunt. com/Paulin5.html

Morris, Denise. "Jesus the Pharisee?" *The Boundless Line.* 6/11/2007. Retrieved March21, 2011. www.boundlessline.org/2007/06/jesus_ the_phari.html

Moule, H.C.G.. "Justification by Faith." Volume 3 ch. XI. From H.C.G. Moule. *The Fundamentals: A Testimony to the Truth*. Baker books. Last updated December 22, 2005.Retrieved March 7, 2011. www.xmission.com/~fidelis/volume3/chapter11/moule.php

"Muratorian Fragment." *New World Encyclopedia.* Retrieved March 7, 2011. www.newworldencyclopedia.org/entry/Muratorian_fragment

Myers, Peter. "The Exodus & the Expulsion of the Hyksos-Archaeology of the Bible." *Neither Aryan Nor Jew website.* Canberra, Australia. June 3, 2004. Last updated March 30, 2010. Retrieved March 3, 2011. mailstar.net/archaeology-bible.html

N

*Nicene and Post-Nicene Fathers.*Vol. 5. book1, chapter 34. " Treatise on the grace of Christ." Sacred Texts. Retrieved March 16, 2011. www.sacred-texts.com/chr/ecf/105/1051070.htm

"Noah's Ark." Robert T. Carroll.   1994-2010. Last updated 12/09/10. Retrieved March 3, 2011. skepdic.com/noahsark.html

"Nubian Civilization." Retrieved March 7, 2011. shazlyasmail.tripod.com/ new_page_12.htm

O

Olsen,Ken. "Eusebius of Caesarea forged the Testimonium Flavianum ." Mountain Man Graphics. Retrieved March 7, 2011. www.mountainman.com.au/essenes/article_008.htm

Omer, Ibrahim. "Ancient Sudan~ Nubia: History: The Christianization of Nubia." Ibrahim Omer, 2008. Retrieved March 7, 2011. www.ancientsudan.org/history_13_christianization.htm

"Origin and Evolution of the Universe Chapter 1 THE ORIGIN OFMATTER Part 1." *Evolution Encyclopedia.* Vol. 1. EVOLU TION FACTS. ALTAMONT, TN. Retrieved March 4, 2011. evolutionfacts. com/Ev-V1/1evlch01a.htm

P

"Particulars of Christianity: 313 Preterism." *Bible Studying.net* Bible Study Resource. Retrieved March 3, 2011. www.biblestudying.net/ topic_preterism.html

Pearse, Roger. "Shlomo Pines, Agapius and Elmacin (Al-Makin)." Roger Pearse. August 26th, 2008. Retrieved March 7, 2011. www. roger-pearse.com/weblog/?p=33

Pelagius. "Letter of Pelagius to Demetrias A.D. 385." From *The Letters of Pelagius.* Robert Van de Weyer ed. Retrieved March 11, 2011.
pelagius.net/demetrias.htm

"Pharisees." *Conservapedia Encyclopedia.* Last modified October 20, 2009. Retrieved March 3, 2011. www.conservapedia.com/Pharisees

Philo of Alexandria. "The Essenes." Retrieved April 25, 2011. catholicgnosis. wordpress.com/2009/01/01/the-essenes

PINES, Shlomo. "An Arabic Version of the Testimonium." WordIq. com. 2010. Retrieved March 16, 2011. www.wordiq.com/definition/ Testimonium_Flavianum

Pliny the Younger. . "Epistle to Trajan." Paul F. Pavao. 2009-2010. Retrieved March 7,2011.
www.christian-history.org/pliny-the-younger.html

"Polycarp, Bishop of Smyrna (ca. 70—ca. 155)." Christian History Institute. 2007. Retrieved March 3, 2011. www.chitorch.org/index. php/in-context/Polycarp

"Polycarp." Biography from Answers.com. "Date of Martyrdom." Answers Corporation, 2011. Retrieved April 20, 2011. www.answers.com/topic/polycarp-saint—

" Postmillennialism." *Wikipedia*. Last modified January 2, 2011. Retrieved March 9, 2011. en.wikipedia.org/wiki/Postmillennialism—

Preston, Don K. "Full Preterism, Every Eye Shall See Him." Don K. Preston. Ardmore, Oklahoma. Retrieved March 7, 2011. www.almac. co.uk/personal/renaux/static/eye.htm

"Preterism." *Theopedia Encyclopedia of Biblical Christianity*. October 28, 2006. Retrieved March 8, 2011. www.theopedia.com/Preterism

Price, Christopher. "Did Josephus refer to Jesus?" Christopher Price. 2004. Last updated December 8, 2009. Retrieved April 25, 2011. www.bede. org.uk/Josephus.htm

"Pseudepigraph." *Wikipedia the free encyclopedia*. Last modified February17, 2011. Retrieved March 15, 2011. en.wikipedia.org/wiki/ Pseudepigraph—

"Ptolemy II Philadelphus." *Wikipedia the free encyclopedia*. en.wikipedia. org/wiki/Ptolemy_II_Philadelphus

R

"Radioactive dating." *Dictionary.com*. 2011. Retrieved March 10, 2011. dictionary.reference.com/browse/radioactive+dating

Ramesh Manocha, Anna Potts. "Synopsis Holger Kerstein Jesus lived in India." Retrieved March 4. 2011. www.spinninglobe.net/jesusinindia. htm

Reardon, Patrick Henry. "Susannah." Conciliar Press. Retrieved March 8,2011. www.orthodoxstudybible.com/index.php/articles/Susannah

Reid, George. "Canon of the New Testament." *The Catholic Encyclopedia.* Vol. 3. New York: Robert Appleton Company, 1908. Retrieved March 15. 2011 www.newadvent.org/cathen/03274a.htm

Remsberg, John E. *The Christ.* Chapter 2. "Silence of Contemporary Writers" *Positive Atheism website.*Retrieved March 3, 2011. www.positiveatheism.org/hist/rmsbrg02.htm

Rich, Tracy R. "Judaism 101: The name of G-d." Tracey R Rich 1995-2008. Retrieved March 7, 2011. www.jewfaq.org/toc.htm

RJMI. "The Final Position of St. Augustine on Baptism." From RJMI *The Baptism Controversy.* Retrieved March 8, 2011. www.romancatholicism. org/augustine-final.htm

Roberto, John Rocco. "Flavius Josephus and the Jewish Wars." John Rocco Roberto. 2005. Retrieved March 21, 2011. www.historyvortex.org/Josephus.html

Robertson, A.T. "The pharisees and Jesus. The Stone lectures." Victoria University Library, Toronto, Ontario. Retrieved March 21, 2011. www.archive.org/stream/phariseesandjesu00robeuoft/.

Robinson, B.A. "Estimates of the age of the earth." *Religious Tolerance. Org.* Retrieved March 7, 2011. www.religioustolerance.org/ev_date1.htm

Rusbult, Craig . "Common Sense about Schrodinger's Cat and QUAN TUM PHYSI CS, Principles Interpretations,New Age Speculations andJudeo-Christian Theology." Craig Rusbul. 2007. Retrieved March 8, 2011. www.asa3.org/ASA/education/views/qm-cr.htm

Russell, J. Stuart. *The Parousia: A Careful Look at the New Testament Doctrine of the Lord's Second Coming* Free Online Books. *PreteristArchive.com.* Retrieved March 8, 2011. www.preteristarchive.com/Books/1878_russell_parousia.html

S

"Sadducee." *Indopedia.* Last modified December 1, 2004. Retrieved March 4, 2011.
www.indopedia.org/Sadducees.html

"Sadducees." *New World Encyclopedia.* Retrieved March 7, 2011.
www.newworldencyclopedia.org/entry/Sadducees

Sasson, Remez. "Self Control." Success Consciousness.com, 2001. Retrieved April 5, 2011. www.successconsciousness.com/self_control.htm

Saunders, Dean. "The Great Controversy, Lucifer's Rebellion." The Bible Study Collection. McDonald Road Seventh-day Adventist Church. November 3, 2006. Retrieved March 8, 2011. mcdonaldroad.org/bible/study.html

Saunders, William."The Missing Books of the Bible." Arlington Catholic Herald. 2003 . Retrieved March 15, 2011.
www.catholiceducation.org/articles/religion/re0134.html

Schaff,Philip. *History of the Christian Church.* The Electronic Bible Society, Dallas. 1998. Retrieved March 8, 2011. www.ccel.org/s/schaff/history/About.

Schiffman, Lawrence. "Essenes." *Encyclopedia of Religion.* 2005. Retrieved March 23, 2011. www.encyclopedia.com/article-1G2-3424500952/essenes.html

"Second Ecumenical Council." *OrthodoxWiki Encyclopedia.* Last modified May 16, 2010. Retrieved March 15, 2011. www.orthodoxwiki.org/Second_Ecumenical_Council

"Seventh-day Adventists Believe." *At issue magazine.* Retrieved March 8, 2011.
www.sdanet.org/atissue/books/27/27-24.htm

Setzer, Claudia Tikkun. "The Historical Jesus." Reprinted from *TIKKUN MAGAZINE*. July 17, 1995. No. 4, Vol. 10; Page. 73. *Frontline*. April 1998. Retrieved March 4, 2011
www.pbs.org/ . . . /frontline/shows/religion/jesus/tikkun.html

" Shepherd of Hermas." *Early Christian Writings*. . Peter Kirby. February 2, 2006. Retrieved March 9, 2011. www.earlychristianwritings.com/shepherd.html

Shepard, John. "The kingdom of Israel." John Shepard 2007. Retrieved March 8, 2011. www.northforest.org/Eschatology/index.html

Smith, Mahlon H. "Ptolemy I Soter." American Theological Library Association Selected Religion Website. 1999. April 15, 2011. virtualreligion.net/iho/ptolemy_1.html

_____. "Ptolemy II Philadelphus." *American Theological Library Association Selected Religion Website*. 1999. Retrieved April 15, 2011. virtualreligion.net/iho/ptolemy_2.html

_____."Ptolemy III Euergetes."   Retrieved April 15, 2011. virtualreligion.net/iho/ptolemy_3.html

_____."Ptolemy IV Philopator." Retrieved April 15, 2011. virtualreligion.net/iho/ptolemy_4.html

"Spread of Christianity into early Britain." *Historical Stuff.*, Retrieved March 15, 2011. www.lundyisleofavalon.co.uk/history/spreadofchristianity.htm

Sproul, R.C. "The Spiritual Kingdom of God pages 53-55." *The Last Days According to Jesus.* Retrieved March 8, 2011. www.truthandgrace.com/Kingdom2.htm

Spurgeon, C.H. "Statement on Premillennialism." James Dearmore. *Gospel Web.* 2009. Retrieved March 8, 2011. www.gospelweb.net/SpurgeonSermons/spurgeononmillennium.htm

Still, James. "Critique of New Testament Reliability and "Bias" in NT Development." *The Secular Web.* 1995. Retrieved March 16, 2011. www.infidels.org/library/modern/james_still/critbias.html

"Story of Africa." *BBC World Service*. London. Retrieved March 3, 2011. www.bbc.co.uk/worldservice/africa/features/storyofafrica/

Streich ,Michael. "Cluny and the 10th Century Reform Movement." *Suite101.com*. Retrieved March 8, 2011. www.suite101.com/content/cluny-and-the-10th-century . . .

T

Tacitus, Cornelius. *The Annals*. Book 15, chapter 44. Alfred John Church, William Jackson Brodribb, Eds. Perseus Digital Library. Retrieved March 8, 2011. www.perseus.tufts.edu/hopper/text?doc=Perseus%3Atext

"Teacher of Righteousness." *Encyclopaedia Judaica.* The Gale Group. Jewish Virtual Library. 2008 . Retrieved April 13, 2011. www.encyclopedia.com/article-1G2-2587519666/teacher..
"Teacher of Righteousness." *Wikipedia.* Last modified April 11, 2011. Retrieved April 13, 2011.
en.wikipedia.org/wiki/Teacher_of_Righteousness

"Tertullian." *Wikipedia.* Last modified March 2, 2011. Retrieved march 9,2011
en.wikipedia.org/?title=Tertullian

"Testimonium Flavianum-Definition." Wordiq.com., 2010. Retrieved March9, 2011. www.wordiq.com/definition/Testimonium_Flavianum

"The 39 Articles" Full text. Britain Express, London. Retrieved March 31, 2011.
www.britainexpress.com/History/tudor/39articles-text.htm

"Thomas Aquinas." *Wikipedia Encyclopedia*. Last modified March 7, 2011. Retrieved March 7, 2011. en.wikipedia.org/wiki/Thomas_Aquinas

Thurston, Herbert. "Aelfric, Abbot of Eynsham." *The Catholic Encyclopedia.* Vol. 1. New York: Robert Appleton Company, 1907. Retrieved March 15, 2011
www.newadvent.org/cathen/01171b.htm

_____"The Venerable Bede." *The Catholic Encyclopedia.* Vol. 2. New York: Robert Appleton Company, 1907. Retrieved March 15, 2011.
www.newadvent.org/cathen/02384a.htm

U

Untener, Kenneth E. "What Catholics Believe about The End of theWorld." Franciscans and St. Anthony Messenger Press. 1996-2011. Retrieved March 8, 2011. www.americancatholic.org/Newsletters/CU/ac0993.asp

Ussher, James (1581-1656).*Annals of the World.* London, 1658. Retrieved March 6, 2011.
www.swartzentrover.com/cotor/E-Books/christ/ussher/

Ussher-Lightfoot Calendar—Definition. WordIq.com.2010, Retrieved March 10, 2011. www.wordiq.com/definition/ Ussher-Lightfoot_Calendar

V

Varner, William C. "Jesus and the Pharisees A Jewish Perspective." Personal Freedom Outreach. Saint Louis, Missouri 1996. Retrieved March 9, 2011. www.pfo.org/pharisee.htm

Vlach, Michael J. " What is Amillennialism?", TheologicalStudies. org. Retrieved March 21, 2011." www.theologicalstudies.org/ amillennialism.html

Voltaire. "Poem on the Lisbon Disaster." Online Library of Liberty. 2011. Retrieved April8, 2011. oll.libertyfund. org/?option=com_staticxt&staticfile=show

_____Letter to Rousseau. English translation CEW. Retrieveed April 25, 2011. reflectionsonlandusetranslationsmorebycew.com/Frenchin

Voonwide, Stephen. "Formation of the New Testament canon." Vox Reformata. 1995. Retrieved March 10, 2011. www.bible-researcher. com/voorwinde1.html

W

Ward, Dan Sewell. "Gnostics." Dan Sewell Ward.2003. Retrieved March 9, 2011. www.halexandria.org/dward269.htm

Warfield, Benjamin. "The Origin and Nature of Pelagianism." Retrieved March 9, 2011. pelagius.net/pelagian%20controversy.htm

Warren, Tony, "What Does God mean, I create Evil." Tony Warren. 2001. Last Modified 1/19/01. Retrieved March 9, 2011. www. mountainretreatorg.net/faq/create_evil.html—

Welburn, Andrew. "Christianity as Mystery Religion." Michael Hoffman. Retrieved March 10, 2011. www.egodeath.com/ ChristianityAsMysteryReligion.htm

Wesley., John. "Sermons-Numeric Index." Global Ministries, United Methodist Church ."Evanston, IL. Retrieved March 9, 2011.gbgm-umc. org/umhistory/wesley/jwesley3.html—

WESTMINSTER CONFESSION OF FAITH. 3rd Edition with Corrections . The Committee for Christian Education & Publications. Presbyterian Church in America. Lawrenceville, GA, 2000. Retrieved March 24, 2011. www.pcanet.org/general/cof_contents.htm

Whalen, Robert K. "Premillenialism." MedLibrary.org. Retrieved March21, 2011. medlibrary.org/medwiki/Premillenialism

White,Ellen G.."Through Faith Alone Part 1 A general manuscript." Ellen G. White Estate. 1999. Retrieved March 9, 2011. www.whiteestate.

org/message/through_faith_alone1.asp

_____*The Great Controversy between Christ and Satan.* On-line edition Ellen G. White Estate. Last Modified March 24, 2000. Retrieved March 9, 2011. www.greatcontroversy.org/books/gc/gc.html

_____*Justification and Sanctification.* "THIS IS JUS TIFICATION BY FAI TH." Adventist Biblical Truths Website. Retrieved March 17,2011. dedication.www3.50megs.com/egw1888_2.htm

"Why did contemporary writers not mention Jesus?" Tekton Education and Apologetics Ministry. Retrieved March 8, 2011. www.tektonics.org/qt/remslist.html

Wilde, Stuart. "Where did humans come from? (The Fourth Alternative). Stuart Wilde. 2009.Retrievede March 9, 2011. www.stuartwilde. com/ . . ./where_did_humans_come_from.html

Wilson, Tracy V. "How the earth works." *HowStuffWorks.* 1998-2011. Retrieved March 9, 2011. howstuffworks.com/earth6.htm

Wronsk, Peter. "MONTSEGUR |History Part 1." Peter Wronski 2002. Retrieved March 9, 2011. www.russianbooks.org/montsegur/ montsegur2.htm—

Wynants, Eric. "The Church's War on the Cathars." *New Dawn Magazine.* 1995. Retrieved March 9, 2011.www.newdawnmagazine. com.au/Article/The_Church_s_War_on the

YZ

y de la Torre, Walter Reinhold Warttig Mattfeld. "Yahweh-Elohim's Historical Evolution (Pre-Biblical)." Walter Reinhold Warttig Mattfeld y de la Torre. Retrieved March 9, 2011. *www.bibleorigins.* netYahwehYawUgarit.html

"Zealots."That the World May Know Ministries. Holland, MI., 2007. Retrieved March 8, 2011. www.followtherabbi.com/

Brix?pageID=1482

"Zealots." *LookLex Encyclopedia.* Retrieved March 5, 2011. lexicorient. com/e.o/zealots.htm

"Zoroastrianism." *New World Encyclopedia.* 2005. Retrieved March 9, 2011. www.newworldencyclopedia.org/entry/Zoroastrianism

Zwingli, Ulrich. " Huldrych Zwingli, Swiss Reformation." *BELIEVE web-page* . Last updated January 7, 2011. Retrieved March, 2011. www.mb-soft.com/believe/txc/zwingli.htm

INDEX

Edwards Brothers, Inc.
Thorofare, NJ USA
October 5, 2011